Clinical Understanding

About the Author

Gail S. Reed, Ph.D., is a training and supervisory analyst at the New York Freudian Society. She is a member of the Editorial Board of *Psychoanalytic Inquiry,* an editorial reader for the *Psychoanalytic Quarterly* and author of *Transference Neurosis and Psychoanalytic Experience: Perspectives on Contemporary Clinical Practice.* She maintains a private practice of psychoanalysis and psychotherapy in New York City.

Clinical Understanding

Gail S. Reed, Ph.D.

JASON ARONSON INC.
Northvale, New Jersey
London

Critical Issues in Psychoanalysis

CIP4

Editors:

Steven J. Ellman, Ph.D.
Arnold Wilson, Ph.D.

Editorial Board:

Director of Editorial Production: Robert D. Hack

This book was set in 11 pt. Bell by Alpha Graphics of Pittsfield, New Hampshire and printed and bound by Book-mart Press, Inc. of North Bergen, New Jersey.

Copyright 1996 by Jason Aronson Inc.

10 9 8 7 6 5 4 3 2 1

Library of Congress Catologing-in-Publication Data
Reed, Gail S.
    Clinical understanding / by Gail S. Reed.
        p.   cm.
    Includes bibliographical references and index.
    ISBN 1-56821-855-9 (hc : alk. paper)
    1. Psychoanalysis—Philosophy.   2. Psychotherapist and patient.
I. Title.
    [DNLM: 1. Psychoanalytic Theory.   2. Countertransference
(Psychology) 3. Transference (Psychology) 4. Psychoanalysis.
5. Empathy. WM 460 R324c 1996]
RC506.R386 1996
616.89'17'01—dc20
DNLM/DLC
for Library of Congress   96–12367

Printed in the United States of America. For information and catalog write to Jason Aronson Inc., 230 Livingston Street, Northvale, New Jersey 07647-1731. Or visit our website: http://www.aronson.com

FOR TOM

De la musique encore et toujours!
Que ton vers soit la chose envolée
Qu'on sent qui fuit d'une âme en allée
Vers d'autres cieux à d'autres amours.

Que ton vers soit la bonne aventure
Eparse au vent crispé du matin
Qui va fleurant la menthe ou le thym . . .
Et tout le reste est littérature.

    Paul Verlaine, Art Poétique

Contents

Part II: The Clinical Uses
of Comparative Understanding

Foreword

In this book, Gail Reed confronts a central question of psychoanalytic technique: How does an analyst come to understand a
patient? It is an important and obvious question, but one that has
not been adequately addressed. Dr. Reed brings us closer to an
answer by rigorously scrutinizing her own technique and the
theoretical underpinnings of the classical position. In the process,
she examines other theoretical perspectives as well, using the same
careful manner she applies to her own clinical efforts. The result
is a series of well crafted, well thought-out conceptualizations that
clinicians from any perspective will find informative and thought
provoking.

Developing her approach around a contemporary version of
classical psychoanalytic theory—although in her hands all theory
is examined and reevaluated—Dr. Reed describes a methodology
that enables the therapist to understand a patient's central unconscious organization in the clinical situation. She puts forth the
view that classical theory describes rules of transformation of
unconscious processes and she shows us how to use these rules to

arrive at in-depth understanding that is unique to each individual. Dr. Reed forcefully (and clinically) argues that classical theory provides us with the most flexible, least rigid method of discovering meaning in the analytic situation. Further, she shows that this approach is applicable to the needs of even quite vulnerable and difficult patients. These assertions are sure to raise controversy, but Gail Reed states her views clearly in this compelling and superbly written volume that addresses some of the most critical issues in psychoanalysis today.

Steven J. Ellman
September, 1996

Acknowledgments

The chapters in this book span my career in psychoanalysis and in one instance precede it. Between "Radical Simplicity and the Impact of Evil," originally part of my doctoral dissertation for the Department of Comparative Literature at Yale University, and "Clinical Truth and Contemporary Relativism," written last year, I have accrued many debts, beginning with that acknowledged in my dedication. Those not yet mentioned are debts of friendship and of the intellect, and I am most blessed in that the two so frequently are one. In my earlier training as a literary critic, the late Professor Isabel Gamble MacCaffrey, then of Bryn Mawr College, inspired my first attempts to write coherently about the sources of emotion in literature as well as my love of Renaissance poetry. The late Professor Lowry Nelson, Jr. directed my doctoral dissertation with patience and tact and became a firm friend. The late Professor William K. Wimsatt taught me to write about theory with discipline.

Given my somewhat unusual foundation in literary theory, my psychoanalytic career has always seemed to me a series of happy accidents. The first was the felicitous founding of the Interdisciplinary Colloquium on Psychoanalysis and Literature at the New York Psychoanalytic Institute at just the time I was starting analytic training. This group, which continued for seventeen years, allowed me access to the disciplined and imaginative minds of excellent, experienced and informed clinicians. I would particularly mention with gratitude my now collaborator, Francis Baudry, as well as James Spencer Jr., Marc Rubenstein, and the late Donald M. Kaplan. The second was the enthusiastic reception by the *Psychoanalytic Quarterly* of my paper on methodology by its then Editor, Dale Boesky, and his subsequent encouragement.

That publication led to a request for a paper on empathy and most importantly for me to Warren Poland, whose generosity and intelligent support cannot be adequately described. Theodore Shapiro, then Editor of the *Journal of the American Psychoanalytic Association* and its Editorial Board awarded me a Journal Prize for 1985. The opportunity to work for several years with Jacob Arlow and William Grossman has been invaluable as has been my profoundly affectionate and respectful association with all the members of the Group for the Study of the Psychoanalytic Process. Other debts shall remain unspoken, but not unrecognized.

Clinical Understanding

The sighs, groans and laments at first were so loud,
  Resounding through starless air, I began to weep:
  Strange languages, horrible screams, words imbued
With rage or despair, cries as of troubled sleep
  Or of a tortured shrillness—they rose in a coil
  Of tumult, along with noises like the slap
Of beating hands, all fused in a ceaseless flail
  That churns and frenzies that dark and timeless air
  Like sand in a whirlwind. And I, my head in a swirl
Of error, cried "Master, what is this I hear?"
                              Dante, *The Inferno*, III:25

Psychoanalytic understanding is defined by the principle that the dynamic unconscious is ubiquitous and determining. So humbling is this principle that we are always trying to deny it, forget it, or find exceptions to it. It diminishes the value we tend to place on self-consciousness, introspection, intention, and apparently informed action. It holds that none of us knows him- or herself except partially, that each of us knows his or her motives only by approximation and inference. It reduces our subjective, conscious sense of self to a problematic compromise among contending forces.

But when Freud deciphered the secret of dream formation, he identified the basic mechanisms by which the unconscious metamorphosed into consciousness. He discovered how condensation and displacement transformed childhood wishes into dreams and illicit impulses into symptoms and how, working backward from verbal associations, the analyst could identify the transformations of unconscious wishes into their conscious expression and retranslate them. Today, we speak more of compromise formations that include unrecognized and unconscious drive derivatives than of the transformation of unconscious wishes, but the existence of a potentially discoverable unconscious impulse is common to both and more important than the differences.

Subsequently, Freud discovered transference, adding a crucial and complicating clinical principle to those involved in reversing the work of condensation and displacement. It was complicating because it revealed that the psychoanalytic work of translation could not be intellectual and detached: it took place within an affective relationship. Most fundamentally, the material for retranslation comprised aspects of affective relationships from the past that manifested themselves, with predictable reordering, in the treatment present. That is, the unconscious was understood to speak through our words and actions to a desired, but unknown other, even if that other might be an unacknowledged version of oneself. The analyst assumed the position of that other and interpreted from it the unconscious but unrecognized wishes that spoke through the patient's affectively saturated words and actions to him or her. In clinical psychoanalysis a tension thus exists between the position to which the patient unconsciously assigns the analyst and the latter's material reality in the session. Transference is largely unconscious. It utilizes the same mechanisms of transformation that are present in dream work and in symptom formation. Moreover, it is not, as Freud originally supposed, the property of illness. It is a universal characteristic of humankind so that to some extent a reciprocal tension to the one just described exists in the analyst's attitude toward the patient.

Once the universality of transference was acknowledged, the analyst could never be separated from the uncertainties of his or her own unconscious. No matter how Freud sought to objectify the analyst, how he sought to bracket his analytic experience from his personal life, how he agreed to analyze Ferenczi and let him eat meals with his family but not play cards with him, the analyst had to contend with his own affects and his own unconscious. His or her knowledge was therefore approximate, his or her objectiv ity only relative, wrestled temporarily, by unceasing inner struggle, from the affective maelstrom of the engagement of patient and analyst. Freud recognized this, if only intermittently. He spoke of the therapeutic procedure of psychoanalysis as one in which the analyst unleashed demons and struggled with them to the best of his ability; he realized the dangers of overly personal involvement and warned against them. Eventually he recommended a prophylactic reanalysis every five years.

The reciprocal vulnerability of the analyst in his or her own transference to the patient also raises the specter of a fundamental antagonism between the principle of unconscious determinism and the possibility of the analyst's authoritative (*not* authoritarian) understanding. The question becomes, how does the analyst, buffeted as he or she is by his or her own unconscious, know how to understand and what to interpret?

In this book, I elaborate on some of the ideas that have been helpful to me in understanding patients. One such idea, which is extremely controversial and unpopular these days, is to take seriously a contemporary version of classical psychoanalytic theory. I do not mean the version of this theory and its consequent practice that makes the analyst out to be a bogeyman who is rigid, unyielding, and cruel. That vision developed out of particular unresolved transference conflicts. It is as far from my experience and practice as conceivably possible. Leaving aside the fantasies about the theory and its conduct, the many misunderstandings about it that exist today, its inevitable weaknesses, and its undoubted misuse by individual analysts, especially during the decades when the ideal of the anonymous and silent analyst was at its most grotesque height, I find classical psychoanalytic theory the most potentially inclusive, integrative, comprehensive, and the least doctrinaire of available theories, though also the most difficult to understand and utilize. It is flexible enough to treat quite vulnerable patients as well as more traditionally neurotic ones. Indeed, many of the alternative theories offered today seem to err in offering themselves as alternatives. Rather, they are potential developments of isolated aspects of contemporary Freudian theory, lacking not in what they offer but in their failure to integrate their insights consistently into the concept of the dynamic unconscious.

Although theory is an invaluable organizer of a clinician's perception, it does not tell one what to do in the clinical moment. For that one must rely on one's own capacity for self-understanding as that capacity has been sharpened and developed by experience, including, most importantly, one's own analyses. One who does rely on theory to tell one what to do in a clinical moment enters the realm of the psychopathology of authority. The theory each of us adopts, however, subliminally organizes the way we hear material, the questions we ask, the interpretations we make. Many theories tend to dictate a specific understanding of the content we hear. These work, as I point out in Chapter 7, allegorically. Surface elements may be susceptible to interpretation, but the arrangement of elements remains the same in the interpretation as in the original disguise. Classical theory, instead, describes rules through which transformation occurs in content and form alike. It shows us how to use those rules of transformation to arrive at the depth without dictating a specific content or assuming that a specific arrangement of the surface will indicate anything about the depth. Surface form does not remain the same, but is transformed by the same mechanisms that transform content.

Moreover, in Freudian theory, the meaning of clinical material is multivalent and the levels at which it is understood to reverberate limitless. This factor makes the analyst's task more daunting and difficult perhaps, but it also implies, with great optimism, that the individual is infinitely creative and resourceful. The esthetics of unconscious transformation; the delicate structure of wish, substitution, and symptom; and the kaleidoscopically patterned shifting of elements that occurs during a well-progressing analysis have always seemed beautiful and admirable to me. They are evidence of a capacity for creativity in each of our minds.

Theory is an accretion of principles that have been worked out by repeated clinical observation. Thus, if Freud early deciphered the complex disguise of an illicit sexual impulse that expressed itself in the more acceptable fainting spells of a particular woman and found that these principles of disguise corresponded to the mechanisms at work in the symptom of paralytic contractures of a second patient, the obsessional symptom of a third, and the dream imagery of a fourth, there has been established a principle by which specific mechanisms may be said to transform a specific, unacceptable, unconscious impulse into an acceptable symptom or dream fragment. In Chapter 1, I illustrate how the principles of condensation and displacement manifest themselves in the pattern of a patient's free associations and how, taking the transference as an organizer, it is possible to work backward from the patient's associations to reconstruct a central unconscious childhood fantasy. In this case, this fantasy was at the root of the patient's dangerously suicidal behavior.

But theoretical principles need to be distinguished from clinical circumstance. Circumstance has to do with whatever interferes clinically with the application of a principle. The analyst's transference to the patient might be such a circumstance. Another might be his or her fantasy about being an analyst, a fantasy that accounts for much of the rigid misuse of Freudian theory alluded to above. The distinction between principle and circumstance is important because modern thinking has contributed to the erosion of clear, clinically useful categories. We have begun to confuse a past event with the form in which it is narrated, interpretation with the authoritarian imposition of an opinion, and the impossibility of knowing something exactly with the idea that it does not exist. In Chapter 2, I take up confusing ideas about meaning and narration in psychoanalysis. By pointing out that meaning for a patient is not relative, and the logical necessity that an event—including the event of making a fantasy—that is being narrated in some derivative form must have occurred before it is narrated, I make it possible to explore the components of a patient's screen memory.

Theoretical principles, of which these distinctions partake, furnish, first and foremost, a way of inquiring with the patient into his or her difficulties. Free association, for instance, is no arbitrary tool. It is the logical consequence of a principle that holds that wishes for gratification are displaced from things to words and from words to words in a chain of substituted meanings. The analyst tries to interpret not only these wishes but also the defenses, anxieties, guilt, and frequently maladaptive behavior such wishes engender and tries to interpret them in terms of the unconscious attitudes toward him or her as a transference figure. But the patient too has a job: he or she needs to be willing to face unpleasant truth gleaned from his words and actions about his or her way of avoiding anxiety and then attempt to tolerate that anxiety. Otherwise, there will be no change. The articulation of this partial goal for treatment, another principle, allows me to delineate patients who use the analysis continually to avoid anxiety. Thus, in Chapter 3, with the concept of the transference perversion, I describe patients who seek to use the analytic situation to seduce the analyst into continuing a secret and sexualized gratification constituted by the action of analyzing and being analyzed itself.

These patients are avoiding the unconscious terror that the idea of penis absence in women creates in them. Indeed, the concept of penis absence, especially as it defines women in these patients' view, figures not only in my explication of the transference perversion but also in the two cases that follow. It is important to make clear that such a definition of women, by adults of both sexes, has its origin in the pathological perpetuation of an unconscious, originally childhood fantasy of the female as castrated. This fantasy, the consequence of a great deal of early and unresolved destructiveness, is reinforced, in individual cases, by a variety of object relational contexts. In Ms. X. in Chapter 4, for example, the births of a string of male siblings, one after the other, and her belief that her parents favored her male siblings were such contexts. Moreover, the meaning of the penis for these individuals is complexly overdetermined. It functions primarily as a sign of difference, differentiating one person from another, presence from absence, male from female. As such, it is, par excellence, the organizer for the acute anxiety that occurs when omnipotent control of the object fails. The fantasies around penis absence in no way should be taken to represent a mature or desirable understanding of what constitutes a woman.

The analyst's ability to understand is inevitably circumstantial as well as guided by principle. Patients elicit responses both in general and in particular, and in no way more immediately yet covertly than through the form of their free associations. By removing, as much as possible, requirements for logical discourse, the method of free association gives the patient's unconscious organization the opportunity to reveal itself in the contiguities and similarities of his or her language. But the way the patient associates also constitutes an action, one that has important reverberations in the analyst and important unconscious meanings for the patient. In Chapters 4 and 5, I describe the uncovering of the unconscious transference meaning of the way in which two very different patients associated.

If theoretical concepts can be helpful, however, they can also hinder clinical understanding. They can become more connected to narcissistic ideas about being the right kind of analyst than they are responsive to the exigencies of the clinical situation, for instance. As a result of their connection to narcissistic ideas, they sometimes become untouchable, a response to historical and political imperative, contorting clinical practice and no longer modifiable by clinical observation. That is, they participate in the psychopathology of authority mentioned earlier. The transference neurosis has become such a concept. I conclude Part I by offering a modern, not a received view, and one that takes into account the changing quality of the therapeutic object relationship as well as the shifting nature of compromise during the psychoanalytic process.

The second part of this book develops the use of comparison as a way of both illuminating psychoanalytic principle and sharpening the understanding of the nature of the psychoanalytic clinical method. Comparisons of theory have been far too geared to variations of content. They have not evaluated the relative approach to the understanding of meaning that a specific theory affords or fails to afford. Yet, for a psychoanalytic theory to stand on its own, the model of mental functioning it proposes must provide a rationale for the psychoanalytic method as well as for the clinical understanding of meaning. That understanding of meaning may then also be assessed with respect to the freedom, variety, repetition, or dogmatism the theory encourages. I am not discussing technique per se; rather I am approaching the question of what freedom of meaning inheres in a theory and whether the method adopted to uncover meaning is accounted for in the theory itself. If it is not, the theory is incomplete and relies on another, unacknowledged theory. In Chapter 7, I explore the comparative rules of clinical understanding in classical psychoanalysis and in self psychology. The result yields an unrecognized and extremely significant property of classical theory: the specificity of an individual's life experience furnishes the individual's symbolic universe. Unconscious meaning is thus specific to the individual and, not as in self psychology, a general property of development. Since meaning cannot be anticipated by a theory, *a modern, classically informed psychoanalysis is the exploration of the individual's ways of signifying.* This insight is of enormous clinical importance because it affects how we listen and how we formulate interpretations.

These two contrasting assumptions about an individual's way of making meaning are explored further in Chapter 8. Here I explore the nature of language and communication within the classical psychoanalytic dyad by contrasting it with assumptions about the communication of theoretical ideas. To illustrate this delicate and elusive distinction, I turn to an analogy in poetry. A similar difference in assumptions about meaning and interpretation can be found in comparing a seventeenth-century poem by Andrew Marvell that contains its own theologically agreed-upon interpretation with a nineteenth-century poem by Stéphane Mallarmé in which meaning is elusive, evocative, imbued with affect and uncertainty, and constantly shifting. This chapter is actually built around parallel contrasts: the relation of clinical meaning to theoretical meaning and the relation of the seventeenth-century poem to the later one. Each contrast illuminates assumptions about two ways of understanding and interpreting. Each contrast illuminates a way of conceiving of the unfolding of clinical meaning that is different from any other type of communication.

Polyvalent meanings, however, exist in theoretical discourse as well. When these contradict each other, a clinical approach to the phenomena may yield unexpected insights. In Chapter 9, I explore the multiple meanings of the term "empathy" in psychoanalytic writing. The exploration reveals repetitive contradictions in usage, which represent the unacknowledged presence of two unrecognized and frequently contradictory attitudes toward the patient and his or her meaning on the part of the analyst, one penetrating, the other supportive. A reciprocal relation exists between the advocacy of too one-sided a technique and clarity of expression. That is, the disregarded aspect asserts itself in unanticipated fashion in the figurative language of the text.

Pondering the difficulty of legitimately using psychoanalysis to understand literature proves an invaluable stimulus to considering what is essential about the clinical process. In order to find a method of dealing with unconscious meaning in literature, Chapter 10 grapples with finding an analogy that mirrors, without distorting, something intrinsic in the clinical situation. The analogy arrived at is the relation of text, reader, and the latter's critical discourse to a specialized and documented relation among patient, therapist, and supervisor, the so-called parallelism phenomenon. The method proves capable of tracing a repeated disavowal and of locating the unconscious fantasy that organizes both text and the disavowing response.

The last three chapters continue the effort of defining clinical psychoanalysis by distinguishing its work from applications of psychoanalysis to literature. In the process, I examine the ways in which an observer might identify conflict, a step preliminary to exploring its constituents, in the product of culture and in the individual (Chapter 11) and then assess the difference in the conventions of interpretation present in a literary study and during a clinical exploration (Chapter 12). Finally, in Chapter 13, I examine the effect of the narrative structure of *Candide* on a hypothetical reader's affective response, an exercise that approaches, from a different angle, the issues raised in the exploration of the effect of the formal properties of a patient's free associations on the analyst. Chapters 8 and 10 to 13 also stand by themselves as contributions to the relatively neglected subject of the methodology of applied psychoanalysis.

I The Clinical Uses of Understanding

1   On the Value of
Explicit Reconstruction

The use of explicit reconstruction within the psychoanalytic process based on data generated by that process has markedly diminished (Curtis 1983, Greenacre 1975), to be replaced in many quarters by what Friedman (1983) has described as a focus on current process with "pictures of the past giving form to latent meaning" (p. 203). The focusing on current process has largely involved the here-and-now transference, a technical emphasis discernible across a very broad spectrum. This spectrum has included analysts influenced by Klein through Strachey's (1934) concept of the mutative interpretation or various of Winnicott's works, by Kohut's technical concerns (e.g., Schwaber 1983), by Loewald's emphasis on the analyst as a new object, and by psychoanalytic ego psychology (e.g., Gray 1982). Various assumptions about the role of a past event and its lesser importance in cure relative to other factors have influenced this technical change.

The diminished emphasis on the role of the specific past event has also partly been an artifact of the need to rid classical analysis of oversimplified vestiges of the early hysteria theory and owes much to Kris's (1956) influential paper warning that the path from past event to present substitute trace(s) is so complex that the original event must remain uncertain. Confluent concerns about suggestion, the transference meaning of arrogating the right to pronounce upon historical truth, and questions about the onto-logical status of the reconstructed past have also contributed to a turning away from explicit reconstruction (Schafer 1982, Spence 1982).[1]

Where the past is given weight, the emphasis on current pro-cess tends to encourage the interpretation of the meaning of a past event over the specific delineation of the event or its attendant fantasies themselves. Since the meaning of the past event is re-garded primarily, as Friedman suggested, as giving form to the present, the interpretation of the event or the fantasy connected to it is subordinated to an understanding of the present and often remains impressionistic. Bergmann (1991) recently asserted that analysts today interpret only the symbolic meaning of screen memories, for instance.

Although the psychoanalytic method imposes limits on the de-gree to which specific reconstruction of past events and the fan-tasies connected to them may be possible, it does not preclude being as explicit as possible (Hanly 1990). Moreover, it is my con-tention that specific reconstruction of memories and/or fantasies is sometimes the crucial therapeutic element in a treatment. The situation in which explicit reconstruction of events and fantasies, as well as their particular meaning, is called for may arise when disavowed memories have become the nidus of organizing uncon-scious fantasies. Such combinations of memory and fantasy may represent the core of a patient's difficulties and continue actively

---

1. These trends are not, of course, universal. See, for example, Blum (1977, 1978, 1980, 1986).

in patients' minds to affect their behavior, character, and present perception while remaining sequestered from conscious awareness (Arlow 1969a,b).

Beyond the establishment of the unconscious meaning of a past event, explicit reconstructions of fantasies and/or memories may be necessary in order to enable a patient to understand how he or she has organized meaning for himself or herself. I believe it is frequently patients' understanding of the mechanisms they have employed to organize meaning, as well as their understanding of the meaning of those events, that is therapeutically illuminating and freeing.

Explicit reconstruction, as I understand it, evolves from within the psychoanalytic process, particularly from within the transference; it is integral to that process, an exploration on the part of both analyst and analysand of the relations among disparate clinical events such as enactments, transference attitudes, and the patterns of the patient's free associations. Without reconstruction or recall, these disparate clinical events would remain discrete because the fantasy/memory complex generating them is sequestered by a powerful defensive organization that is not resolvable by dynamic interpretation alone.

Reconstruction is an ongoing series of partial restatements in more and more precise language of memories and/or fantasies that have been disguised by specific, demonstrable mental operations. It is a reasoned technical procedure utilizing general principles of interpretation of verbal derivatives (Arlow 1979a,b, 1980, 1987) that reverses those mental operations. Reconstruction is also an act of the analyst that becomes part of the transference and must be analyzed as such. However, the purpose of reconstruction is not, to my mind, the isolated delineation of these fantasy/memory organizations. The point is to specify the way they have been fashioned by the patient, including as far as possible, the specific materials he or she has used in their creation. The reason for such specificity is that the way they have been constructed explains how they organize meaning for the patients.[2]

The Interrelation of Theoretical Assumption and Psychoanalytic Methodology

The relation of primary process mechanisms (Freud 1900) to figurative language suggests certain guidelines that can help us arrive at formulations of those specific events and the fantasies elaborated around them that inform the patient's present discourse. Relations between conscious and unconscious presentations are organized either according to similarity or to a combination of contiguity and displacement. These two major organizations of experience appear in the patient's discourse as metaphor and metonymy, though only one part of the figure is manifestly and consciously available.

Primary process relations based on similarity take the rhetorical form of metaphor. Just as the primary process may treat injury as identical to castration so that a particular individual may react

---

2. The impact of an event on the psyche, particularly a shocking or traumatic event, may be different enough from the fantasy about it to assume different classifications within the mind (Terr 1991). From that point of view, one function of reconstruction might be that of differentiating as much as possible the defended registration of a (specified) historical event from the (specified) fantasy elaborated around it. When reconstruction is explicitly attended to, as in recent discussions of childhood sexual abuse, such important distinctions tend to be blurred. A focus on recovering the past rather than on the past as the basis of the system by which an individual has established meaning for himself or herself often predominates. In that regard, insufficient attention is sometimes paid to distinguishing the recovery of a reputed historical event from the memory of acquiring that knowledge later in childhood. See Steele (1986) for such an example.

to a scratched finger with anxiety, metaphor treats two disparate nouns as identical. For example, the phrase "my love is a beautiful flower," however trite, treats love and flower as identical.

Primary process relations based on contiguity take the rhetorical form of metonymy (Jakobson and Halle 1956). In metonymy connections between words and the events they represent are based on contiguity alone. Tammany Hall comes to stand for municipal corruption. Moreover the contiguity at the base of metonymy leads to condensation—all municipal corruption is represented by one group—and to displacement—a meeting house comes to stand for the political venality transacted within it.

The same primary process mechanisms that can be demonstrated in the formation of metonymy, namely contiguity, condensation, and displacement, are at work in the reorganization of memory: a chance happening immediately before a trauma can provide the apparently indifferent screen material that substitutes for the memory of the trauma (Fine et al. 1971, Katan 1969), denying the shocking memory and concomitant affects and wishes and preserving it without conscious emotion at the same time (see also Freud 1937b). The manifest content of screen memories so formed may have neither an obvious symbolic meaning nor even manifest traces of the disavowed event. Moreover, as this example reminds us, repression is not the only defense that opposes remembering. While all defenses contribute, denial, isolation, and disavowal common to the formation of a fetish are frequently employed in dealing with disturbing external perception (Freud 1927, 1940b).

The type of primary process organization represented by metonymy makes explicit reconstruction therapeutically necessary. Because they are originally determined by proximity in time or space only, relations between significant events and their representations based on contiguity are dependent on *specific* life experiences. Such apparently arbitrary connections, particularly but not only from childhood, form an important part of the private system of signification of each patient. That is, a patient's private system of meaning is partially composed of metonymies of which he or she is unaware. When we reconstruct explicitly, we help patients re-establish the contiguous links they have lost so that their private system of meaning becomes clear to them.

Sometimes, the verbal representations of such idiosyncratic connections emerge rather directly through sequences in the patient's associations. More often than not, however, a patient's associations reveal a mixture of metaphoric and metonymic reworkings of the original experience. To take a hypothetical example (one modeled after one from my practice) for purposes of illustration, a particularly garish shade of purplish pink mysteriously produces a state of anguish in a young woman. The color was that of a book jacket that she was holding as a child when she was told of the death of her mother. The relation between the color and the shock is based on contiguity and is therefore metonymic. Only the color and its unaccountable associated affect remain conscious, while the memory that explains their connection does not. Let us imagine, however, that the young woman's associations to the color go not to the original shock, but to a scene of loss and unhappiness in a movie where a wall is painted a similar color. The relation between the unknown childhood memory and the movie scene is based on the similarity of color and of loss. That is, a metaphoric link intervenes. Metaphoric connections disguise and reveal aspects of the original contiguity.

One of the many functions of the analyst is to help patients realize that their associations actually represent one part of more complex metaphoric and metonymic organizations and to discover what constitutes the hidden, specific verbal tenors of their metaphors, the contiguities implied by their metonymies, and how the relation between the two has led to the formation of organized and pathogenic fantasy/memory complexes. When the analyst intervenes, it is partly in the hope of modifying the patient's current verbal organization so that it moves closer to the original contiguous links established in the past. To make the hypothetical young woman referred to above aware that she has linked the purplish pink color with a scene of loss is to underline for her the contiguity in her associations. The analyst next listens for the patient's reaction to such an intervention with particular reference to what shifts occur that expand our knowledge of her metaphoric and metonymic disguising of the underlying unconscious organization. She might, for instance, associate to her mother or make a more displaced reference to an admired teacher.

The point I want to emphasize is that to make her aware of the way she has attributed meaning to the color, if she does not recall the original event, we may ultimately need to use her associations to attempt to reconstruct, as far as possible, the original contiguity. Such activity is neither the forging of a mutual narrative nor the interpretation of an impressionistic symbolic meaning. Rather, *it is an attempt to re-establish with the patient the original steps in her creation of a private symbol.*

Clinical Illustration

In presenting this example, I wish to underline the presence in the patient's associations of words linked to significant fantasy/memory complexes and the role of therapeutic intervention in reversing the operations of primary process that conceal those complexes. I also wish to illustrate the beneficial effect of such intervention: to enable the patient to become aware of the operation of these processes in his original construction of meaning. To those ends, I shall report specific material that emerged over a one-month period, emphasizing verbal sequences, interventions, and responses that highlight the gradual uncovering and reconstructing of an organized pathogenic fantasy/memory complex. The material emerged in the seventh month of a five-times-weekly analysis. I select the sequence from a much more complex psychoanalytic process to emphasize a progression that begins with a transference interpretation, includes a reconstruction of childhood fantasy, and ends with the recall of a childhood event that partly organized a pathogenic fantasy/memory complex and of

which the reconstructed fantasy was also a part. I choose to describe aspects of a month's work to emphasize the fact that reconstruction is essentially interrelated with all other aspects of the
psychoanalytic process, particularly with transference.[3]

Despite a presentation full of verbal pyrotechnics, joking, and
facile associations without much affect, Mr. M. was evidently
depressed and could not control self-destructive trends. He continuously disregarded his medical regimen and would roam dangerous neighborhoods late into the night. Although he had many
friends, some of long standing, he limited his contacts with them,
could enter into no intimate relationship, and avoided any sexual
activity. His brother had been killed at the age of 3 by being catapulted out of a neighbor's convertible during an otherwise minor
accident. Mr. M., who was not present, was 5 at the time.

Mr. M.'s hypomanic self-presentation entertained me and defended against affect. When I pointed out his propensity to amuse
me, he began to talk about the time after the accident. Nothing
reminding his depressed mother of the dead child could be mentioned. Instead, throughout latency and adolescence, he enter-

---

3. I restrict myself to reporting sequences, interventions, and responses
that reveal the process of transformation of enactments and associations
at the beginning of the sequence into knowledge of the unconscious meaning of those derivatives at the end. One artifact of my presentation is that
it emphasizes both genetic and cognitive aspects of the work at the expense of transference interpretation, affect, and intuition; a second is its
necessary condensation that leaves out much evidence, excursions, mis-
directions, the full impact of the patient's characteristic resistances, and
the verbatim wording of many of my interpretations. I will not be able to
convey adequately at the same time the transference work, the intense affect
that was almost continuously present, or other aspects of the work that
came to be subsequently elaborated. This material is offered only in the
service of my thesis and should be taken neither as a model of the clinical
work per se nor as a case presentation to be discussed beyond the points
I use it to illustrate.

tained her with his musical ability. As these associations accumulated, patients who had the hour following Mr. M.'s began to wonder what I was doing to cause him so much suffering. He eventually reported that when he left my office and re-entered the waiting room, he would lean against the door opposite to where the next patient sat waiting, close his eyes, exhale, and wipe his forehead with a handkerchief.

Transference Interpretation

Shortly after describing this enactment, Mr. M. came in declaring that he was in a good mood and did not want me to ruin it by making him suffer. Taking into account both his actions in the waiting room, by which he seemed to be calling the next patient's attention to his suffering, and the negation of a wish to be made to suffer by me in his present declaration, I responded, "You want me to make you suffer." "You're laying a package in my lap. What am I supposed to do with it?," he complained. Ultimately, with a significant change of affect, he said sadly, "I don't want to feel guilty anymore."

Mr. M. began the following session with a description of how he had defied his doctor's orders. He referred to the previous day's interpretation that he wanted me to make him suffer and to a visit by his parents that had temporarily interfered with his disobeying his doctors. He became anxious waiting for them to leave. He complained about his mother's attitude of entitlement, made a pun about guilt, referred to two brothers and to a painting of a baby that he said was his mother's favorite. Then he began to joke. I pointed out that he had started to entertain me after he talked about guilt and his mother loving the painting of a baby; I said that it also followed mention of his not taking care of himself and my telling him that he wanted me not to take care of him.

"I survived. Guilty," he said again sadly and reported smelling smells that reminded him of kindergarten. With his sadness growing, he thought of being closer to the ground when he was little, then of dirt and graves. He imagined one of his brother's favorite toys burned up, thought of a photo he'd seen of a mother holding her baby's burnt, dead body and refusing to let it go. Then with horror he remembered a latency nightmare in which his mother turned him into ashes.

I said to him, "You want to be the dead baby." He burst out: "He got attention without doing anything. He got off easy!" He was shocked that he felt that way toward his brother and angry at me for making him aware that he wanted to die.

Dream

Shortly thereafter Mr. M. reported a dream. He was riding in a cab with friends trying to do errands in preparation for a concert. He was late for a rehearsal and went home to a house he was living in rent free because "there'd been a murder in it and they were making a movie about it. I could live there rent free during the production of the movie, even though I wasn't in the movie. Robin was there. He had done the murders, or they were using him in the movie to act the part of the murderer. The producer wasn't there. He had another house that he was living in. He had two brothers. I was one. One was shadowy. I went over to the producer's house. They said that he might not forgive me for being late and making him angry. I had to explain I was a space cadet."

The patient associated to the accident. He felt very guilty and fervently wished that his brother had held on inside the car. Beyond identifying Robin as a friend, Mr. M. associated neither to "Robin" nor to "space cadet"; with the benefit of hindsight, however, I wish to underline those verbal traces as well as one additional feature, the murder or the movie rehearsal within the dream in which a murder "took place or was going to take place" involving Robin. The work that followed gradually elucidated those elements.

Screen Memory

There was an interruption in the treatment for most of a week owing first to his and then to my schedule. In the hour following the interruption, Mr. M. began by mentioning a recurrent dream from childhood in which "I'm looking out a door at a path made of concrete and can hear a scary tap tap. Like a heartbeat noise." The sound was "scary, like someone was coming." He thought his mother was looking out the window, only she wasn't. She was not comforting to him. On the way to my office, he'd seen a delivery man carrying a parcel and tapping with an umbrella on the sidewalk. "Tap tap." The house was the one they lived in at the time his brother was born, he added. This account was followed by angry remarks about teachers and friends that upon exploration, turned out to be transference references. Mr. M. spoke of having wanted to be with me and having felt angry at me for having been unavailable. The approaching end of the session felt like it would be a banishment for his being so angry.

In the next session, Mr. M. continued to express strong feelings about my not having been available, then mentioned again the childhood dream and his fear of the intruder. Referring to the dream, and thinking of the associations in the previous session about the parcel delivery on the way to my office, his mother's lack of concern over his fear of the approaching person, and the baby's birth, I told him he felt angry at me in the same way he had felt angry at his mother for not paying attention to him when an intruder, the baby, was coming. He remembered the feeling of wanting his mother to look for him after the baby was born and continued, "I don't want to own this sibling rivalry. I don't want to say it. It makes sense without feelings. I wanted my mother's attention. . . . I'm looking up and seeing my mother changing diapers. This is very vague, I'm a lot shorter and smaller, far away from the table, low. I have this feeling of being stood off, watching, of it not being part of me."

Reconstruction of a Childhood Fantasy

Several sessions that occurred about one week later provided the material for the reconstruction of a childhood fantasy. The first session began with this sequence. Mr. M. thought that I was turning my back on him when he entered my consulting room. He pictured himself going through a laundry chute into space, to total isolation, into magic warped time. When I asked about his associations to the laundry chute and space, he thought of an astronaut in a space suit, a space cadet attached by a line to the space ship, a mother ship, then an umbilical cord. As he was walking to my office, he continued, he had been angry at a thief he saw stealing a plant from a garden of the house down the street. He saw it ripped out.

He stopped and began to criticize himself. I pointed out that he had expected punishment from me when he came in, that he had the idea of being attached to a mother ship, that he had a thought about ripping out a plant, and that he then attacked himself.

"I didn't drive the car! I didn't kill my brother!" he burst out. I interpreted his wish to get rid of his brother. Fantasies of guilt, retribution, and self-punishment followed, including: "I'm seeing dancing feet; that's what people do when they hang. Guilty. I picture taking my head and bashing it against the floor. How that must have hurt to be thrown out and crushed on the street." I told him he now wanted to make himself into his brother to take the impact of the pain himself.

"I looked inside something that looked like a tinfoil oven; inside there's an abortion, or a fetus with small legs. Something else dead. All the pets we had always died [he elaborated].... I knew they would. Knew I'd caused it, like I'm a curse." I told him that when he was little he had believed that his thoughts of wanting to kill his brother had killed his brother. Sounding both contemplative and puzzled, he said: "Wishing is not some innocuous thing. It doesn't make sense, but there's no difference to me between wishing and acting."

In a session a few days later, he spoke of being afraid of me, feeling guilty about his brother's death, being afraid of being destructive, and again thought of himself as a space cadet going into the laundry chute. I told him he was afraid of my punishing him the way he had been afraid of his mother punishing him for his destructive thoughts toward his brother. Then taking account of the previous associations about the astronaut in space, the mother ship and umbilical cord, and the thief ripping out the plant, I reconstructed his childhood fantasy: "You envied the baby when the baby was inside your mother's stomach. You wanted to rip the baby out so you could get inside your mother, like the space cadet you imagined going into magic warped time." "Oh God," he responded, "Throwing him out in space! That feels like an indictment."

Memory

Two sessions later mentions of me appeared, followed by a reference to danger from a devouring shark and thoughts about his brother being dead. He next imagined himself projected off a car seat. Then, for the second day in a row, he had a rush of memories of a place he didn't recognize that looked like an underground garage and his basement playroom at the same time. Suddenly he remembered: "I had a Batman car with an ejector seat! I'd totally forgotten about it until now. You pushed the button and Robin would get popped out through the roof. No wonder it's so cemented in my mind I did it. I had a toy that did it. I loved doing it! I was pushing that button all the time! [pause] It's so wild, thinking about how . . . It seems so blatant, it was so satisfying. It was fun. No wonder life isn't allowed. It makes me cry."[4]

---

4. From the time Mr. M. recovered this memory, he believed that his play preceded the accident. Other memories, confirmable and never forgotten from the same time, tended to substantiate his belief, but there is always, of course, the possibility the play was an attempt at mastery of the accident and only later became conflated with his rivalrous wishes.

Discussion

Primary Process Transformations and Their Reversal

Explicit reconstructions become possible when interpretations touching active conflicts result in shifts in the patient's dynamic equilibrium. These shifts in turn are reflected in changes in the quality and patterning of the patient's associations, so that, optimally, associations approach ever closer to the original metaphoric and metonymic connections. A particularly dramatic reconfiguration of material occurred once Mr. M. had become conscious of his guilt about his rivalry with his dead sibling: he had a dream that included in its manifest content both references to the memory he would later recover and traces of the fantasy I would reconstruct. Robin, who is, of course, Batman's companion, appeared in the manifest content of the dream either as a murderer or an actor used in the murder. The form of the dream suggests that it might be related to a dream within a dream, which, as Freud remarked, frequently represents an actual memory that is being denied (Freud 1900, p. 338). The actual memory denied was the child's play pushing the button that activated the ejector seat of the Bat car. Greenacre (1956) added, as possible formal criteria for dreams within dreams, the play within the dream. To include this dream in that category, we would need to add the movie or movie rehearsal within the dream to the variants Greenacre listed and to understand that the historical uncertainty of the child about whether he had actually killed by ejecting Robin over and over from his toy car was represented by the uncertainty about whether Robin had committed a murder or was going to be used in the murder that was going to be played.

In retrospect, it is possible to see that the space cadet element in the dream stood metonymically for the entire childhood fantasy/wish to be inside the mother in the sibling's place and to eject the sibling from the mother's body, which ultimately made the historical play so significant. Whether the spaceman fantasy was a childhood fantasy elaboration of that wish or a later (adolescent or adult) vehicle for that fantasy, verbal traces of the significant memory and fantasy constellation appeared in the manifest content of his dream.

Following the appearance of the dream, the transference, sometimes in a configuration in which sibling rivalry was uppermost, sometimes in one in which terror of retaliation dominated, provided a continuous context for the subsequent reconstructive work. In its context, Mr. M. became aware of his rivalry with his brother *before* the accident. The memory of the changing table that emerged at this juncture I understand as a screen memory *in statu nascendi* (Boesky 1973). The screen memory both confirmed the rivalry with his live sibling and isolated and denied powerful emotionally laden perceptions and conflicted wishes from the past, here the envious and destructive wishes toward the intruder/baby, gestated, held, fed, and cared for by Mr. M.'s mother. That is, the memory of the changing table was in part a protestation of innocence screening the wish to eject the sibling from the mother's womb. He was saying, in effect, "I was only a helpless, neglected child looking on." Later in the analysis it became apparent that this defensively detached onlooker constituted the conscious self-representation at times when Mr. M. acted self-destructively.

When the space cadet, first mentioned in the dream, reappeared in a sequence that included going into total isolation, going into magic, warped time, and being attached to a mother ship by an umbilical cord, their sequence led me to construct the patient's childhood fantasy/wish to be inside his mother's body. The connected ejection of the intruder/fetus became probable in the further juxtaposition of the story of the thief ripping out the plant, which Mr. M. related he had observed on his way to my office. To understand that this sequence could be translated into a childhood fantasy as I did at the time, I had to supply the probable missing similarity between the plant and the fetus. I did not immediately interpret this fantasy. Related material in the following session included fetuses and abortions, adding weight to my hypothesis.

When I did reconstruct the explicit childhood fantasy as I understood it, Mr. M. recovered his childhood memory. In contrast, the interpretation of the less specific wish to do away with the baby, which I had already made, did not produce that result. While it stimulated a further realization of his guilt and further associations involving fetuses, the space cadet fantasy reappeared in the next session in the same dynamic configuration as before. Such a repetition to my mind is evidence for the need of a more explicit reconstruction. In reconstructing, I emphasized specific nodal words that had appeared in the derivative associations: for instance *ripping* the baby out of his mother's body as in a recent session he had reported the thief ripping out the plant. Mr. M. linked the words "ripping out" to throwing out into space. Throwing out into space resonated both with his play with the ejector seat of his toy and with the actual accident in which he understood the toddler to have been catapulted out of the convertible. Forcibly getting out something that was originally inside was the similarity upon which condensation of accident, play, and earlier wish had been based. That similarity, together with the unhappy contiguity of the accident duplicating the child's play, formed the unconscious belief that he was responsible for the death of his sibling and the pathogenic unconscious fantasy/memory complex that emerged in the transference in the form of an enactment representing a wish to be made to suffer.

While some of the dynamic components of this complex could be hypothesized on the basis of clinical theory, *its particular metaphoric and metonymic organization could not be predicted by any theory, including a theory of development.* Theory in classical psychoanalysis does not provide such specific content. It predicts that some kind of a metaphoric and metonymic organization will exist and that our data about what to reconstruct must be found in the sequence and content of associations. It further offers guidelines based on knowledge of the laws of primary process mechanisms for the understanding of those associations (see Chapter 7).

The particulars of this organization were uncovered through

a combination of reconstruction of a childhood fantasy and the patient's subsequent recollection. The value of uncovering the specific metaphoric and metonymic structure through explicit reconstruction of verbal derivatives is that discovering the components of the structure allowed Mr. M. to understand not only that he had come to equate wishing with doing and pleasure with destruction in many facets of his life, but *how he had come to equate them*. The work reported here led to a much more direct expression of Mr. M.'s hostility. It initiated a prolonged and intense negative transference that could ultimately be connected to various objects, events, and fantasies from his childhood.

Reconstruction and Transference

One of the objections to reconstruction is that it lessens the intensity of the transference. Of course, overly complicated reconstructions can dissipate any affect by virtue of their length and complexity and are probably not advisable in any event. Moreover, a well-timed explicit reconstruction may reduce the intensity of transference by contributing to its resolution. That is what we set out to do, after all, but such reduction need not be an immediate result of mutual ongoing reconstructive work.

On the contrary, effective reconstruction requires a perceptual context congruent with that which formed the original pathogenic fantasy/memory complex, and that ongoing perceptual context is usually furnished by the transference. Whether or not that transference context is the explicit subject of discussion in the treatment at the moment—and there are times when concentration on the transference would cooperate with a resistance to remembering—in ongoing productive work on the past, transference will optimally remain active and relatively intense (though not necessarily always conscious).

In the case of Mr. M., growing positive transference feelings led him to perceive other patients as his sibling and to envy them. His resentment activated unconscious fantasies around his brother's death. Part of that network of fantasy was his conviction about his responsibility for his brother's death. He anticipated my punishment. The transference wish to be made to suffer functioned both as a way of preventing a worse, unanticipated punishment and as a way of atoning for his supposed deed. The transference thus duplicated in a highly condensed way the emotional conflicts that held sway around the birth and death of his baby brother and directed the flow of his associations. Thus, it paved the way for the reconstructive work that eventually also elucidated it.

The fact that the analyst makes a reconstruction will likely be perceived by the patient in accordance with his or her current transference fantasies. That perception also needs to be analyzed. In the course of reconstructive work, Mr. M. experienced the intervention in which I repeated the sequence of his associations, which were derivatives of his central childhood fantasy, and linked them to his subsequent self-criticism as an accusation of murder. His response was a transference enactment: verbal denial. It is, of course, technically important to take such a reaction up with the patient, all the more so because reconstructions of traumas often recreate the traumatic situation for the patient (Le Guen 1982). But the principle of paying attention to the patient's reaction to a reconstruction not only as content but as an action by the analyst extends beyond such obvious instances. It would be equally important to pay attention to a sudden access of conviction that what the analyst says is correct.

Explicit Reconstruction and the Analyst's Technical Stance

Greenacre (1975) advocated active cognition in regard to reconstruction. Noting the ineffectiveness of asking associations to screen memories, she instead advised listening to the associations that occurred around each mention of the screen memory, thinking of those patterns of juxtaposed configurations between sessions if necessary, and using those associations that occur around screen memories to reconstruct appropriately.

The rationale behind her technical point becomes clear if we consider that, besides its other functions, a screen memory is the product of a particular defensive operation. That function accounts for the observation that a screen memory will frequently reappear almost stereotypically when the original fantasy or memory threatens to emerge (Arlow 1990). Since the original defensive process by which the unpleasant memory and its attendant fantasies are screened frequently employs isolation and displacement, pointing out the associations contiguous to the screen memory counteracts the defensive process and allows the other, more expressive aspects of the screen memory to be more easily elaborated.

The dream within the dream may also represent a phenomenon in which a disturbing memory defended against by isolation and denial requires the analyst to synthesize the derivatives of the warded-off material and to present the patient with them, not merely to wait passively for a memory to emerge (Silber 1983). The dream within the dream is similar to certain screen memories, at least to the extent that it constitutes an attempt to deny an unpleasant past perception and to isolate it by formal means. What is absent in the dream within the dream is that part of the process of screen (and fetish) formation involving displacement from the traumatic perception. It may be that dream formation permits a less disguised representation of the warded-off material and that the two phenomena are on a continuum.

For Mr. M., interpretation of his specific fantasy led him to remember his deadly seeming play. Where such specific interpretation of the fantasy does not lead to recall, a reconstruction as specific as possible of the forgotten event may be required. Reconstruction under those circumstances is probably best effected when an intense transference dynamic identical to that represented by the screen memory toward past objects is active and the screen memory itself appears in the patient's associations in place of the forgotten event (Arlow 1990).

The elucidation of such a fantasy/memory complex as I have illustrated is not, of course, the end but the beginning of much important analytic work. The arduous task remains of tracing both the vicissitudes of this organization in the development of the patient, the antecedents that contributed to its acquiring such power, and its effects on subsequent conflicts and their resolutions.

Conclusion

Explicit reconstruction is a therapeutically useful clinical tool. It is most usefully conceived of as part of a larger psychoanalytic process and as a mutual activity of analyst and analysand. The mutual activity comprises an exploration of the original creation of central, organizing fantasy/memory complexes. These organizations originate in part in apparently arbitrary events linked by contiguity that are endowed with private meaning by the patient. Their rhetorical representative is metonymy.

The purpose of explicit reconstruction is not the isolated discovery of past events or even of these more complex organizations, but a specifying of the way these organizations have been fashioned by the patient, including, as far as possible, the specific materials he or she has used in their creation. Verbally specific reconstructions of past fantasies and/or events may be required, and need to be based on an understanding of the primary process mechanisms as they are manifested in the patient's associations. The reason for such specificity is that the way these pathogenic organizations have been constructed explains how they have acquired meaning for the patient in the past and how they continue to organize meaning in the present. Knowledge of the way the patient has constructed private meanings in the past allows the patient to free him- or herself from their tyranny.

2 Clinical Truth and Contemporary Relativism: Meaning and Narration in the Psychoanalytic Situation

Postmodern thought has had a major, if often indirect effect on contemporary psychoanalysis. It has given impetus and intellectual ballast to a deidealization of authority by challenging absolutist ideas that psychoanalytic theory is uncontaminated by the observer's assumptions, that phallocentric formulations are necessarily primary, and that interpretation itself consists in the imparting of an objective truth to a patient (Chasseguet-Smirgel 1964, Renik 1993, Schafer 1980). The new thinking challenged concepts of hierarchy (Culler 1982). Rejecting the traditional hierarchical categorization of "literature" as separate from expository writing, it fostered literary readings of Freud (Culler 1975, 1981). The literary commentaries on the rhetorical composition, narratology, and philosophical underpinnings of Freud's texts provided a more direct connection for analysts between familiar theory and philosophical ideas that might otherwise have seemed remote and abstract; brought to light heretofore unrecognized prejudices and assumptions whose revelation had a demystifying effect (Brooks 1979, Hartmann 1978, Kofman 1980); and offered nonpsychoanalytic literary tools that could be brought to bear on psychoanalytic thinking (Schafer 1980, Spence 1982).

Perhaps because theory can be treated as a text much more easily and with far fewer direct consequences than a person can be, little consideration has been given to a careful assessment of the *clinical* effect of the importation of many of these ideas. Yet generative ideas inevitably change the observer's perspective, and a new perspective inevitably changes the categories used to organize perceptions. If our perception of a clinical interaction is altered by the introduction of a new but nonclinical viewpoint, it is possible to lose sight of the fact that the new perspective, while intellectually arresting, will also change the configuration of categories the distinctions among which are either useful or requisite as regards clinical work. Indeed, it is my impression that many of these imported ideas have been selectively applied to specific clinical concepts lifted out of their individual contexts, be they theoretical or clinical.

In what follows I discuss some of the implications of two concepts imported in different ways from contemporary literary theory into psychoanalysis. The first concept is that of narrative. Applied to clinical reconstruction, it has led to the idea that reconstruction of the patient's past can be only a narrative creation of the here-and-now interrelation of analyst and patient. The second is the idea that meaning is absolutely relative. Applied to the clinical situation, it has led to a questioning of interpretation as a technical tool.

If the concepts of narrative and relative meaning are to be useful in clinical psychoanalysis, certain categories—and therefore certain hierarchical distinctions that these concepts tend to blur— need to be clearly maintained. *The first of these distinctions is between an event and the narrative through which the event is recounted.* By definition, an event, which in psychoanalytic thinking would include the making of a fantasy, must occur before it is narrated. If it seems self-evident that an event exists independently of a subject's account of it, or of the analyst's exact knowledge of it, analysts nonetheless are uneasy according reality its necessary place in clinical practice. As Loewald (1949) acutely noted, reality appears in psychoanalytic theory as "an outside force . . . most typically . . . represented by the paternal figure" (p. 8) who interferes with the child's obtaining gratification from the mother. That is, the idea carries with it the connotation of arbitrary authority and unpleaure.

Moreover, the idea of reality imports with it a hierarchy of perceiving. Someone may be more right than wrong or more wrong than right about an event, and the contemporary thinking that seeks to level distinctions and abolish hierarchies dislikes the potential for authority that this implies. Yet, whether we acknowledge it or not, hierarchy is inherent in the psychoanalytic situation (Hoffer 1993). Patients, after all, come to us because we have a specialized way of perceiving. I suggest that it is not hierarchy or authority that is the problem, but the meaning we attribute to them.

The second distinction is that between fixed unconscious meanings that govern perception and the more flexible attribution of meaning that the former impede. This distinction too implies hierarchies of meaning. I do not invoke these hierarchies to engage in what I believe is a barren dispute between so-called one- and two-person psychologies. Hierarchies of meaning are intrinsic to all communication. Indeed, the position I shall later refer to as advocating the absolute relativity of meaning ironically exemplifies, in its frank assertion of authority, this necessary hierarchy. The categories maintained by the two sets of distinctions I have drawn make possible what I believe are the clinically necessary techniques of reconstruction and interpretation.[1]

---

1. Although the points I try to make about the arbitrary application of contemporary ideas apply to clinical concepts that grow out of any psychoanalytic theory, I confine my discussion to contemporary Freudian theory in order to stay within the paradigm with which I am most clinically familiar. For simplicity's sake, all references in what follows to psychoanalysis or to clinical work, unless otherwise specified, are to Freudian psychoanalysis.

The Clinical Perspective

Clinical practice depends on a perspective that permits certain discriminations. From a literary theoretical point of view it may be logical to conceive of the analyst's interpretation uniquely as rhetorical strategy. Spence (1982), for example, sees analysts functioning "as artists and storytellers in the analytic hour"; it is in their "interest to build a seamless web of belief ... in which all findings can be captured" (p. 23).[2] If, however, the analyst's interpretations are conceived *only* as rhetorically strategic, then interpretation in the clinical setting is reduced to the analyst's imposition of his subjective view on the patient. Although such a viewpoint is useful in exploring one aspect of the here-and-now interaction, it is easy to see that the flexibility to investigate other possible motives, less easily discernible, is eliminated.

When instead we discriminate among motives for interpretation in clinical work, it is possible to consider whether a distrustful attitude toward interpretation might be the result of patient or analyst having become caught up in sadomasochistic fantasies of treatment. Thus, we can say that, beyond the general intellectual category that sees interpretation as a part of rhetorical strategy, a clinical perspective differentiates between interpretation as a potentially nonauthoritarian analytic instrument, in *principle*, and specific *circumstances* such as a countertransference dilemma, through which interpretation becomes in fact enmeshed in a sadomasochistic interchange with the patient. Clinical truth—that is, an insight that is also already a measure of change—may emerge out of the discrimination between circumstance and principle (Reed 1994, p. 197).

---

2. That he exempts his own theoretical statement from the category to which he assigns clinical interpretation is another example of implicit hierarchy.

Clinical work requires a frame of reference strong enough and flexible enough to contain in identifiable form the kind of differentiation I have just illustrated. Consistency in point of view establishes the frame and the rules for making discriminations within it. Point of view is established by consistent use of a theory to identify and organize data, though, it is important to emphasize, such consistency does not preclude modification of the theory with the accumulation of data. Clinical insight is not the objective property of the analyst. Such an assertion would take us back into sadomasochistic fantasy. Nor, for the same reason, is it the subjective property of the patient. Rather, it is continuously modifiable through the understanding of the subjective by relatively more objective capacities in each party to the dyad.

Work toward clinical insight consists largely of differentiating circumstances from principles in the way I have illustrated above. There is a principle underlying the idea that the analyst's intervention is potentially helpful to the patient. The analyst's understanding of the patient, which is imparted to the patient, is assumed to convey or move toward a truth about the workings of the patient's mind that will allow the analysand a new perspective on him- or herself.[3] Various circumstances, such as transference fantasies in the patient or countertansference conflicts in the analyst, interfere with the patient's ability to hear the intervention and the analyst's ability to carry out this principle. Thus, differentiating that principle from circumstances that interfere with it is an important part of the clinical work for both analyst and analysand.

---

3. An interpretation can be stated directly, as in "you believe that . . . ," or indirectly. The indirect form includes more tentatively worded observations or various series of interventions that group certain associations or phenomena together for the patient's consideration. We err, I think, when we confuse the manifest form in which the analyst intervenes with the unconscious message conveyed to the patient.

Reconstruction as Narrative

Narrative has been analyzed in contemporary literary theory in conjunction with diverse authorial strategies through which written texts, especially fictional ones, create meaning for a reader. Narratives are seen as composed of interchangeable and transformable units analogous to parts of speech that combine according to specific "grammatical" rules (Propp 1928, Todorov 1971). They are understood as a form of discourse consisting of a history, or sequence of events, and the narrative in which the events are organized and recounted (Culler 1981). The events of the history are arranged in a particular sequence and told to an audience by a character or impersonal "voice," however effaced, which observes events from a particular focal perspective (Genette 1972). This perspective may be variously omniscient or limited. A narrative thus requires the assumption of events prior to its recounting and combines the formal elements of presentation—the words and situation of the narrator—and representation—the events the narrator designates and arranges (Scholes 1982). Narrative always implies a differentiation in fictional space and/or time between the narrator (or point of view of the narration) and the events narrated. In addition to the internal differentiation, narrative impels a similar activity in the reader. It forces "the interpreter to make a distinction between his own immediate situation and some other situation that is being presented" (Scholes 1982, p. 57).

When Schafer (1980) introduced ideas of narration into psychoanalytic discourse, it was without such minute attention to form and with the intention of continuing his attempt to find a language less abstract than that of metapsychology to describe what people do. He was not contending that the analyst's distinctions about what may or may not have happened were unnecessary for the nitty-gritty of clinical work. For him, narration is "not an alternative to truth" (1992, p. xiv). Nevertheless, his statement, "each account of the past is a reconstruction that is controlled by a narrative strategy" (Schafer 1982, p. 77), blends into contemporary formulations that undermine the analyst's authority to reconstruct.[4] For example, Viderman (1970, 1977), like Schafer a serious Freudian who also makes exemplary *clinical* use of interpretation and reconstruction, describes the analyst's reconstruction as an entirely new creation. Most radically, Spence (1982, p. 165) argues that the only truth relevant in the analytic situation is a narrative truth concerned with "finding a verbal expression for the anomalous event" and "finding a narrative home for the verbal expression." For him, there are only esthetic constructions, never reconstructions.

These formulations about narrative in the psychoanalytic situation emphasize the commonalities among the patient's recounting activities, the analyst's construction of the here-and-now transference, and the analyst's reconstruction of the infantile past. At the same time, they de-emphasize crucial differences between the analyst's and the patient's motivation. A patient's motivations for shaping the accounts of his past have to do mainly with unconscious conflicts and the need to defend against affects connected to unacceptable unconscious wishes. But when these writers discuss the analyst's motivations for *his* narrative strategies, they emphasize *conscious* desires that a reconstruction make coherent the clinical data the patient offers. According to Spence (1982, p. 25), the analyst, "probably listening with a bias toward coherence and continuity," hears "a finished narrative." Applied unspecifically and globally to all clinical events, such a formulation fosters a view of the analyst as manipulator striving to create a coherent construction that will move the patient by its esthetic coherence and creativity and leads easily to neglect of the independent existence of the patient's unconscious motivations.

Although the intention in minimizing differences in patient's and analyst's narratives is to show patient and analyst as laboring under similar difficulties, and thus to abolish the hierarchy that holds the analyst's narrative as authoritative, the distinction that

---

4. Mitchell (1993, p. 74), for instance, believes that Schafer's view is more radical than Schafer contends.

emerges is hierarchical in a different way. As Schafer expresses it, "reconstruction of the infantile past is a temporally displaced and artificially linearized account of the analysis in the here-and-now" (Schafer 1982, p. 81). The contrast of a rhetorically tainted, linearized *account* of the past with the *experience* of the transference here-and-now elevates present, as yet unverbalized experience to a privileged place. Viderman (1977) also implicitly elevates present experience over a hypothesized past, though for him it is through reconstruction that present experience is created: "To say that the sniffing of the adult Freud has on his couch *is* the transformation, twenty-five years later, of panting in the primal scene is literally to *create*, by the word that speaks the interpretation, an entirely new and radically heterogeneous reality from that which is historically designated" (p. 18; my translation). The difficulty resides not with the idea that new meanings are created in the analytic present, but with the elevation of the present creation above the historical creation of personal meaning from which present meaning arises. This elevation of meanings created in the present separates the newly created meaning from and elevates them above those meanings created in the past.

This timeless present has primacy over necessarily inexact attempts to discriminate among and describe its constituents: Viderman goes on to argue that Freud's reconstruction limits a multiplicity of virtual meanings contained in the symptom, and Schafer writes that the "then-and-there constructions of the vicissitudes of early development remain part of the here-and-now of the analytic narrative enterprise" (Schafer 1982, pp. 80–81).

The advantage of the unintended hierarchy in which timeless, non-narrative present experience is given ascendancy over a past considered as exclusively narrative is that it places what is non-narrative *beyond the verbalized and beyond chronological time*, thus beyond the possibility of articulation in the clinical setting. Instead it locates all that is clinical within narrative strategy and contrasts it with an unattainable, "untainted" alternative. In effect, a reality that is difficult to know exactly or to describe, or that exists in different, not entirely coincident versions, is treated as if it did not exist. This elevation of present experience over verbalized insight or, in the case of Viderman, of meaning created in the present over the possibility of verbalizing meaning created in the past is most common in those today who see the therapeutic function of relation as separate from and superior to interpretation (Mitchell 1993).

To be sure, the statement, "each account of the past is a reconstruction that is controlled by a narrative strategy," is unobjectionable in and of itself. It observes clinical occurrence from a vantage point outside of the clinical, that of literary theory, and applies that discipline's definition of narrative: an account of anything by a speaker to a listener about events within the speaker's experience must by definition be a narrative and is therefore controlled by a shaping strategy that includes differentiation in time and/or space between the presenter and that which is represented. It follows that any reconstruction of an aspect of the patient's past that emerges out of a transference present is a "temporally displaced and artificially linearized account of the analysis in the here-and-now" (Schafer 1982, p. 81). That is precisely how a narrative of the events that furnish the reasons for the patient's current behavior would be described by the literary theory of narrative summarized above. In fact, any interpretation by the analyst of a patient's motivation, including one restricted to the here-and-now transference, is a narrative,[5] thus a "temporally displaced and artificially linearized account of the analysis in the here-and-now" because the here-and-now is past by the time it is discussed. Consider, for example, a recent clinical intervention of my own: "When I pointed out to you that there was more to explore in what you said, I got the impression that you experienced me as making a demand of you. At that moment what you probably wanted from

---

5. Schafer applies the concept of narrative to any number of clinical categories, from resistance to character, as well as to the theory that establishes clinical categories itself.

me was not a demand but praise for the work you had already done. Since I didn't give you that praise you became angry with me." The analyst/narrator represents to the analysand/audience events that occurred between them in the past and imposes a sequence on those events as a way of clarifying the reasons for the patient's current angry state. That is a description of the intervention from the point of view of literary theory.

To actually *do* the analysis, however, all of us practicing Freudian psychoanalysis adopt a dynamic clinical point of view rather than an essentially descriptive literary theoretical one. Thus, in describing the successful analysis of a male patient, Schafer (1982) made clinical distinctions between (a) the fantasies the patient arrived at in the past and (b) the present situation to which he unconsciously ascribed them.

This shift to the clinical point of view obliges the analyst to perceive the relation between past and present differently from its description, ex post facto, from a literary theoretical point of view. From a literary perspective all accounts are timeless narrative creations, and no one account has precedence over another. From a dynamic, clinical perspective, however, we see a person living out in the present some interpretation arrived at in the past. If it were otherwise, there would be no here-and-now transference, since transference means a carrying across from past to present, from primary object to analyst, and therefore no reason to reconstruct motivations in the past for present experience and perception.

From a clinical perspective, then, it makes sense to confine what we identify as narrative to those perceptions governed by unconscious fantasy/memory complexes, rather than to apply the idea of narrative as broadly as it is applied in literary theory. If we then designate a "temporally displaced, artificially linear" construction of a time period, *that time period will refer to the present as it is shaped and brought to life by an unconscious fantasy constructed in the past.* We thus understand the (narrative) present in which the patient lives to be organized by a signifying fantasy/memory complex, formulated in the past and ever alive in the patient's understanding. In the case Schafer reported, the signifying structure was a fantasy/memory complex in which the patient believed that his mother would kill him if he revealed his talents and abilities by displaying his accomplishments. In this framework, the analyst helps his analysand by helping him perceive the existence of the account as separate from the present, to understand the conditions under which this account was constructed, and to grasp the reasons for its construction (to the extent to which they can be established), thereby changing the patient's present experience. By so doing, the analyst helps the analysand separate this account from the narrative present in which the analysand locates himself. Since the therapeutic process depends on the disengagement, from the present the patient constructs, of a way of perceiving imported from the past, the explicitness of the delineation of the imported signifying structure is not a matter of indifference (see Chapter 1).

Both literary theory and clinical psychoanalysis confront a similar problem about the past. In order to function therapeutically, the analyst must understand his patient as *suffering from an artificially constructed account of the present*, the cause of which is the way that present is influenced by unconscious signifying structures, or fantasy/memory complexes, organized in childhood. Even if one focuses on fantasy, the events that are both its context and its stimulus accompany and often precede it. That is, the priority of the event, including the event of making a fantasy, must be assumed. Similarly, the literary analyst must also assume the priority of a *history* to its narration. Even when entering the fictional world and exploring the narrative strategy of a protagonist-narrator, the literary critic assumes a fictional series of events anterior in fictional time to their narration. As Culler (1981) points out, "Narratological analysis of a text requires one to treat the discourse as a representation of events which are conceived of as independent of any particular narrative perspective or presentation and which are thought of as having the properties of real events" (p. 171).

In both cases, this assumption of a specific, sequential past that must be approximated is conceived not as a rhetorical strategy but *as a requirement for analytic work within the discipline.* That is, a crucial distinction of *principle* between analytic work and rhetorical strategy is necessary for insight into the form of the narrative to take place. The work of literary analysis, insofar as it involves the study of rhetorical strategy, requires the separating out of the prior history so that the nature and sequence of its events can be compared to their rhetorical arrangement. In clinical analysis we make a similar distinction de facto every time we interpret underlying wishes and defenses or reconstruct events that have led to the creation of unconscious fantasies. We assign to the category of narrative the analysand's experience (and therefore unconsciously motivated construction) of the here-and-now, as that experience is presented, particularly, but not only, through free association. We understand analytic work, the province of both the analyst and the analysand, to be constituted by the separating out of prior signifying events—both those of the transference and those of the childhood past—and the identification of the form that constitutes their silent but powerful present influence. To establish the latter requires that the reasons for the specific construction of the here-and-now by the individual analysand be uncovered and verbalized. From the viewpoint of the internal workings of the specific clinical discipline, as opposed to general questions of philosophical interest, that analytic thinking, which, among other things, identifies prior event, needs to be established as a category separate from narrative.

Meaning as Absolutely Relative

Spence's emphasis (1982) on a truth that is entirely narrative and exists in the present moment without reference to the past depends on a general philosophical position that meaning is relative. Viderman (1977) makes the point more directly: the analyst creates meaning through the words of the interpretation. The work of the late Paul de Man (1969) furnishes the intellectual basis for this assumption. De Man's argument is highly important to questions about authority and interpretation in psychoanalysis because it connects the idea of fixed meaning with authoritarianism and relative meaning to a lack of that hierarchy in which authoritarianism is always implicit.

His argument begins with a reconsideration of allegory. In its familiar medieval and Renaissance form, allegory was an indirect narrative that functioned to illustrate abstract qualities such as grace, greed, and charity. The allegorical narrative depended on communally shared conscious referents considered to be matters of divine revelation. That is, allegorical narrative depended on a hierarchy of meaning. In that hierarchy, divine meaning is always the ultimate referent. De Man's new concept of allegory, by contrast, depends on the absence of a hierarchy anchored by the Word that embodies Divine Truth. What replaces the Word as the carrier of fixed meaning is what is known as the *infinite displaceability of the referent*: there is always another meaning (the signified) to be ascribed to a word, concept, feeling, action, or definition (the signifier) and yet another one after that.

To simplify, in the statement "I am in love with John," the signifier *John* refers to an earlier boyfriend, to a brother, to an uncle, to a father, to a mother, to a part of a mother, to anything that would satisfy the speaker's wish to "love," without any one meaning being assumed to be more basic or powerful or more valuable than any other. The signifier *love* would equally refer to possession, to sensual pleasure of various kinds, and to an infinity of substitute meanings. This infinite displaceability of referent creates a perpetual movement. De Man contended that its reality contradicted the illusion of eternal oneness, presence, and temporal transcendence afforded by belief in a hierarchically superior divine meaning that was fixed. In that hierarchical meaning, the signifier *John* would inevitably refer to God, but it is easy to recognize other, more contemporary versions of transcendent meaning such as Scientific Observation or Experimental Proof.

De Man made his argument about the ubiquity and necessity of this formal and unanchored linguistic allegory in a particular literary context: it had become a truism of romantic criticism to consider allegory a lower form of rhetoric while valorizing the way romantic poets were thought to use the symbol. The symbol was elevated because it was thought that through it the romantics had regained that divine authority of meaning lost to the secularization of the eighteenth and nineteenth century. The symbol was understood as simultaneous experience and representation— atemporal, immanent, and eternal, a sort of oceanic communion with an external object that both encompassed and transcended the subject.[6] The symbol, fusing nature with man's experience of nature, was held to replace the dualism between divine truth and human sensibility. Although the romantics' symbolic use of nature apparently resolved the contradiction inherent in the fact that the romantic poets acknowledged no higher authority yet spoke of the transcendence of the self through the depiction of the landscape, de Man argued that this apparent resolution was illusory and showed that the romantic symbol inevitably had external referents. Further, he contended that the romantic poets at their "most authentic" were aware of this "hard won" truth, and aware as well that man could not use the symbol to escape his temporal existence.

Thus, relative meaning, for de Man, fills the void created by God's no longer being the final authority. The inevitable consequence of the absence of Divine Truth is that since there is no eternity, there is no *final* referent. External referents themselves have other referents. In other words, the price of recognition of the limits on transcendence was recognition of the limitlessness

---

6. The parallel to the timeless, here-and-now transference experience opposed to narrative account discussed earlier is striking.

of referents in time. For de Man, the external referent was infinitely displaceable, never fixed, and allegory consisted in the referential displacement itself. It is this reconfigured concept of allegory, generalized to all verbal communication, that makes meaning absolutely relative.

But clinical work in psychoanalysis is not predicated on the absolutism of relative meaning; it is predicated on the very hierarchy of meanings that the assertion of absolutely relative meaning exemplifies. That is, it is predicated on the assumption that there is something, or many things, the analysand does not know consciously about himself that is more powerfully affecting his perceptions, actions, and present experience than what he consciously knows. The existence of a hierarchy of meaning implies neither an absolute referent nor the analyst's unfettered access to it. The further assumption is, rather, that the analyst, by virtue of his ability to observe in particular ways, can help the patient discover unknown but influential meanings. The analyst's observations and interventions, however subjective, thus carry affective import and significance.

To illustrate the shift in frame necessary to move from general intellectual play with ideas to clinical work, I shall shift perspectives on de Man's academic writings, with their heady insistence on the absolute relativity of meaning, by juxtaposing them with de Man's activities as a Nazi collaborator in Belgium (Lehman 1992a). During the war, de Man was the literary critic for the collaborationist newspaper *LeSoir*. At least some of his articles there followed the Nazi line, endorsing the concept of a French literary canon purified of Jewish contributions, most notably of Proust, and invoking the Final Solution as the vehicle of purification (de Man 1988). De Man was silent about these articles for the rest of his life, even though his critical and philosophical stance during his brilliant postwar academic career in the United States was founded on facing negative self-knowledge and identifying the authentic voice that does so.

Once we juxtapose his academic and Nazi writings, our focus

shifts to an awareness of contradictions: Nazi propagandist vs. academic spokesman for the relativity of meaning, advocate of the authentic voice that faces negative self-knowledge vs. concealer of shameful secrets about himself. The moment we notice these contradictions, our focus shifts also to de Man, the man, like all men seen from a psychoanalytic clinical perspective, driven by unconscious motives that we assume governed his anti-Semitic as well as his intellectual writings. That is, we change the context of our observation and in doing so change the hierarchy of meanings we assume.

We might frame the problem by supposing that de Man's collaboration, an historical fact, can reasonably be described as a submission to higher and stronger authority,[7] personified by Hitler, that ends with the writer becoming his mouthpiece. Whatever de Man's youthful, predominantly conscious motives may have been, ambition, fear, deformed idealism (none of these, of course, mutually exclusive), we assume that some unconscious affective situation motivated his conscious action. His subsequent argument in favor of the absolute relativism of meaning may have been an attempt to render his actions meaningless.[8]

De Man's historical action may nevertheless be seen as contradicting his concept of the infinite displaceability of referents. The moment of action by opportune submission testifies to the subject's recognition in his particular affective state of an absolute authority, with a Final Solution, the power of life and death

---

7. De Man had an uncle with whom he was exceptionally close, Hendrik (Henri) de Man, a well-known leftist intellectual who became a collaborator and had powerful political connections. Hendrik de Man was, for a time, an official of the Nazi government in Belgium. It is possible that he obtained the influential literary post on the newspaper for his nephew (Stephen Koch, personal communication; see also Atlas 1988).

8. If this is so, the actions were not limited to his journalism. For a report on de Man's bigamy and unscrupulous handling of debts, see Lehman (1992b).

over him. From a clinical perspective, at the moment of an action like de Man's Nazi collaboration, there is indeed, in the subject's mind, one final referent, an absolute authority, however much the academic, in his intellectual detachment, may see infinite possibilities, however much the amoralist, in his conscious rationalizations, has convinced himself that action has no one meaning and that moral judgment is meaningless. In just the same way, unconscious conflict fixes meaning; it impedes the movement of displaceability of referents; it imprisons its subject in automatic response. That automatic response can, as seems likely in de Man's case, lead to the perception of danger from a new absolute authority and to the keeping secret of previous action.

The meaning we seek out in the clinical situation is that which unconsciously motivates such contradictory actions on an individual's part. It arises out of moments of *materially real anxiety* (the stimulus for which is exemplified by the Nazi threat—exemplified in that a corresponding inner scenario already exists or the threat would not be recognized) in interaction with idiosyncratic (e.g., drive- and defense-motivated) ideational content. I use the term *materially real anxiety* because the anxiety itself is body-based, and I want to stress the contribution of gut-level response. The anxiety arises in concert with psychic reality, a previously elaborated fantasy, a specific danger situation. The anxiety thus responds to a meaning that the individual automatically attributes to his circumstances. That automatic response prevents the effective functioning of higher capacities and inhibits freedom of choice.

Rather than being part of an infinite chain of referents, meaning in the affectively bound clinical instant represents a break in that chain. It is fixed, automatic, out of the patient's conscious control. It is that meaning that analysts seek to construct and then deconstruct by their interventions, interpretations, and reconstructions. The goal of psychoanalytic work might accordingly be seen as attempting to reduce fixity of meaning and to restore, in situations in which it was not possible for the patient to do so, the analysand's capacity for choosing among multiple meanings.

Clinical Example

I have suggested that two distinctions be clearly maintained for the sake of clinical efficacy: first, that a prior event be distinguished from the various narratives in which it might be presented: second, that meaning automatically attributed in the clinical moment be seen as a category distinct from a general idea about meaning being absolutely relative. I wish to illustrate the usefulness of such categories with an excerpt from a case in which a patient repetitively and automatically attributed unconscious fantasies he had originally attributed to a childhood event to any unpleasant external perception, particularly one he interpreted as a slight. Thus, he looked away and refused to see anything that stimulated an unpleasurable and anxious feeling. The looking away was not only defensive but also expressed the intensely sadistic and vengeful impulses that were partly the patient's reaction to the perception. Disavowal was so prominent that it called in question, though subtly, the minimal collaboration one might assume to be analytically necessary. I made the technical choice to work first on the patient's anxiety about looking. When the opportunity presented itself, I reconstructed what I deemed to be the prior event at the center of the signifying structure. Space will not allow me to describe in detail the work on the sadistic components that both preceded and followed the reconstruction.

Dr. P., a 35-year-old playboy, was blond, good-looking, European, and the youngest of five children. He could not say why he wanted an analysis beyond it being the thing to do in his circle. He did not consciously seek out my help for his potency problems. Instead he ascribed his repeated, sudden loss of sexual interest to "falling out of love," every man's fate. He did not connect this event to his women friends' leaving their previous relationship for him, nor did he recognize any callousness in his sudden and complete loss of interest once he had them to himself. Neither did he consult me about his lack of interest in his profession. Indeed, he regarded his work as an unfortunate interference with his inalienable right to the pursuit of pleasure and did as little as possible. He certainly had not consulted me about the loneliness, dearth of close relationships, or the lovelessness beneath the surface of his cosmopolitan, socially exemplary life. He did not consult about those things because Dr. P. could not look closely at anything that disturbed his positive sense of himself. In fact, he could not look at anything disturbing. If he were made anxious, he immediately turned his attention to something else. An electrical engineer accustomed to confronting sophisticated mathematical problems, he went months without opening his credit card statement.

From the beginning of the analysis, he had fantasies of me as a monster of the deep lurking in wait to bite off one of his limbs. Simultaneously he insisted that he did not care what I did or said. When I pointed out that he was afraid of me, Dr. P. imagined cut-up sausages in tomato sauce, thought of cartoons in which cannibals were about to immerse a luckless explorer in a big pot already on the fire, thought of a childhood fear that a lioness would attack him in a narrow alley, remembered one of his older brothers' friends telling him that male dogs' penises got irretrievably stuck inside the female during intercourse, remembered incidents as a child when his mother had threatened him, and referred to me as turning the heat up. It became clear to both of us that he unconsciously equated me with a vagina dentata and that this transference referred to fantasies he had about his mother. By not looking at me, he protected himself from unbearable anxiety that came from knowledge of the danger that awaited him. Looking at me extended to paying attention to my interventions about his terror and the insights about it that we arrived at together, so he would look away by forgetting what we discovered. The mechanism of looking away extended to all genuine feeling for another human being in whose presence he found himself and was one component in his relating to people in a way that continually disregarded the other's existence.

When I pointed out to him that one condition necessary for his sexual excitement was not to look at a woman's vagina, he disagreed: just the night before, he had rented an explicitly porno-graphic video and was looking at women's genitals with pleasure. When I asked him what he saw, he replied that he couldn't see the details of the woman's vagina because it was completely out of focus, though the rest of the picture was quite clear.

The presence of a male rival was another, related condition for his excitement. Although he lost interest in having sex the mo-ment he no longer had a rival, he did not recognize for a long time that when he had intercourse he was murdering in vengeance. Indeed, sadistic and vengeful impulses pervaded this material and were an important component in his immediately disregarding the insights we arrived at together. In the session following the first summer break of the treatment, he reported a dream in which he saw a stream of water dousing two reeds in front of him. A lighted cigarette lay on the ground. He associated the setting of the dream to a "burning" desert and camels to the cigarette. His associations were dominated by negations ("This has nothing to do with you and your summer vacation") and with looking distractedly to something else ("Which has two humps, a dromedary or a camel? I can't remember").

Rather than looking at his anxiety about me, or his passionate attachment to me, or his rage at me, or his feelings of insignificance in relation to the men he imagined in my life, he took refuge in an unacknowledged belief that he always had my attention and admi-ration. Any change in the analytic frame that drew his attention to the professional nature of our relationship disrupted that belief, was intensely upsetting to him, and called forth vengeful retaliation.

Condensed with this maternal transference was a less immedi-ately visible paternal one. He had a covertly contemptuous attitude toward anyone more successful than he, or anyone with authority over him. He delighted in subtly undermining his boss and fre-quently made condescending remarks about people who worked long hours at a job and then worked at home as well. Although he knew that I saw patients from early in the morning to well into the evening, he denied that his comments referred to me or that he had any knowledge of my long days in the office. A dream of my holding a frighteningly large reptile brought associations to his fear of his father.

Early in the analysis, Dr. P. had described a childhood memory that I provisionally understood as a screen memory. The memory was puzzling to him because he could not understand why his father and not one of the family's servants was involved in the job that was the central action of the memory. In the memory, Dr. P. was watching while his mother helped his father attempt to replace a wire in a lamp that had shorted out after an extension cord had malfunctioned. His father, unaccustomed to working with electric wires, was having trouble doing the repair. Dr. P. was experienced in this kind of task. He knew exactly what to do and how to do it because he was secretly using electric wires to do scientific experiments involving electrical charges. Indeed, the original accident had occurred because he had borrowed the extension cord for such an experiment and the insulation had been damaged in consequence. In this memory, despite his informed suggestions about what had to be done to repair the lamp cord, his mother ignored him and concentrated on his father's apparently futile efforts. He felt humiliated and enraged.

At a time in the analysis when Dr. P. already realized intermittently and in a general way that his play with electricity was motivated by anger at his father for being the successful competitor for his mother, and that his failure to notice and bring to his parents' attention the damaged insulation might have been unconsciously connected to his wish to burn them both up, I informed him that I would need permanently to delay the starting time of one of his five weekly hours. He was furious at me for making him wait and felt slighted by my not putting his needs first. He accused me of telling him on a Friday in order to "insulate" myself from his anger. The following Monday he reported having had sex over the weekend with his current woman friend, the first time in more than six months he had done so. In the ensuing work, I told him that I understood him to be reacting to my changing his

time with pain and rage because his belief that I had eyes only for
him had suddenly collapsed and that he wanted to get back at me
by making me jealous. "If that's the case, I'm surprised that you
didn't check the insulation on your extension cords before telling me about this change," he said. When he referred to the insulation and with it to the childhood memory, I linked the transference rage and wish to take vengeance on me with the dynamic
situation he had described in the screen memory, in which he felt
like taking murderous vengeance on his mother for preferring his
father and refusing to recognize her son's superior knowledge.

The transference feelings of betrayal and humiliation persisted,
as did the resultant wishes to kill me. Neither my clarification of
the dynamic situation in the transference nor my linking of the
present situation with the past *as remembered in the screen memory*
changed his perception that his hurt and humiliation were uniquely
a product of my callous inattention to his needs and that he was
justified in his wishes for vengeance. References to his wishes to
hurt me continued to be prominent in his associations. At the same
time, primal scene derivatives also appeared. He mentioned a love
scene in a movie.

A new reference to the lamp memory appeared ten days later
in the same transference context. The association came up in conjunction with Dr. P.'s not wanting to look at evidence that his
woman friend might be about to leave him for another man. This
time I said to him, "The idea makes you feel like a little boy with
too small a penis to be paid attention to. You also feel that way
here about the time change I made, and you felt that way when
you saw your mother helping your father rewire the lamp. That's
how you remember a time when you saw your parents making
love." Dr. P. responded, "I just had a reaction without feeling
much. I find myself saying to you, 'I hate you! I hate you! I hate
you! I hate you!' I said it a number of times, as if chanting your
words away." To this repetition of the genetic defense against the
primal scene observation in the transference, so prominent in his

character, I pointed out that he always tried not to look at disturbing events. Seeing his parents having sex was terribly disturbing to him, and now he was trying not to hear about it as well as not to look.

He began to report "instances of memory recall. They don't come as thoughts, they just intrude": details from the basement storeroom in which he did his experiments; an incident in latency when he became convinced that his parents had a sexual relationship; his mother on the edge of a high sea cliff near the family's summer home in Northern Spain ("It would frighten me that she'd stand there in the wind: she might be blown off"); and a fight with his woman friend ("I became so angry I threw a lamp at the wall and smashed it. . . . I'm thinking for the first time this is connected to something always starting to go wrong in my relations with women. I'm jumping back to the scene of the lamp repair. I feel excluded, angry at my father, angry at my mother's deference to him. The phone rang at three in the morning. My first thought was that it was my mother calling from Europe to tell me my father had had a heart attack. Now I'm feeling the way I felt Monday here, angry at you. I'm thinking of being on the veranda outside our villa and of looking through the double doors that led into my parents' bedroom"). He next thought of a time on a walk home from school for lunch when one of his schoolmates told him about sex. He never believed that this information applied to his parents. Then he remembered his feeling of betrayal much later, when evidence of his mother's sexual relationship with his father had become undeniable to him. "I suddenly realized there were five of us and we looked like both of them! *Carrai!* Such a terrible feeling!" He went on to remember many humiliating instances of being excluded by his teenaged siblings for being too little, and of instances of being disregarded by girls he was attracted to for being too young. He thought of birds of prey attacking smaller birds with their beaks and returned to feeling vengeful toward me and toward his girlfriend. "I feel like taking retribution by leaving." Then a pause: "I was just lost in feeling. Mother. The lamp cord. The purpose of denying the real. I was the better choice!"

Although my reconstruction was partial, it allowed the analysis to progress. Subsequent work could then address the sadistic, vengeful, and murderous wishes so prominent in Dr. P.'s attempt to chant me away with his hate mantra, in his remembered worry that his mother would be blown off the cliff, and in his belief that the telephone heralded his father's heart attack.

Of course, no clinical illustration can disprove Spence's contention that a reconstruction is only an aesthetic creation in the analytic moment, but my purpose in offering one is more limited: to illustrate that *in doing actual clinical work it is extremely helpful for the analyst to keep categories of event prior to narration and of a controlling unconscious meaning in mind, whatever ontological status he later wishes to attribute to his reconstrution.* My own understanding of what I did, in reconstructing, is that I presented to Dr. P. a shocking realization that during his childhood had crystallized previously existing sadistic wishes in him. He had used these wishes to construct out of the primal scene an unconscious fantasy of destructive violence, betrayal, humiliation, and vengeance. Whether the scene was actually seen, was heard, or was vividly imagined was less important than that his parents' sexual life was a reality that he had not believed and then in some devastating way had been confronted with.

The intervention had a significant impact on the course of treatment. It described and located in the past something that was for him an indiscriminate part of present experience. Reminded through the treatment of something he had been continuously and unsuccessfully trying to forget, Dr. P. gained perspective on his way of perceiving in the present. He became able to look at his relation to women as a problem that was his, not theirs, and could begin to understand how vengeful he was. He began to see how his wishes for vengeance related not only to his sexual inhibitions and to the hurt he had felt about my changing the time of his appointment, but to the terrible blow he had received when he realized he was not the most important person in his mother's life.[9]

By making a narrative of violence, betrayal, and humiliation out of his sudden knowledge of the primal scene between his parents, Dr. P. had created a signifying structure in his mind. The license he believed he had to behave with impunity in romantic liaisons, his inability to look at unpleasant reality, his severe castration anxiety, his sexual inhibitions, the profound sense of inadequacy beneath his desperate attempts to be admired, his need to behave as though others to whom he felt close did not exist—all drew their meaning from that controlling signifying structure, or unconscious fantasy/ memory complex. His paralyzing inability to look at anything that disturbed him also prevented him from becoming aware of what he wanted or needed to work on in the analysis. When some of the meanings he attributed to his shocking realization were put into words, it was possible for him to catch a glimpse of important aspects of the signifying structure motivating his perception.

Distinguishing an event from narratives about it and maintaining a category of unconscious meaning that is more powerful than other possible meanings make possible certain kinds of clinical work that are otherwise not possible. By establishing the possibilities of an event prior to narrative and the meaning likely attributed to it, an analyst is in a position to discern the narrative strategy that informs the construction of the patient's current discourse. By identifying the patient's narrative strategy, the analyst can tentatively see the work of the very signifying structure that it is his or her aim to help the patient discover. For example, Dr. P. substituted a burnt-out wire that can be replaced for the female genital with its apparently missing penis. His screen

---

9. Of course, a psychoanalysis needs also to investigate the reasons why this experience had such a powerful impact on this patient, but that subject is beyond the scope of this chapter.

memory thus allowed the absence of a penis in the female to be disavowed. It also permitted the disavowal of the sexual relation between the parents. Later, when his sadistic wishes were the more direct subject of analytic investigation, it became clear that Dr. P. understood the primal scene as a violent castration, so that sexual relations were for him causally related to the absence of a penis in women. His disavowals, both in the transference and of the memory, were the equivalent of the violent attacks he imagined. By making himself the authority in the screen memory, he became the victor who had violently acquired knowledge and power by robbing the other.

If my reconstruction can be seen as facilitating an eventual retranslation of narration into prior event, painful affects, and fantasy elaborations, however, that is not how Dr. P. experienced it. Dr. P. experienced my reconstruction in terms of the violent sexual act that he envisioned. This led him to the re-enactment of his original disavowal—drowning out feelings of confusion, humiliation, and inadequacy, announcing his hatred of me, and trying to "chant away" what I was saying. My knowledge of the scene at which he could not look and, later in the analysis, his envy that I, now more clearly equated with his father, understood what was involved and knew how to do it, caused him to continue the re-enactment of his disavowal over many, many years. He would disavow my interpretations, often in the subtlest verbal ways: "Your idea that . . . You say that . . . This happened over the week-end. It fits well with your theory that . . ." These verbal disavow-als, defenses against anxiety at one level, castration equivalents at another, also needed each to be interpreted.

Confronted with the disavowal and repression of so disturb-ing a realization, as well as with knowledge of its unconscious meaning, the analyst has a choice: either to reconstruct the event and in doing so appear to the patient to be subjecting the latter to the attack he fantasizes once again in its reconstruction, or to allow the patient to re-enact the attack through the disavowal by not following up the original reconstruction with interpretation of the defenses against the perceptually frightening event and the drives mobilized by it. Although many therapists might argue that there is a third alternative, that of providing the patient with a new and different relationship, a new relationship can become available to the patient only when the signifying structure no longer dominates his or her perception.

Whatever the analyst does, the patient will attribute meaning to the analyst's action or lack of action in accordance with the signifying structure that is activating the patient's perception. Failure to confront the patient with the perception he refuses to see cannot escape being a collusion with the patient's disavowal of differences of gender, generation, and authority, to say nothing of his enacted hostility. Where we interpret the disavowed memory, we must also, of course, explore with the patient the new transference level on which the patient, confronted with the disavowed perception, now experiences the analyst.

Conclusion

General intellectual ideas applied randomly to clinical concepts tend to confuse crucial distinctions necessary for the clinical work. Thus, reconstruction can become confused with the unconscious meaning the patient attributes to it, the hypothesis of an event prior to its narration can be conflated with narrative strategy, and meaning seen as relative can obscure the pathological structures that prevent patients from perceiving multiple meanings.

However limited by our human lack of omniscience, our position as psychoanalyst to suffering patients requires us to discover with them various aspects of their signifying structure. Psychoanalytic theory that permits us to arrive at reconstructions establishes guidelines for the transformation of prior event into its narrative form in the patient. The analyst may then transform verbal derivatives and enactments into their unconscious representations, or signifying structures, whether verbalized or not, to whatever extent is possible.

These guidelines of transformation must include those that sensitize us to evidence of disavowals, which may or may not also enact sadistic vengeance in the transference. In addition, the method that rules of transformation afford us needs to be sufficiently convincing that general fears about inexact interpretation or authoritarian imposition of arbitrary ideas do not prevent us from interpreting to the patient according to the evidence at hand. It is easy to talk about the inexactitudes and mistakes we are prey to. However, we possess a methodology that allows us to reconstruct accurately enough to open up central signifying structures for further work (Reed 1993). It is this opening that seems to be the best criterion of the usefulness of reconstructions, not subsequent exact verification.

The concept of rules of transformation requires the distinction between prior event and narrative elaboration of the event. Events are the stuff of which narratives are made. The goal of analysis is not to tease out the prior event from the narrative, however; the comparison of the prior event with the narrative itself leads to the rules that govern, in a given individual, the transformation of events into narrative. Those transformations are the embodiment of central signifying structures, the fantasy/memory complexes that confine our analysands to the narrow meanings they have made at moments of terror and desire. To discover those structures with them makes it possible for them no longer to be condemned to lives full of fruitless and repetitive efforts to disavow that meaning.

Just as we need the distinction between event and narration, so, while a world of infinitely displaceable referents is a theoretical possibility, in the clinical situation we enter it only so far as we attempt to restore more of that flexibility to our analysands. Meanings for them have been limited and fixed by the affective results of trauma and drive-bound fantasy in interrelation—that is, by their personal interpretation of the events they live through. The analyst's interpretation, construction, and reconstruction all become formulated according to the limited meanings created by the patient at moments when higher, definitive authority is assumed to exist and to threaten. That is why we can postulate, within the clinical situation, that there are correct interpretations and reconstructions to be made, and is partly why we can try to make them.

Clinical work requires the assumption of a hierarchy of meaning in the analysand. The sign of that hierarchy is the existence of persistent rather than displaced referents. Through the affective results of trauma and unconscious conflict, signifiers in psychic life become fixed and limited to unconscious fantasy/memory complexes that confine and severely restrict the possibilities of reference, thus exercising an absolute tyranny over perception and the subject's construction of unconscious meaning. Clinical truth requires not only the recognition of a discontinuity in the infinite displaceability of the signifier but also that the specific unconscious fantasy that constitutes that discontinuity be put into words.

3 The Transference Perversion

The idea of a transference perversion grew out of an inquiry of several years into the concept of the transference neurosis. That inquiry resulted in my recent book (Reed 1994). There, my attempt to restrict the transference neurosis on the basis of the neurotic ego's synthetic capacity allowed me to recognize another group of transferences demonstrating the ego's reduced capacity for synthesis. However inevitable it may have been that the idea of the transference perversion grew out of a struggle with defining the transference neurosis, the clinical phenomena to which I am drawing attention under the rubric of transference perversion are useful to bear in mind in and of themselves. In some measure, they appear in most if not all analyses. In the patients I have in mind, however, this transference picture is pervasive and of long duration. These patients engage in a rather consistent, often sexualized undermining of the defining aspects of the psychoanalytic situation. The development of the treatment is more repetitive and apparently circular than progressive because conflict solutions common to perversion have altered these patients' egos in ways that impede the synthesis characteristic of neurosis. This ego-altering conflict solution may give rise to a distinctive psychoanalytic process that we might call a transference perversion. Etchegoyen (1991) has done so from a Kleinian perspective.

By utilizing Freud's late and extremely creative thinking about perverse mental functioning (Freud 1927), it is possible to integrate recent emphases on narcissism, (part) object relations, and preoedipal pathology into the conflict model. By suggesting that the psychoanalytic process in these patients may differ from that of neurotic patients, it may be possible to disencumber the concept of transference neurosis with its theory of neurotic conflict resolution from confusions that have followed the widening scope of analysis (Reed 1994). The most relevant allied work is by Renik (1992) who described certain non-neurotic patients' use of the analyst as a fetish.

Renik uses the term *fetish* somewhat globally, alluding to but not explictly tying his formulation to the dynamic constellation involving castration anxiety that Freud (1927, 1940a, b) describes in his papers on fetishism. Instead he concentrates on significant aspects of these patients' mental processes, differentiating their functioning from that of neurotic individuals. He describes exceedingly well their blurring of the relationship between reality and fantasy, a characteristic that allows them to actualize wish fulfillment in the transference and to continue to believe the illusion they have created with much more persistence than other patients. He also emphasizes their tendency to avoid anxiety rather than to grapple with it and underlines the problems this tendency causes for the progress of an analysis. Renik recommends that termination be proposed by the analyst in order to deal with the patient's wish to perpetuate the analysis indefinitely.

Renik's description fits the patients I have in mind; however, my emphasis is placed more explicitly on the consequences of a compromised synthetic function of the ego, on the various manifestations, especially deceptive enactments, of the perverse compromise formations in the transference, on the underlying unconscious fantasies informing that transference, and on the technical necessity and difficulty of addressing the contradictions that are the result of the failure of synthesis.

The essence of the character structure of such patients is its patterned changeability. These analysands shift rapidly but not chaotically from more advanced to more primitive structural configurations. That means, for example, that they can move, in short order, from relating to whole objects to treating the other as a fetish or part object. By emphasizing that the perverse solution to conflict that they adopt is organized around castration anxiety, I do not mean the existence of castration anxiety to imply stable, triadic, whole object relations or neurotic-level psychic structure. The perverse solution to conflict organizes anxieties at all levels and permits their *coexistence* by creating a structure characterized by rapid shifts in its composition.

Their transference material has in common a repetitive, sexualized enactment that is often hard to discern. The avoidance and the sexualized enactments utilize defenses common to conflict resolution in the perversions: disavowal, the substitution of something contiguous common to fetish formation, and a splitting of the ego.

Clinical Material

Professor B.

In Professor B.'s case the transference enactment appeared as an undermining of the analysis. An economist in his early forties popular with undergraduates because of his personableness and willingness to be helpful to students in distress, Prof. B. led a fundamentally lonely life. As the treatment he reluctantly engaged in nevertheless helped him become more successful in his scholarly work, he began increasingly to seek out anonymous sexual encounters with men. His pleasure came from controlling his partner by exciting him into desire for his penis. Not surprisingly,

in the transference, he would make significant connections, raising my expectation and interest in the continuation of the work
and then would undermine the continuity with a series of absences.

While exploring the meaning of the sexual encounters, for instance, Prof. B. gradually saw how controlling men by exciting
them both bolstered his fragile sense of his masculinity and reas-
sured him that he could control them and thus prevent them from
attacking him. He then remembered, with great anxiety, how his
father would accost him in fits of rage and threaten to castrate
him. I would feel pleased with the insight he had achieved and
anticipate further productive work. Prof. B would then cancel
several sessions, come back, and describe the anonymous sexual
activities with which he had replaced his sessions. I took up both
his need to avoid looking at his anxiety over his father's threat
and his turning of the treatment into a duplicate of his reassuring sexual encounters with men. Prof. B. welcomed the insight,
connected it to the previous insights about his fear of his father
and the harm he feared his father would do to him if he were successful, and then missed more sessions. I began to address Prof.
B.'s avoidance of looking at his anxieties by questioning in a variety of ways how he thought he might work his fears out if he
continued to subordinate our work to maintaining the transference seduction and control of me. He knew his behavior made no
sense at the same time that, at the moment of acting, he avoided
knowing.

Avoiding knowing or looking at reality was endemic to him
because reality, as the following sequence illustrates, had the unconscious meaning of the female genital as a sign of castration
(Arlow 1971, Lewin 1948). Prof. B. remarked one day that he had
picked up the check for a large group of people in an expensive
restaurant the night before. He did not want to think about his
depleted checking account balance or how he would pay his credit
card bill. He went on to connect his need to be a big spender with
wishes that I look at and admire him. He reported an urge to expose himself to me so that I would see how big his penis was and

be impressed. I linked these wishes to his anonymous sexual encounters and to his preferring to arouse a man with his big penis
than to look with me at how frightened he was of losing his. He
thought about not wanting to visit his mother and mentioned that
he had felt intensely anxious coming to my office that day on the
subway. The thought of the subway made him shudder. It was
dirty, dark, dangerous, sleazy, and filled with germs. I pointed out
that he'd made a connection between losing his penis, coming to
my office, not wanting to visit his mother, and feeling frightened
of the subway as a dirty, underground place that was dangerous
and germ-filled. That sounded like a vagina, but he did not want
to think about all that, he said dismissively. The way he didn't
want to look at his bank balance, I started to say. Prof. B. interrupted me to tell a joke about the wife of a dictator who bought
an astonishing number of shoes. When I pointed out that he seemed
to be trying to drown me out, he stopped talking and fell asleep.

As he gradually felt closer to me in a maternal transference,
his anxiety at entering my office escalated, as did the frequency
of his making exciting discoveries and missing sessions. He declared with bravado that he would solve all his problems directly
and leave the treatment, but as he lay sleeping beside the woman
he had chosen for this purpose, he had nightmares that his father
was attacking him with a knife. He gradually realized that his
avoidance of the sessions was an avoidance of his castration anxiety and that entering my office had the unconscious significance
of vaginal penetration. He was panicked by the thought that his
father would intrude into my consulting room and attack him. He
re-experienced his sense of childhood inadequacy in the face of his
father's power.

He was simultaneously afraid that I would trap him inside of
me so that he would not be able to get out. Associations to that
worry led not only to his fantasy of a suffocating and uncontrol-
lable mother but also to his relating the comfort he derived from
hiding out alone in his house with the blinds drawn, as though it
were a cave, drinking sodas through a straw and seeing no one.

He felt that regressive defensive wish to be inside me as he wished once to be inside his mother to be frightening as well as intensely humiliating. He preferred violent posturing, threats, and controlling me through excitation and interruption.

Controlling me in this way spared him the terror not only of penetrating a woman and finding himself his father's victim but also of being alone, separated from his mother and yearning for and being vulnerable to her. If the thought of being in the power of a woman terrified him, so did terminating. I was his magic amulet, he declared; if I were not available to him, he imagined that he would be emasculated.

Mrs. C.

Mrs. C. also turned the analysis from a search for insight into a subtly enacted, enduring conflict solution in which insight was concretized and its acquisition took on the meaning of acquiring a phallus. In this way, Mrs. C. used the transference to maintain the illusion that she could be both male and female. A 27-year-old married musician and mother, she remembered periods in latency of playing the clarinet in front of the mirror while imagining the instrument was a penis and that her performance was being greeted with wild applause. She excitedly described perverse activities involving urinating standing up. Both the effort to excite me and the sexual activities enumerated were associated with moments in which she believed that I had everything and she had nothing. The effort to excite me proved to be an attempt to contain envious and destructive impulses. A heightening of Mrs. C.'s obsessive concerns about her body being anything other than "straight and long" also accompanied the intensification of envious transference feelings.

She frequently dismissed her own associations, effectively withholding them. Often, moreover, she would reiterate her difficulties, evincing no memory of the unconscious meaning of her doing so, although just the previous day insight into those meanings had been the focus of the session. She would then react to a repetition of the previous day's discovery with great excitement, saying "I never realized that before." The excitement, repetition, and palpable feeling of enhancement that accompanied it signaled that the interaction had important transference meaning. If, however, I sought to explore the reasons for her excitement and subsequent forgetting rather than responding with comparable excitement to her apparently new understanding, she would feel worthless and convinced of my contempt.

Every insight was in this way turned into an occasion to exhibit an acquisition, which was then forgotten and the process of acquisition repeated. Every attempt on my part to analyze either the forgetting, the excitement, or the whole pattern led to manifestly painful depression and suffering on her part. She was convinced of the fact that I was condemning what she had showed me as no good. Eventually she revealed that when she felt excited the excitement was accompanied by a conscious idea that she was exhibiting her penis to me. When I did not show the responsive excitement she desired, she felt disappointed and deflated, and the experience ceased to have the qualities of something real. Forgetting allowed her to repeat the sense that she had acquired and was showing me her penis.

Yet, even while experiencing the interaction as the actualization of her fantasy, Mrs. C. was at the same time conscious that she didn't have a penis and was not going to acquire one, just as she also knew I was not contemptuous of her. This divided state of knowing and not knowing was also present in Prof. B., who knew and did not know that by replacing the sessions with homosexual encounters he was not going to work out the problems that led to his loneliness. Mrs. C. spoke about this mental state of knowing and not knowing at the same time. I had pointed out to her in the course of an hour, that because of the very envy she was talking about feeling, she was stopping me from adding something that might be helpful to her. In a new tone that expressed mild amazement, yet also disapproval of herself, she said, "This has made the analysis much more difficult!" When I asked what she would have come for if she hadn't had a difficulty, she replied, "I never thought there was a problem for me to *work* on. I still don't at the same time that I do. I think I just have to hold out until you make me into what I want to be."

By holding out, Mrs. C. was actualizing her wishful unconscious fantasy that she was omnipotent, omniscient, male and female, and merged with me into a powerful being that wanted nothing. She needed to be invulnerable to separation, loss, and castration. Once, when there was a break in the treatment, she took an object from my office with her. Possessing it made her feel she had me as well as a key that made her competent, adult, phallic. She was no mere dirty little girl, but male and female at once, able to penetrate to the inner sanctums of adult activity. At various times, I pointed out her need to deny the fact of separation from me as well as the reality of her femaleness. To the latter intervention, she burst out, "You're making me choose! I don't want to have to choose."

As her envy was addressed, Mrs. C. recognized the great difficulty she had in holding onto the possibility that her understanding of anything that happened between us might be of interest to *both* of us because it was a product of *her* motivated interpretation. By the time I could point out to her that she had no choice, she no longer felt that I was sadistically taking away her option. She could talk movingly of the deep wound she felt within herself instead. The growing ability to work *with* me marked the progress of the treatment; nevertheless, for a very long time, insight was an opportunity to exhibit her instrument, and her reaction to my attempts to explore that exhibition was to experience me as depriving her of her acquisition. Forgetting was a means to repeat the experience.

Discussion of the Clinical Material

In both patients, transference action and content were related through disavowal. Each turned the psychoanalytic process into a stable, sexualized transference enactment that supported a crucial disavowal of a portion of reality. Mrs. C. acquired insight, exhibited it, and forgot it in order to set the stage for acquiring and exhibiting it once again. In that way she could maintain the illusion that she was both male and female, invulnerable to loss, separation, and castration. Prof. B. protected himself against his fear of his father and the latter's castration threats by duplicating in the transference the control he exercised in his homosexual encounters by exciting men.

From the point of view of content, the reality that was disavowed had at one level the significance of the absence of a penis in women. Prof. B. equated unpleasant reality—the fact of a financial limit—with the knowledge of the female genital. In the transference, he avoided knowledge of his avoidance and the castration anxiety linked to it by enacting reassuring homosexual interactions. Mrs. C. equated her female state with castration, disavowed it, and enacted a fantasy in which she exhibited a penis when showing her insight.

To be sure, these patients' castration concern did not exist in isolation from other issues. It also represented earlier anxieties that had become integrated into it. Prof. B. feared separation from a mother he experienced as engulfing as well as castration at the hands of his father; indeed, the latter fear intensified the former. Analytic work revealed that Mrs. C. had the fantasy of being my phallus or of my being hers so that separation from and loss of the transference object inevitably became castration as well. Such a condensation between separation and castration is typical.

Both patients created out of the analytic interaction a circumscribed world in which the analyst provided a magical solution to those fears or depressive affects that would be stimulated by the recognition of the anatomical and other differences. Prof. B. turned the analyst into a magic amulet under his control. Mrs. C. imbued insight with the significance of a phallus and believed me to be so powerful that I could give it to her and believed herself so powerful that she could compel me to give it to her by holding out.

In each case, creation and re-creation were imbued with sig-

nificant omnipotence and isolated so that the transference enactment was experienced as a circumscribed actuality even after its
unconscious significance was understood. These contradictions
were not experienced as ego-dystonic conflicts. The patients were
unaware of the contradictions and their pervasiveness and strove
valiantly to remain so.

Such contradiction is a sign of an ego organized by conflict
solutions employing perverse defenses, that is, disavowal, splitting, and the creation of a fetish or its equivalent. When Freud
(1927, 1940b) describes how the sight of the female genital with
its lack of a penis made palpable and terrifying the possibility of
castration, he specified that "a rift in the ego which never heals
but increases as time goes on" (1940b, p.276) permitted instinctual satisfaction to be pursued at the same time that external danger is recognized. In the portion of the mind in which instinctual
satisfaction was permitted, a disavowal of the absence of a penis
in women took place. One can note derivatives of this conflict in
Prof. B.'s unwillingness to think about his depleted bank balance
and his attempts not to hear my intervention that he did not want
to look at it and in Mrs. C.'s belief that she had a choice about
whether to be male or female.

Contiguity operates to provide a replacement for the missing
penis not only when a fetish is formed but also when a phallic
equivalent is used to allay anxiety and permit sexual excitement
but not to become implicated in sexual activity that leads to or-
gasm. As the observer averts his gaze, he substitutes whatever
his eyes alight on for the thing that is not. The looking away also
narrows the field to be observed in order to eliminate everything
but the substitute that by its presence denies the missing phallus.
Prof. B. looked away by interrupting my attempt to confront him
with his castration fear. He substituted a fetish equivalent by telling a joke about a woman with many pairs of shoes. Mrs. C. nar-
rowed her focus so that insight out of its analytic context became
a phallus she exhibited. Other analysands pick up tangential details and concentrate on them at the expense of the whole or con-

stantly slide away from an anxiety situation to a tangential subject (Arlow 1971).

The result of this defensive activity is the well-recognized mode of cognitive thinking in which a realistic attitude and one characterized by omnipotent thought coexist simultaneously. In a rhythm of disavowal and the substitution of illusion, the latter replaces the former. Thus after insight into the fantasy quality of the transference enactment and its defensive significance, again and again these patients' belief in the enacted fantasy world was reinstated and the insight into its meaning was obliterated.

General Manifestations of the Transference Perversion[1]

Since analysis requires the patient and analyst to recognize and accept anxiety-provoking situations and unpleasant, even unpalatable truths, there exists a basic discontinuity between mutual collaboration and the operation of an ego that employs perverse defenses. But if the operation of disavowal within a limited sector dispenses with a disagreeable truth, then the analysis cannot be seen in that sector as a mutual search for a truth that will be unpleasant but necessary to confront. Analysis must therefore become something else. It is instead imbued with magic and turned into a circumscribed world unconsciously composed of interchangeable body parts and the sexualized relations between them (McDougall 1985, Roustang 1988) in which the object engages with the subject in a way that obliterates sexual and other related (e.g., generational) differences (Chasseguet-Smirgel 1984). Mrs.

---

1. In describing a transference perversion, I am extending perversion to derivative character manifestations (Arlow 1971) and considering it the longitudinal transference expression of an ego organized to permit the continuing of sexual activity in the face of the disturbing perception (or knowledge of the existence) of the female genital where the latter is taken as evidence of castration.

C., in a rage at my perceived attacks, would turn the tables, becoming male, tough, hard edged, and annihilating. The wish to murder me was expressed immediately as a threat to terminate the analysis.

Analysis is also a metonymic world where part substitutes for the whole, or more specifically, whole objects are replaced by fetishes or their equivalents. Although Mrs. C. fantasied winning me with her penis, there was little distinction initially for her between acquiring a penis, possessing me, and experiencing me as the desired body part over which she exercised omnipotent control. In one interchange in this fantasy world the object is experienced as providing or maintaining the existence of the penis so that separating from the object is synonymous with castration. Thus Prof. B. turned me into an amulet and equated termination with emasculation.

The creation of this transference fantasy world follows the mechanisms utilized in the creation of the fetish. The patient diverts his attention and narrows his focus away from the analyst as a whole to a convenient and ordinarily neutral activity of the analyst, the giving of an interpretation, for example. In fantasy, the patient may turn that activity into the giving of a penis needed to ward off anxiety or into the confirmation of the presence of a penis, as well as turning it into the continuation of sexual activity that the fear or actuality of castration would otherwise have stopped. For Mrs. C., my interpreting was the equivalent of my giving her the penis she wanted. She could then excitedly exhibit it to me. Prof. B. used his ability to make significant connections to tantalize and control me, exhibiting himself sexually in fantasy to gain reassurance that his transference father would not castrate him. At the same time he disavowed his terror of entering my office, which he unconsciously equated with penetrating a vagina since being in my office confronted him with the female genital. The patient maintains the illusion that the fantasy is real through the analyst's necessary repetition of the chosen activity.

Evidence of excitement on the part of the analyst, such as my interest in Prof. B.'s insights, reinforces the disavowal of reality.

The contradictory thinking characteristic of the simultaneous disavowal and acceptance of the woman's lack of a penis is applied to the analyst. For the belief in the perverse transference fantasy world to be maintained, it must be accompanied by a partial disavowal of the fact that what the analyst provides is metaphoric. Thus the patient disavows the as-if or "illusory" relation to the analyst in the circumscribed sphere of the perverse fantasy world. This disavowal coexists with a more apparently adaptable, reasoned approach to the analyst and the analysis; thus my patients' simultaneous seeing and not seeing their contradictory behavior I have already detailed. Where patients find a way to create and maintain a perverse transference fantasy world, the motivation to perpetuate the transference compromise powerfully opposes wishes to terminate. Indeed, *termination becomes the transference equivalent of disturbing external perception* (see Renik 1992). This understanding was the basis of Renik's recommendation that the analyst initiate termination. Although it is essential to find a way of helping patients engage rather than avoid their anxiety-laden conflicts, the action that Renik recommends comes too close to enacting wishes of the patient to be omnipotent and is too easily a reaction in the analyst to the impotence engendered by the patients' persistent avoidance.

Discussion

Of course, every patient to some extent avoids looking at painful conflicts, enacts a fantasy derivative in the transference in which he or she believes, has wishes gratified in it that he or she is loath to give up, and transiently loses the as-if character of the transference; however, the sequestered and delimited illusory world that is maintained as real through a sexualized transference enactment is not something I would expect to encounter *with comparable delineation, persistence, and concreteness* in a neurotic patient. The neurotic ego is more able to recognize and regulate action based on wishes for omnipotence and in general moves more flexibly between fantasies and the recognition that fantasies that involve the alteration of reality cannot be permanently actualized. This relative flexibility is a reflection of defenses that do not interfere so entirely with the synthetic function of the ego, of anxieties less overwhelming, of destructiveness less unmodulated. On the other hand, these are not psychotic phenomena. The *sequestration* of the illusory world, its maintenance as an island untouched by rational considerations at the same time that those considerations are left free to be applied in other areas of functioning differentiates this material from a psychotic transference. Glover (1932) aptly formulates the perverse solution as a sacrifice of a small part of reality in order to preserve the greater part.

The conflict solutions that express themselves as a transference perversion grow out of pathology occupying a middle ground between neurosis and psychosis and are related to other useful clinical conceptions, from pathological dependency (Coen 1992), to descriptions of the vertical splits in narcissistic personality disorders (Kohut 1977), to patients characterized by conflicts of ambivalence (A. Kris 1981), to what Kernberg (1976) has described as the middle level of character pathology. From a dynamic standpoint, patients within these interrelated groups have in common anal–phase conflicts characterized by ambivalence, as well as related conflicts around separation and bisexuality. The anal-stage ambivalence conflicts influence structure and conflict at all future stages. For instance, the failure of adequate libidinization of aggression influences the formation of structure, with the most notable result being the lack of synthesis in the ego that Freud (1940b) notes in relation to perverse organization. Object representations, similarly unsynthesized, are dominated respectively by the aggressive and libidinal drive derivatives so that the split resulting from the heightened ambivalence is perpetuated in superego as well as ego structure. Oedipal-phase conflicts are engaged with this divided legacy, as are all attempts to meet the subsequent exigencies of life. Disavowal is therefore frequently in addition an expression of an underlying sadism and destructiveness. When she had acquired a genuine capacity to observe herself and contain her conflicts, Mrs. C. realized that her forgetting the work of the previous session represented a destructive attack on me. In a related way, Chasseguet-Smirgel (1984) considers the perverse fantasy world to be the product of an anal regression.

Moreover, the hostile side of the ambivalence contributes both to a tenuous connection to primary objects, especially the maternal object, and to an instability in body image and sexual identity (Stoller 1975). The intense destructiveness, instability of body image and attendant tenuous object connections motivate the attempt to use the analyst to actualize a fantasy in which the analyst stabilizes the body image either by furnishing the missing part or by confirming its presence.

Given the overlapping of categories characteristic of continua, the organization described here as a transference perversion occupies a middle ground between transference neurosis and psychosis. On the one hand, the ego is sufficiently integrated to know and recognize reality. On the other, it is sufficiently divided to entertain as real an omnipotent version of reality at odds with the truth. The patient shifts from the more regressed to the more advanced organization in order to maintain them both isolated from each other. The shifting lends the analysis its repetitive or circular character that contrasts with the more progressive evolution characteristic of neurosis.

Circularity should not be confused with a lack of therapeutic progress, however. It is rather part and parcel of the working through of the fundamental shifting from one organization to the other. More specifically, the sense of struggle involved reflects the engagement of the underlying and exceedingly important anal-phase conflicts. Instead of measuring progress by change in content, although change and deepening of content also occur, more fundamental and characteristic is the increasing space for observation or alliance that occurs simultaneously with the repetition of the undermining as its motivations are addressed. In the most successful instances, patients become almost imperceptibly more able and willing to observe their contradictions, address their anxieties, take note of their disavowal and splitting, and explore the destructiveness that fundamentally motivates those defenses. These changes go hand in hand with a modulation of envy and destructiveness. When the envy beneath her need to exhibit insight was addressed, Mrs. C. gradually felt less deflated and derived correspondingly more satisfaction from observing what she was doing with and to me. She became more aware of me as an individual and began to experience painful conflicts about wishing to reduce me to a thing out of hatred. Professor B. over time grew more aware of the moments during which he sought to control me and could observe and explore the anxiety that drove him. In fact, recognition of the transference perversion as a distinct category from the transference neurosis may prove clinically useful *precisely because it helps the clinician focus on the defensive shifting of organizations and to approach through it the underlying anal conflicts.*

When perverse defenses supported by an underlying ambivalence are operating to maintain a split of the type demonstrated by these patients, an emphasis on what the patient presents, *without also attending to what he or she disavows and the way he or she does it*, will not be therapeutically effective. Thus I pursued with Professor B. as far as possible the intervention he did not want to hear about the way he did not look. Another patient, Dr. A., used to attack me by annihilating analytic understanding. She would return to a use of language that was entirely literal and that rendered me completely helpless and defeated. I told her that she seemed to be trying to make me feel as disregarded and helpless as she had felt as a child, an intervention that opened up both her dependency needs in the transference and her recollections of traumatic events that threatenened a defensive idealization of her family. This transference intervention did more than address the phenomenon of her turning passive into active or even reversing a projective identification. It also presented her with a realm of childhood experience related to fantasies and anxieties about being female at which she was refusing to look. It required follow-up work on how she enacted in the transference to maintain her not looking. This follow-up inevitably required the analysis of the transference hostility expressed by wiping out the analysis.

Since the patient maintains a defensive stability by shifting from the reality-oriented ego organization to the omnipotent and disavowing one, a technique is called for that addresses the transference manifestations of the *split* in the ego, the motivations for the split, the operation of the perverse defenses, and the resulting construction of the sequestered fantasy world characteristic of the transference perversion. Interventions need to focus consistently on the contradictions that the split in the ego defends the patient from knowing exist and the fantasies and mechanisms that maintain it.

Such a technique requires kindly and tactful, but nevertheless persistent presentation of the patient with that at which he does not wish to look. It runs counter to an approach derived from self psychology, for example, that emphasizes the patient's need to use the analyst to regulate his self-esteem by *also* stressing the necessity of helping the patient see that his use of the analyst allows him to avoid disruptive anxiety with which it would be more helpful for him to deal.

This technique also, however, runs counter to models of classical analytic technique originally derived from the topographic theory that emphasize the facilitation of regression and thus favor a rather passive analytic stance, including free-floating listening (Arlow 1987). If the analyst considers it wrong to introduce something the patient is avoiding because the patient has not mentioned it in the hour or because the patient's associations appear to be emerging freely as that judgment uses measures of quantity and fluency, it is easy to see how a patient of this type will be able to use the psychoanalytic treatment to please the analyst while continuing to avoid, thus maintaining the transference structure delineated here.

It is *not* easy to maintain such a therapeutic focus without unwittingly enacting one aspect of the transference role to which the patient has assigned the analyst. Persistent confrontation, no matter how gentle, satisfies patients' masochistic wishes. Persistent patience in the face of the undermining of the analysis gratifies his or her sadistic wishes. Since the pathological goal of the patient is to continue the transference perversion and not to use acquired insight to confront disturbing perceptions, the analyst is easily drawn into the fantasy and may easily become countertransferentially trapped in one or the other of the roles to which the patient assigns him. He or she may then feel prey to discouragement, frustration, exasperation, and thoughts of discontinuing the analysis. Regressively revived sadism and reactive masochism are obvious countertransference dangers that these patients easily incorporate into their sexualized maintenance of the illusory world. While continuing the analysis can therefore be perceived of as an omnipotent enactment in the same way as setting a termination can be, such a perception is not necessarily the case and is less drastic and definitive a measure.

It seems to me essential to meet the patient's desperate attempts to turn the analysis into the enacted fantasy I have described with interventions that address those repetitive maneuvers and the anxieties and wishes that make them necessary. In struggling with the reactions evoked by their maneuvers, it helps to remind oneself that the very undermining of the analysis that is so discouraging and frustrating is actually a positive development: it is the transference embodiment of the patient's central conflict and in vivo it awaits analysis.

4 On the Communicative Form of Severely Inhibited Associations

The strength of the classical model as it has been expanded over the years is its capacity to encompass in a consistent theoretical perspective both clinical data and clinical method without in any way limiting Freud's crucial discovery of the unconscious and its laws of primary process (see Chapter 7). That means that all facets of the patient's productions need to be regarded as multifaceted, polyvalent communications that speak of the dynamic solutions to his conflicts. These communications include the form in which free associations emerge or, as the case may be, do not emerge. Associations are never, of course, free. They are rather subject to the same laws of unconscious determinacy as all other mental phenomena. Sometimes, however, as in the case in this chapter, their freedom is so inhibited, their content so apparently sterile, their accompanying affect so flat that the psychoanalytic method is stretched to its limits.

The relevance of such associations to clinical work has four aspects:

1. Clinical material cannot be thought of as possessing a single, encompassing, linear meaning. The material is always multivalent and reverberates on many developmental levels at once. Thus, for example, the tendency in psychoanalytic discourse and in some theories to see oedipal and preoedipal material as mutually exclusive belies clinically observable data.

2. Apprehension of meaning for patient and analyst is a product of their interaction: it occurs through the interweaving of patient production and analyst intervention. Apprehension of unconscious meaning for the patient takes place after the capacity to understand it has emerged. That is, there is a change in psychic structure and therefore in the balance between revelation and concealment that optimally leads to further discovery and change. Apprehension for the analyst implies some resolution of the unconscious conflicts mobilized by the patient and may need to precede change in the patient.

3. Regardless of the seeming impenetrability of the surface content of associations, surface content represents and conceals significant unconscious meaning in the same way as does seemingly less impenetrable content.

4. Interpretation of the unconscious meaning of impenetrable content frequently depends on making conscious and then understanding the meaning of subtle enactments taking place with the analyst that are not directly represented in content.

Clinical Material

Ms. X.

Ms. X. was the oldest of four children and the only girl. Her next brother, Sam, was born 2½ years after her and her second brother, 1 year later. Her mother loomed large, a community icon; her father, who was more maternal, was a businessman. The family, especially through the mother, was infused with a sense of its social and moral superiority.

Ms. X.'s conflicts had evolved into a character structure that posed a major challenge to the psychoanalytic method. From the outset of the treatment, she was vigilant and unable to free associate with any degree whatsoever of flexibility and spontaneity. She followed the basic rule by saying what came to mind, but most of what came to her mind were facts. She talked and waited for something to happen. It was imperative to analyze the reasons for the restricted quality of her free associations because that behavior was the manifestation of a central unconscious fantasy that she was enacting in the treatment (Reed 1994) and that had been crucial to her character development.

Despite the considerable number of indications suggesting analysis was a questionable undertaking—her extreme guardedness and apparent concreteness, for instance—the treatment lasted seven years and fostered observable change. The analysis was interrupted during the pregnancy that led to the birth of her first child, with the knowledge on both our parts that there was still a great deal of work to be done. In this chapter, I do not present a detailed account of the analytic process nor explore the many meanings of the material I do present. Rather, I concentrate on a portion of the analysis of her restricted ability to associate.

When she first entered my office six years or so before the events described in this chapter, Ms. X. carried herself rigidly and was friendly though somewhat remote. Extremely long-legged and very tall, she wore miniskirts, sneakers, and ankle socks. Heavy eye make-up accentuated a detached look. In retrospect, I recognize that she looked panic-stricken, but at the time I was concerned by a quality of remoteness. The effect she made, with her extreme politeness, was somewhere between the incongruous and the bizarre. She was disillusioned: the world was not what she was told it would be in her Father-Knows-Best sitcom family. She was good, but it didn't pay. People in her company cheated, and she was left to deal with outraged salesmen who blamed her; she'd recently discovered that her mother, a self-declared model of perfection and a pillar of the church, had a drinking problem and used to sneak outside to smoke after inveighing against the evils of smoking. Men tried to take advantage of her. Her room-mate too was demanding and sloppy and left all the cleaning up to her. Many years later, around the time of the analytic events narrated here, she realized that she had been desperately de-pressed, but at that time, logical deduction alone had dictated her seeking help. Although she did not tell me until many years later, she could not think then of a single reason to live.

It was not only her depression of which she was unaware but also feelings of all kinds: anxiety, guilt, humiliation, anger. She was also unaware of the contradiction between her complaints about the world's lack of virtue compared to hers and her current affair with a married man. Instead, she suffered in body, with ten-sion headaches, itching skin, occasional wheezing, and most prom-inently, with severe, extremely painful, incapacitating migraine headaches.

For the better part of five years, she came to each session pre-cisely on time and lay down and recited, in detail and impregna-bly, the facts of her work situation. There were few details about her private life apart from work, no dreams, no daydreams, no allowance for irrational phenomena, no acknowledgment that I existed. If I questioned the meaning of this dry recital *as an action*, she reacted with high-handed but ever polite frustration. She was doing what she was supposed to do, wasn't she? Wasn't she say-ing what came to mind? Nor did my interpretations that she was doing something *to me* appear to change this behavior. She was ever politely skeptical and rational. I did not exist, except as an adjunct with sometimes "weird" ideas to a treatment she was undergoing at great sacrifice in order to be a "happy" person.

The impenetrability of these recitals was formidable and daunt-ing. Although I had found her likeable, had seen that she rapidly grasped that her problems were within her, and had perceived in her a gritty tenacity and willingness for hard work, I began to feel helpless, frustrated, bored, and trapped by the unending march of details, a victim pinned to the wall by her words. More insidiously, I eventually realized that her behavior had aroused my hostility. I tended to express my hostility by listening passively, waiting for material I could use, and not hearing or reacting to minute, almost imperceptible shifts in tone that might lead to interventions about her extreme anxiety in my presence. Every hour I had to do battle with myself to overcome the desperate and empty feeling—the manifest signal of my frustration—she engendered in me to make myself intervene in a way that might be helpful to her. I sometimes managed to do so, but often it seemed to me quite awkwardly.

If I did intervene, my interventions led to labyrinthine, rationalized discussions during which I felt like a rat trapped in the maze of her narcissistic defenses. I had to use considerable intellectual ingenuity to find a way to say things to her that she could accept. These discussions often felt like diplomatic negotiations, though there gradually developed a greater and greater common ground.

More than occasionally, I found it necessary to explain the reasons behind analytic rules and interventions to her; her mistrust precluded a more abstinent attitude. Although I did not doubt my clinical judgment in giving these explanations, they reinforced an intellectualization that was already a formidible resistance and therefore made me uneasy. Moreover, they were also the mark of my engagement in a reciprocal countertransference enactment in which I, the victim of her wordless but powerful attack, was too cowed to confront her. The task of intervening seemed even more hopeless when, within the enactment, I was forced to surrender the position I felt most therapeutically useful. I thought many times about the advisability of stopping the treatment. While I was determined to allow her all the time she needed, I often felt guilty that I was taking money under false pretenses.

I was aware, of course, that these intense reactions were data—something she evoked in me, might even unconsciously want me or need me to feel. Why I should have the idea that I was like a rat trapped in a maze or like a criminal taking her money are sound clinical questions that will be elucidated by the subsequent material. At the time, however, knowing intellectually that my thoughts and formulations were clues to unconscious fantasies and wishes occurring in the patient that I only understood in this derivative fashion was not immediately helpful. My feelings were too powerful and uncomfortable.

It was not that I hewed to a technique that is a caricatured version of the classical: rigid, unfeeling, unsupportive, and silent. By nature I engage with patients and err toward the too talkative. Nor do I believe in rigid categories of exploration (psychoanalysis) and support (nonanalytic psychotherapy). Rather, support is, to my mind, intrinsic to a good analytic treatment, a consequence of the patient feeling understood and accepted in his or her deepest unconscious wishes and fears. Ms. X.'s rigidities and inhibitions appeared impervious to any approach and made me feel powless and defeated. When these feelings were particularly strong, I would try to take stock, would struggle to recapture my own analytic identity. I would remind myself that *some* work was being and had been accomplished.

For words had been put to feelings. She had gradually been able to realize some of what she felt during the day. In fact, after three years, the recitals about work always began with something that had made her anxious or angry during the day and were an attempt to explore what that might have been and eventually its unconscious meaning. And she realized too much of what she had consciously felt as a child but that had never been named, a work of integration of conscious memories with heretofore unacknowledged feelings. Adaptive aspects from childhood of her withholding, controlling, and politely provocative character traits had also been a subject of our discussions, with the result that she saw her "perfect" parents more clearly and had become considerably more

separated from them. A great deal of work was done on her proclivity for narcissistic identifications and on the subsequent confusion as to who she was.

Moreover, her life was changing in other ways. As she became
aware of who she was, she had become aware of conflicts within
herself and of contradictions in her behavior. Interpersonal cri-
ses were replaced by apparently more stable friendships. She had
married, although she would say little about the man she chose,
and I suspected that great and disowned ambivalence toward him
was increasing her suspiciousness of me. At the time of the events
I relate here, her dermatitis and wheezing had disappeared; her
migraines, a faint shadow of themselves, appeared very occasionally, could be handled by medication when they did, and no longer
caused her to miss work. She had stopped maddening employers
by her subtle and well-behaved superiority and obvious attempts
at control. Instead, she had become acutely perceptive of others'
motives and used her insight in the service of managing situations
less obtrusively. So we struggled along.

Gradually, like oases in the desert, less available and less conscious memories, connections, and insights also appeared. And
then they appeared with more regularity. They had emerged in
connection with distress at work and for the most part had remained segregated from her emotional experience in the present
with me. Nevertheless, imperceptibly, her associations became less
restricted.

I began to point out her insistence that I fix her while she waited
passively, apparently following the rules. While she continued to
insist that she was only doing what she was supposed to do, her
resentment at being treated as a second-class citizen in her family for being a girl and her concomitant wish to have a penis given
to her for following the rules emerged from a childhood memory
following my confrontation. Convinced that she was following the
rules on the box, she expected to be able to fly like Superman if
she ate a certain cereal daily. She remembered her mother's dis-
counting her illusion and her stubborn refusal to accept her

mother's words. Further confirmation of her wish emerged when she shortly thereafter remembered a childhood dream of a little girl in her party dress with a huge penis just like her father's.

We already knew that, as a child of 3 or 4, she had become terrified that Woody Woodpecker would come through the large picture window at night and peck at her head. Now, following the material about her wanting a penis, a memory of watching a cartoon at a drive-in movie from the back seat of the family car with her parents' heads silhouetted by the large screen in front of her led to my reconstructing a primal scene observation. Her response was to remember her mother, unaccountably upset, warning her always to knock if her parents' door was closed. The experience became connected to states, past and present, of confusion, feelings of exclusion, a sense of being prohibited, and, most feelingly, a sense of being worthless; that same sense of confusion and spinning in space recurred in the transference when she one day perceived that I was not feeling well and might be ill, the first sign she was conscious that I had a meaning to her. She later recalled a repetitive childhood nightmare of logs rolling in on her. It was possible to connect it with her feelings of helplessness and rage over her brothers' births and her mother's emotional absence. The wished-for penis represented the connection she longed for and had lost with her mother.

This insight led to her remembering being moved out of her own room into the hated television room to make room for her brothers and then remembering that she was moved off her comfortable potty too onto a big, white formidable toilet for the same reason. She recalled a childhood dream in which her mother lay dead. She realized that she wanted to kill her boss as well as her mother for being so powerful and having so many rules. She was, I pointed out, trying to kill me too by following my rules and making them useless in the process. She could free associate words without saying anything and deny the usefulness of any interpretation I made by dismissing me as weird. She began to see how she used the frame of the analysis not only to undermine it and attack me but also to insulate herself from feeling in it.

One reason for her insistence on knowing the reasons for analytic rules now became clear, and that parameter could begin to be analyzed: if she knew the rules, she could appear to follow them while furiously and secretly opposing them and rendering me impotent at the same time, reversing the childhood situation of being left out and dispossessed. As her subtle defiance of me and its incapacitating consequences became apparent to her, she recognized its pervasiveness in her life. In her sessions, we understood that she had been enacting various scenarios of obstinate vengeance, particularly the toilet scene, hanging on for dear life, furious at her mother, defiant, hurt, alone, and dispossessed by boy babies.

Defiance was, she decided not long before the words I report below, a tragic way to waste a life. It was destroying her creativity and enjoyment of life and hampering her treatment. She began to struggle with herself. Why was it so important to stay in control? She remembered that as a child she had been terrified of death and that the movie, "Darby O'Gill and the Little People," had played a part in her fear.

Then I went away for ten days. When I returned, she spoke in a high tense voice: "While you were away I had the flu. It was a good time for me to be sick. I tried to pay attention to how I was feeling about your being away. I never miss you, not consciously anyway. I started feeling something was the matter with me. I'm supposed to miss you. Then I thought, 'Why am I feeling guilty?' If I don't, I don't. That's all. I never miss friends when I don't see them, and I think in a way you're a friend to me now. I'm very happy when I see them again, but I know they're there. If I went away for a week I wouldn't miss my husband either. I don't feel a void. I always know I'll see you again. The only time I would consciously miss someone is if a group of friends was getting together and I couldn't go. I'd feel left out, that they'd had fun without me. I think if I knew I wouldn't see you again, I'd feel panic. That's how I know there's something there, when I think of ending I get a feeling, but not for a week and I'd probably get over it, once I got used to it." I pointed out to the patient that she *was* feeling something—she was feeling guilty about not feeling anything. She said "Oh!" with surprise and went back, speculating and dutiful, to memories of a toilet scene from childhood where she "should" be doing something and is too scared of falling in and too angry at having to sit there to do what she's supposed to do. It didn't matter if her mother was there or not because there was "no backup." Her mother was involved with the babies. Her mother didn't understand her panic and didn't pay any attention to it. Suddenly, on her way out, she stopped in her tracks: "Oh! I have to tell you. While you were away I saw 'Darby O'Gill and the Little People.' It was very interesting, my reaction. Wow, I'll tell you tomorrow."

In the context of our previous work, there was much that could be tentatively inferred from the words of her session by removing the minus sign of negation: the longing of a small child for her mother who is imagined as having lots of fun—with babies or by making babies—while leaving her out; the anger and humiliation attending such an exclusion; the unbearable three days past the week-long separation that could not even be mentioned; and the substitution of turbulent feeling by physical illness. The trouble was that she *felt* nothing. And the minus sign was reinforced by the conditional sentence structure. Together they reinforced and represented negation, denial, isolation, and rigid internal compartmentalizations.

As I listened, I struggled. Where was there a handhold to help her link these denied perceptions to alive feelings? Finally amidst a confusion of sentences came an opportunity. She was telling me, rather indirectly, that she had a feeling about me that wasn't a feeling. No matter that what she called guilt was undoubtedly many other things as well. I wouldn't quibble because right *there* in that contradiction was a live spot, one that lent itself to more than intellectual debate and was not liable to lead either to overt battle or to content devoid of feeling. What followed my intervention about her feeling guilty was her attempt to be good—a defensive reaction. Then, with one foot out the door, the salient association to "Darby O'Gill" came.

The next day she arrived twenty-five minutes late, and talking in a way so pressured that I could barely follow her, she delivered a confused account of this movie that she associated with her childhood fear of death. There was an angel of death who looked as though she was on fire who would send a horse-drawn coach with a headless coachman to take Darby's wife or daughter. It wasn't clear which one "looked like she was in flames . . . she'd cover the whole screen . . . I was petrified . . . they were coming to get me . . ." I stopped her to point out that she was talking very fast and frantically, as though she was fearful of something right in the room. "I can remember imagining myself being the victim. . . . You don't know, you could go back to the devil and be tortured forever. . . . It was a frightening experience for me—I had connected with being a sinner—*they* were something I couldn't control, God or the devils. When the angel came, it was part of the they." She began to speak of memories from the age of 2½, all new material. In particular she recalled a doll she had who said a prayer "if I should die before I wake," when she was staying at her grandmother's house. She was afraid to go to sleep, terrified she would die. I interrupted: "Sam was born when you were 2½." Her tone changed, became pensive. "I just thought of something! My mother lost a child before and after me. I don't know how I knew. Maybe I heard it from my grandmother. I think I thought babies slept in their mother's stomachs and then would die."

The condensations in this material were multiple and rich. We can reasonably infer from her reaction to my intervention about Sam a wish to murder her brother in utero and can recognize primal scene revenge fantasies in the confusion and fiery imagery (Arlow 1980). We can understand as well that wife and daughter were one, baby murderer and murdered (punished) child were one, pregnant mother and pregnant child were one, inside and outside were confused.

Although her fear, as she related these events, was searing, she was not at all aware of her experience of me as the threatening angel of death. That connection could only begin to be forged months later when, in an entirely different context, she realized—it felt to her like a revelation—that she had *always* felt "bad" in my presence, guilty and inadequate. This pivotal discovery about her immediate transference feelings led to painstaking and important work on the very subtle ways she had of ridding herself of bad feelings toward me *before* she could become conscious of them and *before* they could disturb her equanimity. The most prominent among these methods was to usurp my analytic functions, to become one with me as a powerful and rule-imposing interpreter.

The next piece of work involved the discovery that she needed to be invulnerable, perfect, and invincible to ward off both a fear of punishment for something she didn't understand and a terrible sense of hurt and loss. By this time, talking of a young acquaintance who was dying, she sounded quite different, more reflective and introspective: "I guess you feel cheated, when life is *taken* and the person isn't ready; somehow I think you cry for yourself; you realize your own grief. Somebody took something. My body is me. His body is him. He has no control over it. . . . At the end my grandmother's body was ready for the junk heap, garbage. When she died, I believed she'd got a prize. But he's a loser, vibrant, young. . . . I can't accept the fragility of life . . . could be me, or anybody, someone who is perfect, just had bad luck." I said to her: "You believed that if you were perfect you would be invulnerable to loss, to injury, to illness, and to hurt; you tried to get every unpleasant feeling out, to be perfect again, because unpleasant feelings made you feel like you were garbage, ready for the junk heap. That's the way you feel here." With anguish, she replied, "I know, but it doesn't work. I try to be better than best and then I'm worse because I can't let go."

Months went by during which her awareness deepened of her fear of sudden loss of her sense of perfection. She came to correlate this fear with fear of the loss of someone on whom she depended—me or, she thought, her mother when she was small. At the same time she began to discover how much she envied various people in her daily life, her boss particularly. Then she discovered her envy beneath the defiant feeling toward me. One day she realized how much her feelings of inadequacy, loss, and envy were connected to Sam, the brother next in age to her. She had always regarded him as living a perfect life, had envied him, and had tried to be perfect—"the good little girl who follows the rules and doesn't lie" in order to get the attention and approval she perceived he had always had from her parents. It never worked. Once he had been born, she had always felt blamed and second rate at home. She felt in fact the way she felt with me—"bad."

The following day she had a dream: "I'm in a room, maybe with you. I was sitting in a chair. A nurse, brunette, longer hair, mother or you, I was pregnant, in labor. The nurse was saying, 'That's right, you're doing good.' The delivery for me was like eliminating, like going to the bathroom. I looked down at my stomach. There was [the outline of] a small child. The legs were sticking out like chicken wings. I'm trying to push down the legs. I'm pushing, like eliminating. I thought, 'Shouldn't I be on the table?' This nurse, not like a hospital nurse, is talking to me, 'Push/relax.' All of a sudden the first thing that came out was green peas and macaroni . . . the kind I wouldn't think of eating myself . . . gurgle, gurgle, that came out! I was on the table. I looked down. 'Macaroni? Food?'"

Among associations she's reminded of the garbage disposal—"You know you run water and there's a hole and it gurgles back up?"; "going to the bathroom, . . . funny position of the kid, baby didn't want to leave, chicken wings, Biafran children, malnourished, potbellies, chicken arms, I didn't want it in, get the bad out with the garbage. . . . That nurse, her outfit . . . did I visit my mother in the hospital? The hat was outdated, the kind nurses used to wear, looks familiar, dark brunette hair, like you only not . . . pulled back." She was struggling with a memory. I intervened: "Friday you were talking about how painful it was Sam was born, that he seémed perfect to your parents while you felt suddenly like nothing. You make a dream in which you're giving birth to a baby, and the baby is shit, garbage. You're getting rid of it." She responded, "Oooo! Sam's nurse! She had brunette hair and she wore that kind of outfit! That was her! she was a witch! bitch! She had that nasty expression in the dream! screwed up, scrunched up. . . . Oh! chicken bones . . . the only kind of bones you can put in our disposal. I'm thinking of the toilet too. It is the toilet too, that's why my mother is coaching me. This is toilet training, and I want to get him out and flush him down it."

She went on to think about her chronic childhood constipation and to wonder what it had to do with this wish to flush her brother down the toilet. She had to hold everything in so she didn't defecate the baby out and kill him! "I can't win either way. Can't hold it in, I get an enema, or let it out. If I want to be good, I get no credit . . . " She talked with venom about the nurse and her mother and then with sadness: " Mother always said Sam was a good baby; he was the star for her, not me. She said I was difficult."

Here, with this dream, we have more than the speculation and inference we had previously. We have the patient's associations and memories and affect. Moreover, we can understand her withholding style: to talk freely was to be the envious, dispossessed little girl flushing the hated boy baby down the toilet or devouring him and grinding him up. To associate freely was also, we would discover in more detail later, to be her mother and give birth to a baby defective because of its incestuous origins. If she let go and associated, she would sin by giving birth and by murdering, and would lay herself open to hell's tortures and the ministrations of the angel of death, her mother/analyst. She *had* to control and monitor every word.

This work did not, however, lead immediately to more freedom of expression. Instead, the next session was full of dry-as-dust details about work. She acted as though the last session had never happened. I brought this fact to her attention. She was waiting for *me* to get rid of her unpleasant feelings, her envy particularly, in the same way she wished her mother to get rid of the baby, to make it unnecessary for her to be filled with murderous thoughts and fear of retaliation, and to prove she was best loved and would never be deprived of food. What is more, if I didn't get rid of the baby, as an expression of her anger and envy she would take *my* baby, the analysis baby, in her mouth/disposal, grind up the work we'd done, and make me feel frustrated, helpless, and incompetent, the way she felt: "You're the parent. You could create with someone else. My mother could make a baby with other people and have children. I couldn't be made without my mother. My mother could have other children without involving me." She did not ever want to suffer that hurt again.

Discussion

Ms. X.'s restricted ability to associate was the outcropping of a central fantasy/memory complex that she enacted characterologically and thus also in the transference. The analysis required that the action be translated gradually into words and its unconscious roots explored. By restricting her associations, Ms. X., in fantasy, was wreaking vengeance on her analyst/mother by sitting on the toilet refusing to go, restraining herself from devouring her brother in utero and defecating him out the toilet in order to restore the world to that time before she had felt so hurt, neglected, and deposed, when she had felt herself to be the apple of her mother's eye. She felt not only hurt and dispossessed but also terrified that she would be punished for the hostile wishes embodied in this fantasy. As a result, she restricted herself and her appetites in many ways, was guarded and remote.

Let me now return to the four points about the relevance of free associations to clinical work made earlier in the chapter and elaborate on each of them.

1. *Clinical material cannot be thought of as possessing a single, en-compassing, linear meaning. The material is always multivalent and reverberates on many developmental levels at once.*

Thus, Ms. X.'s central fantasy about destroying her brother was only one important part of a much more complex interweaving of elements. The immediate work I reported led upward, that is to chronologically and developmentally later transformations of these conflicts. It led, for instance, to her grudging recognition of her mother's role in her own creation, to an increased differentiation of herself and her mother, and to a wishful fantasy that she and her father had created her without her mother's help. Differentiation and the ensuing recognition of her mother's role also deepened exploration of narcissistic issues, leading to the discovery of intense anger toward her mother for (purposely) making her feel less ade-quate than her mother as a woman. She felt so inadequate that she believed that, unlike her mother, she could never have babies. She imagined her mother to have something in addition that made it possible for her to have babies, a phallic power that she, Ms. X., would never have. She envied me in the belief that I too had the power to make her as powerful as her mother and that I refused to do it. She didn't like these feelings. They made her feel like a gar-bage disposal, devouring, envious, castrating, and destructive, but she felt deprived of her mother and, as a girl, wronged and badly treated by her parents. They favored the boys. They had leaned heavily on family votes to decide what to do when the children did not agree. Since the boys always wanted to watch football and there were three of them, they got their way. It was unfair. Rules always favored boys; she would not really follow them, but only appear to do so. She also envied me as she had envied Sam, and did not, as a consequence, want to give me more than I already had.

In a still more regressive direction, the clinical material led her to experience her intense craving to be one with me, to deny her rage over her brother's birth and her loss of her mother, and to restore the feeling she had in memories that began now to return from the time before her brother's birth. She wanted me to fill her

up with answers that would bring her satisfaction and content-
ment, like the milk she had enjoyed and was terrified she would
no longer have after the baby arrived.

The material led also to her perceiving her competition with
me and from there to her wish to compete with her mother. She
despaired about ever being able to measure up to this "angel of
mercy" who, it turned out, had insisted that her small child accompany her on weekly visits to pediatric wards full of frightening little amputees and to geriatric wards full of the terrifying,
screaming senile demented. This was the little girl's vision of hell
and punishment, but any feeling she had of fear or dislike automatically made her bad and sinful and increased her sense of the
impossibility of being like her mother.

2. *Apprehension of meaning for patient and analyst is a product of
their interaction: it occurs through the interweaving of patient production and analyst intervention. Apprehension of unconscious meaning for
the patient takes place after the capacity to understand it has emerged.
That is, there is a change in psychic structure and therefore in the balance between revelation and concealment that optimally leads to further
discovery and change. Apprehension for the analyst implies some resolution of the unconscious conflicts mobilized by the patient and may need
to precede change in the patient.*

After the work just detailed, Ms. X. acquired a female dog. She
enjoyed caring for her and began to express a sense of being cared
for in the transference. She recognized and could put into words
that she had experienced her brother's birth as an internal cata-
clysm and loss after which her experience of the objects in her
world was never the same. Without minimizing her parents' considerable shortcomings, she realized that her angry withholding
had also made it impossible for them, particularly for her mother,
to play any positive role. She remembered how often her mother
would be hurt that Ms. X. seemed to shut her out and recalled
that her parents had even gone for counseling because they could
not "communicate" with her.

She began to review her experience during the early years of the treatment. All that talk was, she decided, a way of trying to get out her bad feelings. Since I didn't make her uncomfortable feelings go away, she would leave the sessions feeling worse than when she came, angry and frustrated at me for my apparent refusal. Then she began to realize that I wasn't trying to make her feelings go away or withholding that relief from her. Rather I was interested in understanding them. It began to occur to her that maybe her feelings were worth understanding, that the point was not to get rid of bad feelings and to get fixed, but to understand herself instead. It seemed that conflicts connected to her not valuing her feces had been modified by my listening to her with interest and trying, despite my discomfort, to understand her. This modification led imperceptibly to a change in the way she approached the analytic task and eventually in the way she associated, but not immediately.

Ms. X. began to experience the pleasure of caring for a creature dependent on her. She did not feel that the dog was contemptible because she was weak. She then began to consider having a baby. Until this point, having a baby was a thought that filled her with dread. Now she thought of it with anticipation. That did not preclude a guilt-induced attempt to run the moment she became aware she was pregnant. During the last few months of treatment, as she worked through more aspects of her wish to damage her siblings and the consequent fear of retaliation and its connection to the baby growing inside her, she became concerned about not damaging her child by treating it as a part of her body after birth. She began to work on her wishes for omnipotence with new determination and understanding. She knew that this work was not finished and did not feel confident that she would be able to continue the work alone once she left. Under the circumstances, such a perception seemed to me a measure of her progress.

Instead of fixing Ms. X., I engaged with her in a psychoanalytic dialogue through which I sought to intervene in the maladaptive balance of forces established by her solutions to her unconscious conflicts. In this dialogue, when the analyst intervenes, he or she selects. An interpretation to a patient is neither an explanation nor, with some exceptions, the communication of a very large picture. It is more like a key one uses in a lock, a tool with which one intervenes in a particular balance of forces in order to change that balance. If one is successful, something about the patient's discourse or behavior in the session will change. The patient may become silent, exerting a counter-force, or remember something or associate in a way that confirms an interpretation and allows its understanding to be deepened and developed. In the first session I presented, my insistence on my patient's experience of what she called guilt overrode her attempted denial of the feeling and led to her remembering having seen the movie.

3. *Regardless of the seeming impenetrability of the surface content of associations, surface content represents and conceals significant unconscious meaning in the same way as seemingly less impenetrable content.*

The assumption of unconscious conflict as it is elaborated in unconscious fantasy means that, regardless of the seeming impenetrability of surface content, it represents and conceals significant unconscious meaning in the same general way as seemingly less impenetrable content. Thus, my patient's initial complaints reverberated with references to the focal and organizing wound of her childhood. She complained of her mother being hypocritical, of her sibling/roommate being sloppy and leaving her a mess to clean up, and, to me, of the world having no more meaning. Implicit in the last complaint was the demand that I do something about it. While there was little way to hear this reverberation without more information, the complaints about her mother doing forbidden things in secret and about her messy siblings were at least suggestive. That is, even in the most defended patient, manifest content is not like a lead apron shielding latent content from the analyst's x-ray vision. Larger or smaller traces of unconscious content are interwoven with and are part of the surface. One of the major goals of clinical analysis is to shift the balance of forces so that the presence of these traces enlarges and their relation to other material becomes clearer.

4. *Interpretation of the unconscious meaning of impenetrable content frequently depends on making conscious and then understanding the meaning of subtle enactments taking place with the analyst that are not directly represented in content.*
Although the dry, work-related details were impenetrable to both of us for years before we began to understand that they encoded complaints about her siblings and mother, their impenetrability did not make their formal characteristics less an outcropping in action of a central, complex, and highly condensed unconscious childhood fantasy in which the patient imagined herself holding in and not acting on her vengeful wish toward her mother of defecating out her brother/son and killing him.

Moreover, the fantasies evoked in me by the patient's behavior eerily complemented my patient's central unconscious fantasy. I felt both like a rat trapped in a maze and like a thief taking her money. Rats are well known representations of those hated intruders—unwanted younger siblings (Arlow 1990a). The words in which I articulated my experience of her argumentative response to anything I dared interpret represented an unconscious, empathic understanding of her murderous wishes toward her siblings and their relevance for the transference. My sense of criminality likewise was my unconscious understanding of the guilt she felt for harboring these wishes. Such responses are not rare, either as complementary unconscious fantasies or as affects. They are usefully conceptualized as part of the parallelism phenomenon (Arlow 1963, Gediman and Wolkenfeld 1980, see Chapter 10). The clinical issue is to recognize their presence and to use them to understand the patient, not perpetually to engage in an enactment with him or her.

Unconscious conflict is often reproduced in new form by the patient using the accoutrements of the analytic situation. For instance, the obligation imposed on a patient by the analyst's enunciation of the basic rule creates a conflict in and of itself: for many patients, the request to say what comes to mind without reflection recreates anal-stage struggles around control or oedipal struggles with authority. The fact of that conflict creates a second register in which the manner of associating becomes the patient's solution to the particular conflict evoked by the demand for free association. One of the things we do clinically is to pay close attention to the solutions patients choose, to point them out, and to explore the reasons for them. In Ms. X., the enunciation of the basic rule immediately brought her overriding and organizing anal conflict into the psychoanalytic situation. It was enacted silently for a long time before it was gradually put into words.

One way to describe the psychoanalytic process is to say that the analyst's interventions foster a change in the balance between revelation and concealment in the patient. Inner change in the individual leads, as it did in the case of the young woman discussed in this chapter, to changes in the material the patient produces in the direction of proliferation, specification, and deepening of material. Inner change for Ms. X. led most obviously to greater freedom of association. Greater freedom of association led to more material, more uncovering, and more change. Deepening of meaning and proliferation of associations are signals of psychic change for the analyst.

Ms. X. gave a particularly trenchant description of the way inner change became noticeable to her. The change she was describing was a subjective sense of greater integration and less compartmentalization:

"Analysis isn't one great revelation. You just start seeing things differently, without realizing it. Before, I used to think everyone was a clean slate. In painting, I realized years ago you don't just paint on a blank canvas. You utilize part of the canvas as part of the painting. Then I realized you could use the structure of the canvas as part of the painting, then the gesso. You could build it up, layers on top of layers, washes, everything, the painting builds up, everything could be part of the painting, the size of the canvas, whether you paint on cardboard or copper. As much as I've had these thoughts about painting, I thought in life you were always starting with a fresh canvas. These past few sessions, what feels different is who you are when you begin."

5 Profuse Sexualized Associations as Enactment

The formal characteristics of a patient's associations are of profound clinical significance even when they do not pose a threat to the psychoanalytic process in the way that Ms. X.'s associations did (see Chapter 4). Formal characteristics are particular to each individual. They testify most generally to an adaptive attitude toward the world and most of the people in it—guarded, generous, naively trustful, or anxiously compliant. At the same time, however, they derive from deeper layers of the hierarchically arranged unconscious fantasies that make up an individual's psyche. Ms. X., for example, was characterologically withholding and guarded. She acted with vigilance toward everyone. But her general guardedness also concealed a particular fantasy: since very early childhood, she had feared reprisals at the hands of her mother for cannibalistic and murderous wishes toward her younger brother and even earlier death wishes toward an unborn sibling.

These less available unconscious fantasies incorporate specific memories, wishes, fears, and ideas about important people from

childhood and adolescence. As with all such organizing unconscious fantasies, they subtly, sometimes silently, but always powerfully influence the individual's interpretation of the world. They
constitute the rules that give meaning to perception.

The formal characteristics of a patient's associations may not
attract the analyst's immediate attention. To some extent, technical variation is a matter of character and individual style; to some
extent it is a matter of theory. Some classical analysts prefer to
address conflict through whatever content is presented, as long
as addressing content bears fruit. They attend to the formal characteristics of associations when these characteristics become a
recognizable transference resistance. Others, notably the contemporary Kleinians, zero in more rapidly on the patient's manner of
presenting himself and his concerns in the hour because they consider the patient's interactions with the analyst to be what is most
affectively immediate.

The subtleties of patients' characteristic ways of associating
often become discernible only when character traits that have not
been noticeable intensify; that is, when the formal characteristics
of the associations emerge as subtle verbal enactments. Frequently,
this behavior has been eliciting subjective reactions in the analyst even before the analyst notices the behavior (Reed 1994,
pp. 186–204). The analyst's reactions, which are countertransferential in the broad sense, may inhibit the addressing of the
enactments and a stalemate may ensue, or the analyst may address
these characteristics in a less than tactful way. These formal characteristics are often the agents for what in some quarters is seen
as projective identification.

The form of a patient's manner of associating does not necessarily pose obstacles as severe and challenging to the analytic
process as did Ms. X.'s inhibitions and concreteness. For a long
while, therefore, it may appear as a simple accompaniment to fruitful work with content until, as with Mr. Y., whose treatment is
described in this chapter, his way of associating figuratively hit

me on the head. Mr. Y. volubly disgorged florid and detailed sexual and aggressive fantasies. For some time, their content was helpful for him to analyze and understand in the context of the transference and of his past without my addressing their form, despite the control of me that their form attempted to maintain.

Where the formal characteristics of associating represent an adaptive response to conflict that is not adequate to its chosen task, the impulses beneath the adaptive compromise will seek discharge more imperatively. The defenses arrayed against these impulses will intensify correspondingly. The importance of the form of associating will then loom larger, and its function as a resistance will become clearer. When Mr. Y.'s associations acquired more of a hammering quality, the value of the associations as content diminished. It was then that I became conscious of them and attempted to bring them to the patient's attention.

The centrality and importance of the form may show itself by the patient's reaction when the analyst attempts to include an exploration of the formal characteristics in the analytic investigation. The way Mr. Y. spoke constituted a hidden gratification that was not to be broached. Bringing that manner of speaking to his attention constituted an infringement on a secretly maintained gratification. A treatment crisis ensued. Such characteristic expression is ego syntonic, and questions about it feel subjectively startling and even intrusive to a patient who is unwittingly expressing something he or she wishes more to conceal than to explore. Although the crisis is sometimes a result of a countertransferential lack of tact elicited by the nature of the subtle enactment itself, more often the patient's affect is the expression of precisely what he or she seeks to conceal. Since the fantasies comprising the adaptive behavior organize central aspects of the patient's psyche, their analysis provides access to significant and valuable material and is essential to pursue. The upheaval is the analysis, not a problem to avoid.

Clinical Material

Preliminaries

Bronze complected, broad, short, muscular, compact, and boyish, despite the beginning stages of baldness, Mr. Y. appeared in my consulting room dressed in shorts, sandals, a tie-dyed T-shirt, and a red baseball cap. Staring at me fixedly as though he were seeing a ghost, he spoke in a way both anxious and tearful, his conversation filled with nautical metaphors. Single and already 32, he wanted to acquire an MBA and to pursue a business career, but had been barely able to complete college, so great were his difficulties doing mathematics, organizing his thinking, or developing his ideas. He also suffered from such symptoms as intermittent impotence, fears of being attacked by men, and various compulsions. At the time of consultation, he was working part-time at a menial job and taking postgraduate courses at night in accounting.

His parents had immigrated from Cuba and settled in the South where his father worked at a boat yard. His father spoke English poorly and resentfully catered to his mother, Mr. Y. told me with barely concealed scorn. His mother spoke better English and was better educated and more supportive of Mr. Y.'s ambitions. There were suggestions that his picture of her was more halcyon than the reality, however. He mentioned that when he was quite small she had developed a lung condition. It had been considered life threatening, and she had left her teaching job and spent a great deal of time bedridden. She had mysteriously recovered, given birth to a little girl, only to begin suffering from various other problems, including a skin allergy and back pain. He dimly recalled her lying ill in bed and remembered throughout his childhood her constant preoccupations with chiropractors and skin lotions.

Besides Mr. Y.'s younger sister, an uncle, 6 years his senior, the son of his father's much older half-sister, had lived with the family. His uncle was killed when a motorboat crashed into the boat of a friend on which he was a passenger. Mr. Y. was 9 at the time. The event proved to be traumatic. The children were packed off to out-of-town relatives for a week. His memories were, improbably, of being stronger than his uncle. After the event, he tortured frogs, but let himself be beaten up in fights with peers. Academic difficulties occurred when Mr. Y. reached the age of 15, but his parents seemed not to have noticed.

Associations as Content

If the preliminary consultations were filled with sadness and poignancy, once on the couch, Mr. Y.'s anxiety and tearfulness disappeared, and he began to free associate in an intense, pressured way. Within two months of the beginning of the analysis, before an hour in which he was suddenly curious about what was behind a closed door in my waiting room, he reported picturing me beaten, bound and gagged on my hands and knees. Thereafter, in hour after hour, he poured out a steady stream of perverse and sadistic sexual fantasies about what he would do to me or what men would do to him.

A few weeks later, associations to a dream in which he'd had a victory over a rival led him to think about his uncle and then about driving a motorboat. The night before the dream, he was unable to stop washing his shirt, thinking there was a stain that he had to remove. He had felt shame, anxiety, and the compulsion to "undo what he had done," whatever that meant. I pointed out that he had connected thoughts about his uncle, about driving a boat, the compulsion to remove stains from his shirt, and the feeling that he had to undo what he had done. "The stains must be him," he burst out. He began to feel very sad. It wasn't his fault that his uncle had died, he said. Sometimes, he continued, he imagined himself in a boat crash hitting an object in the water with a dull thud. He reported hearing an internal voice accusing him, saying over and over, "Guilty, guilty, guilty." It had become clear that he felt responsible for killing his uncle.

The profuse associations now shifted to memories and fanta-

sies about his uncle and connections between those thoughts and
his current behavior. Associations tumbled out with a mixture of
relief, anxiety, pain, and an increasing eagerness to figure out the
puzzles of his life. He remembered his night-time fear as a child:
a wet figure covered in seaweed would come to his bed and strangle
him. The seaweed reminded him of the ghost clanking chains in a
movie of *Hamlet* he had once seen. With a shock it then occurred
to him that this was his uncle returning, that, in fantasy, he
had kept his uncle alive by making him a watery ghost seeking
vengeance.

In conjunction with the first summer separation, he mourned
his uncle while being alternately terrified I wouldn't come back
and furious that I was leaving. Separations from me, especially at
moments during which he was attempting to advance himself,
were extremely painful and fraught with anxiety. He had to imagine that I sat next to him, a seaweed-draped revenant. At times,
he alternately felt dead as he attempted to put himself in his uncle's
place.

Then he began to feel both sexual energy and fierce competition. He remembered taking his uncle's baseball bat and being
extremely possessive of his own toys. He suffered intensely from
guilt at his selfishness. The thoughts of boat crashes returned. His
associations revealed a link between the recurring obsessional
image and wishes he had recently become aware of to have intercourse with me. If he were aggressive he was afraid he would kill
me. After all, he'd already done in his uncle. He connected me with
his mother and connected not doing well in school with the fatal
accident. He had to fail in order not to benefit in any way from
his ugly deed. Thereafter, he took a full-time job, did much better
in his accounting courses, and became less dependent on and involved with his parents. He also stopped wearing the red baseball hat to his sessions.

Then, Mr. Y. began to feel increasingly rivalrous with a tenant he had spotted leaving for work in the building where my office
was located when he came for his early morning appointments.

He decided this man was my husband. He worried increasingly about accidentally tracking wet sand into my office. Contiguous with this symptom were sadistic primal scene fantasies and memories involving his parents—he remembered thinking as a boy that his father had made his mother sick—thoughts about stepping into his uncle's decomposing body as he imagined it washed up on the beach, and resentment of his father's position with his mother. These and other associations allowed me to connect his worry both with his resentment at being excluded and with wishes to penetrate me vengefully and damage me.

The clinical material led next to his difficulties doing mathematics. He was connecting his learning block with his fear of penetrating women's bodies, I noted to him. In response, he began to express castration fears more directly, dreaming that he was swimming through rocks into a narrow passage and struggling to capture and confine a vicious shark. He thought the shark would get hurt if he didn't confine it quickly. He then thought of damaging my body with his penis by creating orifices in it, saw his uncle's propeller-torn body, and was afraid of some man puncturing him and tearing him up as punishment for his transference wishes to penetrate and damage me.

Associations related to his castration fear continued. He remembered his anxiety and confusion as a child when he learned in school that girls had different sexual organs from men. He hadn't believed it. In fact, he said with surprise, he still didn't—sort of! Of course he had seen his little sister being diapered, he added. He felt panic at the realization that women did not have penises. He remembered an early accidental observation of his nude mother and the way he had shifted his attention to a white bathrobe she held in her hand. He had concentrated on the bathrobe to take his mind off her genital area, just as he had concentrated on the diaper with his sister. The knowledge that women did not have penises made him so anxious that he couldn't stand to imagine it! I linked his way of handling this unwanted knowledge to his handling of the knowledge about his uncle's death. Ultimately we were able to connect his reluctance to see to his guilt over his own impulses to penetrate and harm his analyst/mother, and to his fear that he would suffer an analogous punishment. His anger and castration anxiety diminished sufficiently for his intermittent impotence to disappear. His associations continued to proliferate and to contain abundant sexual and aggressive fantasies without much accompanying affect, except for a pervasive and ever-present anxiety and his own reports of feeling guilty.

He began to talk about wanting to have intercourse with me while simultaneously fearing that my husband, the tenant in the building, would burst into my office while he was there and shoot him. A more adequate aspect of his father emerged. He had been a guerrilla in the mountains fighting the dictator under most difficult circumstances. As Mr. Y.'s anxiety increased, he imagined his father breaking into my office with intent to do harm, as though on a sabotage mission to blow up a bridge, had thoughts about a pre-emptive attack upon his father, and then felt guilty about thinking of attacking his father. He imagined that his uncle had been his father's illegitimate son and not the son of a shadowy, now dead couple from a country he didn't know whose faces he'd seen only in a faded photograph. He felt sorry for his father. He paused. He was imagining himself a scuba diver in a watery cave demolishing with a saber-toothed weapon a giant sea serpent that tried to gain entry. That sounded as though he wanted to attack his father and prevent him from sticking his penis into his mother in the place where he—Mr. Y.—was the sole occupant, he said. He felt more guilty. I pointed out that that wish and the belief he was responsible for killing his uncle were, in his mind, identical. We were able to connect the appearance of these guilt-laden wishes to defeat and kill his father with the approaching summer vacation that was making his longing for his analyst/mother more intense. He was openly jealous at being excluded by me.

He entered business school, feeling driven to outshine his peers and his professors by making good grades and millions of dollars, and became almost paralyzed by fears of criticism from professors and students in the classroom. In his associations, he equated academic and financial success with wooing and winning his mother and fears of attacks from professors and peers with his fears of his father's retaliation. He further equated his ideas of his father's attack with expectations of retaliation for murderous wishes toward his uncle that his uncle's death had made appear real actions. This work reduced his anxiety over succeeding and allowed him to do mathematics, organize, and complete his course work competently, if not with the brilliant success he desired.

Associations as Enactment

At this point in the analysis, I became aware both of the extent of his exhibitionistic pleasure in his dramatic associations and their driven, sexualized intensity. I noticed that he revelled in producing sexual fantasies that were elaborations on and repetitions of previous work. This activity now filled his hours. His speech rhythm was increasingly repetitive and its effect assaultive. I felt bludgeoned.

I pointed out his difficulty in associating spontaneously and his tendency, instead, to become lost in the elaboration of sexual fantasies that had been the subject of previous work. Momentarily disrupted, he responded with a memory: his mother, a former second-grade teacher, had secretly taught him and later his sister the answers to his school lessons in advance of their second-grade classes. He remembered that she had feigned amazement at how he came to know the answers, and basked in the praise showered on him by neighbors and teachers as a budding genius, *el genio.* He associated the power and invulnerability that he felt with a happy time before his uncle's death. In contrast, after the accident, he had felt frightened, alone, and powerless.

The profuse, sexualized associations began again. When questioned, he said that he wanted to produce answers that would impress me as he had pleased his mother in second grade. He felt too anxious to associate more spontaneously and to reveal a wider range of feeling. Since he spoke of this desire to impress me with the same anxious intensity as when he repetitively expressed his desire to be the best in his program or to make millions of dollars, I pointed out the similarity in affect and asked him to analyze these wishes too.

Mr. Y. became suddenly furious and exceedingly anxious, quit his job, and threatened to leave treatment. I was taken aback by the violence of his reaction, a response on my part that in its intensity both afforded me a glimpse of the extent of his anxiety and told me we had engaged something together that was central to him. He said he felt as though I were drilling holes in him. New material emerged about his mother. She was scathingly scornful toward his father. She told Mr. Y. terrifying stories about little boys who were mutilated and murdered by "an evil man from the mountains." From these, he had fashioned a fantasy of her as an extremely terrifying, dangerous, phallic mother. That image of his mother had become the currently active transference fantasy.

As we learned more about his fears for his penis at the hands of this terrifying and envious mother, he became able to talk in a less defensive and exhibitionistic way about his transference feelings. All along, Mr. Y. had been appeasing me, as he had tried throughout his life adaptively to appease his mother—and all the world. He had set out to be the best possible patient, to mollify me by producing the right associations, in just the way he'd been able to recite his second-grade lessons and please his mother. He needed to do this because he was terrified she would otherwise dominate him, control him, take over possession of him, and castrate him.

In subsequent work, we learned about other ways he had protected himself from his anxiety about what she would do to him. He maintained to himself that certain key fantasies were real, among these that women and men were not different from one another by virtue of their gender, but were the same and therefore interchangeable. The wish that the sexes be interchangeable and their genitalia uniform was expressed in a variety of ways.

He imagined women to possess a phallus, relating with embarrassment that he had to hold onto his partner's preferably dirty foot during intercourse and that he became sexually excited when he found that a woman he was interested in had a substantial sum in her bank account. He also imagined himself as a woman and arranged the sheet around himself, during masturbation, to approximate his wearing of a negligee. He connected this fantasy to a recurrent childhood dream in which he was omnipotent and invulnerable. Further work showed that since the loss of his uncle made more terrifying the threat of castration at the hands of the phallic mother he so feared, his maintenance of the fantasy of gender indeterminacy also allowed him to re-create his uncle in his female sexual partners and in this way doubly to reassure himself.

Now the analysis focused on this fearful mother imago and his attempts to defend against the anxieties associated with it. He became overtly provocative and defiant toward me. He rearranged my waiting room furniture and imagined taking over my office. He wanted to smear me with excrement. He wouldn't associate and refused for three months to pay me. He wondered if he had struggled with his mother during toilet training and felt very sad, once again, about his uncle's death. With these and other associations there seemed enough material to connect the loss of his uncle and the transference loss attendant upon the approaching summer vacation with earlier experiences of loss of his feces and current transference fears of loss of his penis at his mother/ analyst's hands. I pointed out to him that he seemed to be dealing with the vacation loss in terms of trying to withhold and control and to take possession of me in this earlier way to preclude the danger he feared when he was alone and vulnerable. This interpretation led to much important and fruitful work on his constant attempts to control omnipotently the important objects in his life and how difficult that made it for him to have a good relationship with anyone. Particularly, he tried to turn the women he was interested in into what he imagined his uncle would have become.

The impulses to torture women that his early transference fantasies had presented as content devoid of affect now emerged as barely controllable wishes. He thought of times he had ganged up with friends against his uncle. He then realized it wasn't a physical fight he was remembering, but the fact that he used to get his uncle in trouble with his mother. He now again felt extremely guilty. He had used his uncle to protect himself. He had done so by taking the part of his destructive mother of whom he was so fearful. He thought it possible that his uncle had become so disheartened over her incessant critical attacks on him that he had not made any attempt to save himself. When he wished to torture women, he realized, he was imagining himself as the mother whom he was afraid would torture him.

When we resumed after the August break, he said defiantly that he wouldn't let me control him or his body the way his mother had wanted to. He had developed a fear that intruders would break into his apartment. He now sought out a new protector, a former philosophy professor from his college days who was in training to be a therapist. He had long talks with him, telling him with longing and sadness about his uncle. He experienced my attempts to analyze these visits as my wanting to rip this person away from him. He recalled the humiliation and rage he had felt when his mother gave him enemas—something he now revealed for the first time. He was aware of an intense sexual attraction toward this man and saw me as the intruder who would violently separate this man from him. Eventually, the feelings toward this professor proved to be related to longings toward his uncle and then his father.

A shift then occurred so that the wishes toward the uncle appeared in the transference. He spoke feelingly of wanting to be filled up by me and to be held and comforted by me and did so in a way that made oral feeding and pleasurable gentle anal penetration interchangeable. When I pointed this out to him, he said that he never wanted to let go of me. He recalled times he felt neglected by his mother. I reconstructed that he had experienced his mother as ill, depressed, preoccupied with herself, and using him for her own needs, not in response to his. He had created a better mother for himself in fantasy by imagining his *uncle* as a superior substitute, thus also protecting himself from the menace he associated with his mother.

Another way of protecting himself was thus to create a split between this good uncle/mother and the dangerous phallic mother he hated and feared. The transference moved back to the latter. He was afraid that I would "get rid of him" once he showed that he could function independently or that his analyst/mother would castrate him. He didn't want to talk because, he said, I'd interrupt him and "cut him off." He concealed independent work he was accomplishing out of fear that I would immediately terminate the analysis. Attempts to turn passive experience or fear of loss into active abandonments multiplied. He left for a vacation before I left for mine. He behaved increasingly as though he were entitled to special treatment, became demanding, asked for schedule changes, and missed sessions when I didn't comply. There was a resurgence of academic difficulty based on grandiose fantasies that "geniuses don't have to study." He recounted stealing pocket money as a child, incidents in which he had run up debts and never paid them, and incidents in which he had appropriated other people's work without acknowledgment. As we worked together on this material, he understood that the fear that I would castrate him was also a projection of his regressive unconscious wishes to devour and incorporate all organs of supply so that he could be the biggest and smartest, never want for anything, and be immune to abandonment and harm. He connected his guilt over this appropriating of other people's work to the inability he was encountering and had encountered in the past to work effectively in a job. These entitlement wishes proved to be an identification with the "devouring" and dangerous mother who stayed in bed, reduced his father to a servant, was the center of attention in the family, and seemed to receive everything she wanted.

This identification provided ultimate protection because it

meant to him that he was invulnerable. To speak the associations he assumed that I expected was not only to appease the dangerous mother he imagined would hurt him but also to be what she wished to be and wished him to be, all-knowing and perfect. To speak his feelings as a separate entity was to invite her terrifying wrath and scorn. Being different—in body, being, and gender—meant exposing himself to her destructiveness. Better to take refuge in this secret and reassuring identification. It was terrifying for him to relinquish the fantasy of being so powerful. The loss of his uncle had proved to him the consequences of his vulnerability and her power.

Discussion

If the analysis of the form of Mr. Y.'s associations was a crucial moment in the analytic process, it was not because it moved us from the uncle's death, a latency event, to a temporally earlier, central preodipal and oedipal fantasy complex, enabling us to leave the uncle's death behind. Rather, it allowed the death to inform and explain the power of the earlier fantasy complex. It provided a bridge to the most important unconscious meaning that Mr. Y. ascribed to his uncle's death and illuminated the reasons for the tenacity with which he held onto his uncle. Thus this bridge was not a one-way thoroughfare toward a chronologically earlier and therefore presumably more valuable time. The events had reciprocal effects on the content and force of an organizing unconscious fantasy. Mr. Y.'s uncle's violent death reinforced his fantasies about the danger he feared at the hands of his dangerous and envious mother.

Traditionally, latency trauma has been considered primarily in its role as a resistance in the analytic process. Glover (1929) showed how such a trauma served as a screen for and resistance to the recollection of oedipal events and conflicts. Greenacre (1950) followed Glover when she reported on conscious, isolated memories of traumas occurring during the prepubescent period in women. She found them related to preoedipal material and used to defend against both the renewal of oedipal wishes and excitement in the adolescent period and their remembering and re-experiencing in the transference. However, she significantly revised her conclusions in a second paper (Greenacre 1956). There she reported cases in which a repressed latency trauma unconsciously represented to the child the enactment of forbidden oedipal wishes. Until the uncovery of the trauma, which was precipitated by the child's curiosity, no analysis of the preceding oedipal conflict was enduringly therapeutic. The repressed enactment carried with it a guilt far greater than that of earlier fantasy, however charged, and in that sense the infantile neurosis may be said to have reorganized itself around this subsequent historical nucleus.

The death of Mr. Y.'s uncle was not repressed. His unconscious fear of his mother was so strong, however, that Mr. Y. could never wholly accept it. His uncle's death confirmed for him his mother's power to damage and destroy. He remained caught between loss and terror, in a never-never world that was constructed to deny each. The form of his associations with their secret appeasement of his mother, even more secret hostility toward her, and identification with her was a silent testimony to the unspeakable. To conceal these secrets, he resorted to a solution common to pathological mourning and to perversion: he both accepted that his uncle was dead and at the same time denied the death. To do so, he isolated knowledge of the death and kept his uncle alive in a number of ways reflecting different developmental stages. He made him into a watery ghost and an avenging peer in the classroom about to punish him for successful competitiveness; more defensively, he let his uncle stay ahead in school by failing. He identified narcissistically with his uncle, wearing his hat, becoming himself a dead body, letting himself be beaten up, or damaging himself by preventing himself from thinking. He re-created the nephew–uncle dyad in many forms, most notably in the transference, with various women, and with the philosophy professor.

This re-creation that expressed homosexual and narcissistic wishes related to both negative oedipal and preoedipal issues was accompanied by a fluidity of self and object representations so that he sometimes experienced his partner as his lost uncle and sometimes experienced himself as his uncle and his partner as himself. He re-created the relation with his uncle in a still more regressive way between himself and an internal body part, a fecalized penis/breast that he desired to possess to meet all his narcissistic wishes and strivings for grandeur and that he feared his envious analyst/mother would rip away.

The motives for this denial are related to the various ways in which the trauma was suited to represent earlier conflict and the way it revived and reinforced earlier conflict. It actualized a positive oedipal victory. This victory had to be denied so that any progress or success in life would not be the occasion for unbearable guilt. First, in terms of rivalry, the uncle stood for himself, for the father, and for the father's penis. Competition became equated with castrating and actual bloody death so that rivalrous impulses were translated into real murder. Second, retaliation on the talion principle was imagined to be similarly bloody, and thus fear of it was paralyzing. The uncle's death acted as a macabre cautionary tale: "This is what will happen to you if you act in an aggressive, masculine way." Third, the accident and death actualized phallic wishes toward the mother that were already colored by sadistic and vengeful impulses. These had been occasioned partly by rage over primal scene exclusion and partly by his experience of her self-preoccupation, her tendency to use him to satisfy her own narcissistic needs, and her unavailability. The penetrating penis was equated with the smashing boat, and entry into a woman was assumed to end with the woman being castrated and killed on the model of the accident. Fantasies about the cause of his mother's early illness in her sexual activities with his father created a fallow ground for the fantasy connection between phallic aggression and death that the trauma accentuated. Given these unconscious connections, Mr. Y. kept his uncle alive in order to defend against paralyzing oedipal guilt for sexual and aggressive deeds and their regressive sadistic expression. Denial of the uncle's death also enabled Mr. Y. to maintain a homosexual bond with his uncle, part of which had its source in a negative oedipal constellation. In this constellation, the phallic and intrusive mother assumed the role of rival ready to rip the uncle away. The uncle here functioned not only as the masculine love object to Mr. Y.'s feminine one but, given the narcissistic identification with his uncle, also as a defense against castration anxiety associated with his passive, feminine wishes. Whenever Mr. Y. became involved with a woman, he feared that intruders—that is, his analyst/mother—would break into his apartment and separate him from his female partner/uncle, a castration fear as well as a fear of the mother as rival. Further work revealed the representation of the desired father behind that of his desired uncle. Denial of his uncle's death also served to defend against guilt over wishes to incorporate his uncle's phallus. Here the uncle also screened the father.

Preoedipal factors also contributed to the motivation for this disavowal. Rage over the mother's early unavailability and general self-preoccupation was displaced onto the uncle. Mr. Y. began the treatment with memories of being stronger than his uncle, an unlikely happening given the difference in age. After his uncle died, he tortured frogs. When he became more aware of his anger at his mother and no longer needed the defensive displacement, his memory changed. His uncle had allowed him to win. These hostile wishes toward his mother displaced onto the uncle were a considerable, additional source of guilt.

More than guilt was involved, however. Given the fact that Mr. Y. had made his uncle into a good mother, the latter's death made real the fear that, if he expressed his hostility, he would lose the very object he depended on for sustenance. His attempts to hold onto his uncle through re-creation of the dyad, through narcissistic identification, and through control of an incorporated part object that would supply his narcissistic needs and could be treated as part of his body all defended against this anxiety over loss. This anxiety took on forms corresponding to the stage implied by the defensive maneuvers. There were oral-stage fears of losing inner contents and maternal supplies and of being precipitously abandoned and helpless, an anal-stage fear (from another point of reference a rapprochement fear) of being abandoned the moment he had begun to show he could function independently, and a phallic-stage fear of being castrated for independent masculine ability. All these fears were related to imagined punishment for not complying with the wishes for control of the dangerous and devouring maternal object representation, a representation formed partly out of his rage at his mother's early unavailability, partly out of his negative oedipal rivalry with her, partly out of a regressive condensation of positive oedipal rivalry with his father, and partly out of the fear occasioned by the reality of her envy of men and her unstable and controlling personality.

Not only did Mr. Y. displace his anger toward this representation onto his uncle but he also used his uncle as a barrier that protected him from the mother's perceived envy, competitiveness, and acquisitiveness. The trauma intensified these fears of his mother because he believed her to be responsible for the accident. He saw his father, in his resentful passivity, as having already succumbed to her destructiveness and felt himself as powerless to resist overtly. Keeping his uncle alive continued to provide him with a good maternal object and with protection, in fantasy, from the dangerous object. It also represented a silent masculine rebellion, a stubborn, touchingly faithful refusal to comply with his mother's prohibition against remembering his uncle.

One factor, in particular, favored the multiplicity of meanings accorded the trauma and therefore its power to reorganize earlier conflict. The object representation of the uncle was endowed with a fluidity that allowed it to represent a range of objects and part objects from different stages of psychic development, from the father as oedipal rival at one end of the spectrum to the maternal breast at the other. One source of this fluidity was in the oral- and anal-phase conflicts around the mother's unavailability and unresponsiveness, which left Mr. Y. with a tenuous disidentification from his mother (Greenson 1968). Another was in the substitution of uncle for mother. This substitution not only had an adaptive function but also *the substitution of the uncle for the mother crucially defended against knowledge of the anatomical difference.* It made penis and breast into equivalents.

It would be a mistake to regard the centrality of the uncle in Mr. Y.'s unconscious fantasy life as caused by the influence of early factors on later ones only. It was the *interaction* of the traumatic event with the patient's earlier defense against knowledge of the anatomical difference that ultimately made the uncle so central. That is, the uncle became so central a figure because he had first functioned to defend against the fears of loss and castration that the child's early hostility and the mother's indisposition and character had stimulated. Therefore, when he died his death made those fears appear real.

Both this substitution and the factors in the mother's personality that necessitated it fostered the blurring of distinctions between the sexes and between sexual organs—that is between anal and vaginal orifices and between penis and breast—that in any event also warded off his terror of his mother. Marked polymorphous perverse trends characterized Mr. Y.'s sexual fantasy life. This blurring of sexual distinction and unstable sexual identity in turn led to a fluidity in Mr. Y.'s self and object representations that facilitated narcissistic identifications with his dead uncle and with his devouring mother and re-creation of the uncle–nephew dyad in which Mr. Y. could enact either the role of the caretaker or his own self. This fluidity of self and object representations also defended against castration anxiety attendant upon his assuming the female position in the fantasied homosexual relation with his uncle because he could narcissistically identify with the active, masculine penetrator and simultaneously be the passive, receptive partner.

However, turning his uncle into his nurturing mother also increased his sexual wishes toward his uncle and therefore his castration anxiety. Since that substitution of uncle for mother also defended against his rage at her unavailability, and since that rage, projected onto her representation, contributed to his fears of castration, a circular process reinforcing the need to defend against knowledge of the anatomical difference that meant to him the existence of castration as a danger was also set up. The defense against the anatomical difference, the disavowal that leads to the splitting of the ego Freud (1927, 1940a, b) describes in cases of fetishism, became the mechanism for the defense against knowledge of his uncle's death. In seeking a partner, Mr. Y. unconsciously turned every woman with whom he was sexually involved into the person he imagined his uncle becoming, one built on his own, rather grandiose ego ideal. He required that they be intelligent and have attended a prestigious institution. By making these demands, he both satisfied his unconscious homosexual wishes and defended against his castration anxiety. He also defended against his castration anxiety by maintaining the lack of difference between the sexes. His partner was manifestly female, but, "really," he was saying, "there are no sexual differences." Money in a bank account or a dirty foot provided women with a phallus; imagining himself wearing a woman's negligee made him like them, unisex. If there was only one gender, then castration was not a danger.

The major source of his castration anxiety was a dangerous secret, however, one hidden in his profuse and compliant associations. Only when I began to question both his expressions of his ambition and his transferential exhibition of his "right answers" did the extent of his castration anxiety in connection with the maternal object representation emerge. It was accompanied by terror, rage, and the wish to flee the analysis. To be differentiated was to acknowledge the anatomical difference and to put himself in grave danger of what he imagined was his mother's penis envy. At a more evolved level, from which he had retreated, it would also acknowledge the force of his positive oedipal wishes and the danger of castration from the father.

The nature of the trauma was different from the latency traumas Greenacre (1956) described. These seem to have been overtly sexual in nature and directly precipitated by the child's curiosity. The child's unconscious participation undoubtedly contributed to the degree of guilt experienced. Mr. Y., on the other hand, did nothing to precipitate his uncle's death, no matter how much he may have occasionally wished it. *Rather, the trauma had the quality of a shocking and unwanted perception forced on him from outside.* It not only reinforced the dangers of castration and loss he already feared at the hands of the terrifying mother imago but also confronted him with them in reality. Guilt at having caused the death was more comforting in that it gave him power and control not only over arbitrary events but also over the imagined power of the fearful mother representation. The analysis of the form of Mr. Y.'s associations opened up the existence in him of this terror.

6 Notes on Transference and Transference Neurosis

Perhaps no concept in psychoanalysis carries with it so many emotionally charged meanings, yet has remained as obscure as the transference neurosis. Although psychoanalysis has evolved, the transference neurosis has too frequently retained its creaky historical definition. At the same time, my investigation of the current meaning of the term showed that its working meaning varies enormously from analyst to analyst (Reed 1994). It frequently retains the sense of central psychoanalytic experience, however, so that it is linked with the most intimate and moving of present analytic experiences. Its indeterminacy and its centrality combine to offer us an unusual freedom in understanding it that is the ironic counterpart of its long role in the institutional evaluation of young analysts.

The transference neurosis was conceived by Freud as part of a theory of cure. That theory of cure also established the scientific status of psychoanalysis. Psychoanalysis was deemed scientific because it resolved the transference. Cures by suggestion that did not resolve the transference were designated as unscientific. By virtue of this connection, the transference neurosis in later years began to function as the signifier of the science of psychoanalysis. That is, it functioned, as an external entity, to shore up claims to the scientific unassailability of psychoanalysis.

If, historically, external claims of "scientific" correctness occasionally lend status, only hard-won inner conviction about the power of the unconscious can help a clinician facilitate a patient's self-understanding. But that stops none of us from yearning for external validation, especially today, when the idea of the dynamic unconscious is asserted to be unmeasurable, unprovable, and in the eye of the beholder and interpretations that are based on this idea are held to constitute suggestion. The transference neurosis that once served as the guardian of the scientific purity of psychoanalysis, however, can no longer do so. It has itself been called into question. In fact, it is not going too far to suppose that the panel that originally occasioned this chapter was partly a response to the loss of status that the concept of the transference neurosis was called on, extra-clinically and fallaciously, to provide.

Every contribution that attempts to define the transference neurosis is likely in one way or another to be a reaction to this current loss. One way to deal with the problem of suggestion is to agree that the influence of the observer on the material observed is profound. Clinical observations can then be used to describe a transference neurosis, based on the concept of transference as denoting an inference about the past that influences the individual's experience of the present. However, such a statement appears to me to be inaccurate. True, transference *involves* an inference, but it does not *denote* one. To denote means to stand for or signify.

The concept of transference does not signify or stand for an inference. It is, of course, true that each of us draws inferences from what patients imply about the past they are reliving in the transference present, and all of us are partly motivated by our own character and conflicts in the choice of intervention we do or do not make. Indeed, we infer all unconscious phenomena from what we take to be their clinical implications. From a point of view *within* the set of principles of mental functioning to which most psychoanalysts subscribe, however, transference is more than an inference. That theory hypothesizes the dynamic unconscious as existing independently *in each of us* and holds the transference to be one of its manifestations. Its existence is implied by its effects. Patients have transferences; we do not merely infer them because they are dictated by our theory. Our theory influences our observation by enabling us to see them.

I assume therefore that unconscious processes including those that prompt transference exist independently of my inference. To be sure, that assumption will influence my clinical work and shape the process itself. That is, after all, the point of having theoretical and technical precepts. The fact of that influence, however, does not invalidate the truth I believe to reside in the principles to which I subscribe. Although the transference neurosis, as I define it, remains for me one possible sign of a well-progressing analysis, I am reluctant to define it as a concept existing exclusively in the analyst's mind.

The emphasis on the transference neurosis as a concept that delineates the successful analyses of neurotic patients and organizes the analyst's observations is an extremely useful corrective to another historical legacy, that of extreme reification. Freud (1914a, 1917) described the transference neurosis as an artificial illness that evolved organically during the analysis. It was the analyst's business to destroy this illness. His formulation placed the analyst outside the field of influence of the transference neurosis, removing him or her from having a part in its emergence. This perspective, excluding the observer and meshing so well with requirements for so-called scientific status, would be difficult to sustain today about any endeavor.

In addition to describing the transference neurosis in terms of its parts, it can be defined as a whole: "a *mutable organization constituted by the patient's simultaneous, affect-laden perceiving of the analyst as entwined with the core, organizing, unconscious fantasies (as-*

sumed to include relevant memories) from childhood and gradual disengaging of the object representation of the analyst from those core fantasies" (Reed 1994, p.229). This definition does not consider the transference neurosis as distinct from the psychoanalytic process nor does it confine it to one moment in an analysis.

There is at least one relatively reliable subjective criterion for *when* these central object representations and the fantasies attached to them usually begin to emerge in a clearer way that can be considered a property of the transference neurosis itself. There is no one moment, but an accretion of instances, during which the analysand reveals with relatively greater immediacy painful and humiliating conflicts to the analyst. This change occurs when more narcissistically protective, pain-reducing, distancing, defensive fantasies connected to these conflicts have been sufficiently worked through and are no longer needed as frequently by the patient in his or her interaction with the analyst. For example, there was a marked change in one patient's engagement in the psychoanalytic process after he recognized his contempt and what motivated it. Instead of idealizing the analyst as invincible and trying to imitate his success, this patient thought of his analyst more realistically as a person with limitations and strengths, who was interested in him and wished to be helpful. He felt love and gratitude in return.

The transference neurosis may thus be characterized by *a progressively more intimate or intense therapeutic and thus also libidinal involvement. The increasing libidinal investment permits the engagement within the dyad of intensely shameful and/or hostile wishes as well.* I do not, however, mean that the patient must make the analyst the exclusive center of his *conscious* preoccupation. The transference process is multifaceted. From one perspective it is a productive means of bringing unconscious conflict to light; from another, once the conflicts are revived, their transference to the analyst becomes a resistance to remembering the original conflicts with primary objects. It is more accurate to say that one of the signs of a transference neurosis is that the patient becomes progressively more interested in exploring *with* the analyst, who is experienced as a whole object, *all* areas of life where conflicts interfere, including the transference. We need, however, to understand that the interest in exploring with the analyst is a sign of the more intimate transference characteristic of the transference neurosis.

Reference to the ability to treat the analyst as a separate and independent whole object brings me to the concept of psychic structure. I take seriously the limitations implied by the word "neurosis." If the capacities associated with neurotic-level functioning vanish during the most intensely unreasoned moments of an analysis, they must nevertheless reassert themselves. The degree of ego development and the freeing of these capacities partly account for a patient's increasing ability to work with the analyst.

Just as these criteria represent a change from the historically defined transference neurosis, so I would replace the historic concept of the infantile neurosis with one that emphasizes *integrated* conflict solutions reflected by *adequate structure and functions* (Tyson 1993). Preoedipal conflict and compromise determine whether an ego will be sufficiently integrated to meet the challenge of oedipal conflict in a way that synthesizes earlier conflicts and their solutions.

This formulation leads to a central distinction between transference as a more general internal process and transference neurosis as one possible result, given an analysand with sufficient ego and superego capacity. Other possible results with potentially different but progressive trajectories may occur when patients have differently organized character structures. In what I have elsewhere described as a transference perversion, for instance, perverse conflict solutions—involving the defense triad of disavowal, the splitting of the ego, and illusory substitution (formation of a fetish or its equivalent)—lead to a character structure stamped by rapid shifts in organization that maintain the disavowal of disturbing external perception. The transference is predictably less linear and more circular, with solid, neurotic-seeming work suddenly and repetitively undermined by being turned into a gratification that asserts a protective omnipotence. The analyst is not maintained as a whole object, but in these shifts is reduced to a part object. When the process moves favorably toward a termination, the repetition of the undermining shift in organization and attendant disavowal gradually diminish (see Chapter 3).

Distinctions, of course, are much easier to make on paper than in the affectively suffused clinical interchange. The most interesting but confusing cases are those we are least certain about how to characterize. It is possible, for instance, that structural transformations in patients during treatment may lead to transformations in the results of transference processes. Thus a transference neurosis, as I am defining it, could conceivably occur late in the treatment of a previously non-neurotic individual. We would not need to force the previous treatment into conforming with the definition by overusing the concept of regression, for example. To give clinicians maximum flexibility, I prefer to sever the transference neurosis from its exclusive connection to cure.

So far, I have focused on the internal process in the patient. However, for the patient to understand and work through those perceptions of the analyst based on conflict solutions arrived at in the past, he or she must also differentiate the object representation of the analyst he or she has fashioned from previously constructed primary objects. The construction of the analyst arises as a result not only of the patient's internally motivated perception but also of the contributing actions and character of the analyst. In this sense the patient and analyst together may create resistances (Boesky 1990), as well as insights and perhaps the most irrational moments of a transference neurosis. The perception of difference between the analyst and primary objects at times, depending on the patient–analyst pair, may become difficult or transiently impossible, even for the patient with adequate structure. Some actualizations arise from the analyst's doing his job in a characteristic way. The fantasy of a physical fight with the analyst that may represent a derivative of a male patient's homosexual longing can be actualized by a verbal tussle over some trifling, otherwise unimportant incident.

In addition, the increasing distillation of core conflicts in the patient in the course of a transference neurosis especially tends to exert a regressive pull on the analyst, frequently reactivating aspects of his or her own conflicts and therefore making possible the analyst's unconsciously motivated enactments. Thus an analyst may enact with the patient in any number of subtle or not so subtle ways—answering questions, for example—without realizing the meaning of what the patient is asking for. Such an interchange has its own meaning for each participant and will affect the subsequent process. Such moments may paradoxically facilitate understanding, but they also possibly limit access to other areas that it might be advantageous to explore. Intersections of unconscious conflict in analyst and patient may be inevitable, but do not influence the principle that the transference to be analyzed originates in the patient.

As process, the transference neurosis is characterized by a distillation and clarification of conflicts, unconscious fantasy, and affect. This concentration, distillation, and clarification may be considered additional criteria. They occur as part of an interaction, the analyst's synthesizing functions interacting synergistically with the patient's construction of the analyst and with his greater capacity to integrate unconscious material and thus to bring it forward.

They also occur, however, because analysis of specific transferences requires analyst and patient to focus on the latter's private and automatic systems of meaning. Such systems confine patients to fixed patterns of affect, understanding, and behavior. Organized unconscious fantasy/memory complexes are systems that automatically and repetitively attribute fixed meaning. They have been constructed by the patient at moments involving terror, internal drive arousal, and/or unwished-for external perception. At these moments, only one meaning out of a plethora is possible for a given individual. The univocal meaning attaches itself to a similar situation or contiguous object, to name only two possibilities, and persists with its univocal meaning and affect charge to affect current perception. Such instances of private meaning dictate the rules by which the patient perceives the analyst. That is, they are the material out of which specific transferences are formed.

Work on these inflexible units facilitates integration of the experiences they isolate into the adult ego. The greater the integration made possible by the mutual work of analyst and analysand, the greater the patient's capacity becomes to integrate larger units of his system of meaning within his adult ego, thereby removing the repetitive, fixed, autonomous invocation of univocal meaning described earlier. The transference neurosis is the sign of this progressive integration. It is, finally, more than the sum of its parts.

II The Clinical Uses of Comparative Understanding

7 Rules of Clinical Understanding in Classical Psychoanalysis and in Self-Psychology: A Comparison

While many authors have examined the theoretical and clinical tenets of self psychology (Coen 1981, Friedman 1980, Grossman 1982, Kris 1983, Levine 1977, London 1985, Rangell 1982, Richards 1981, 1982, Rothstein 1980, Schwartz 1974, 1978, Ticho 1982, Treurniet 1980, 1983), little attention has been paid to the potential impact of self psychology on psychoanalytic understanding. In order to undertake such a critical examination, I think it useful to compare self psychology and classical psychoanalysis with reference to one very narrow, but influential, area, that of exegesis, or the rules that govern interpretation in each. I intend interpretation in its broadest sense to cover all understanding of the patient by the analyst, not just what the latter says to the patient. I shall contend that self psychology adheres to a system of interpretation that is contrary, not complementary, to that of classical psychoanalysis and that the two systems are incompatible.

I shall not concern myself with the content of self-psychological interpretations. Whether they are valid or not, or whether, indeed, they could be arrived at within a classical framework is a matter outside the concern of this chapter. My focus will be on the different rules of interpretation that each theory favors. These rules are often not articulated; rather, they exist as both potentialities in and as results of those theories. Nor am I concerned with the work of individual practitioners. Some may have integrated the concerns of self psychology in such complex and creative ways that my description of interpretation in self psychology will seem foreign to them. In fact, one of the conclusions that follows from this study is that experienced analysts attracted to the psychology of the self and finding its perspectives helpful to a greater or lesser degree are in a potentially different position from contemporary candidates at institutes where the self-psychological paradigm is favorably regarded and introduced early into the curriculum.

If Kohut, however, has acknowledged the applicability of classical psychoanalysis to those patients who do not suffer from a "disorder of the self," how can it be suggested that self psychology is inconsistent with the practice of classical analysis? This question needs to be addressed in the context of a critical examination of Kohut's characterization of classical analysis as well as of the relation of his conclusions to his method of observation of data: introspection and empathy (Kohut 1959). Grossman's treatment of introspection as an analyzable behavior, the content of which reflects the motives for undertaking it, is relevant here (1967, p. 17), for Kohut's insistence on the maintenance of subjectivity toward the patient's productions determines what may and may not emerge as data. Indeed it is conceivable that Kohut's and his followers' empathic-subjective stance will prevent clinical data relevant to unconscious guilt from emerging and eliminate classical analysis as a treatment in all but name. This position is, apparently, the obverse of Kohut's characterization of classical psychoanalysis as imposing its "objective" theory on data and thereby preventing contradictory data supporting the psychology of the self from emerging. But only apparently. As I shall present his own work to demonstrate, Kohut's characterization of classical analysis is more a misunderstanding than an accurate characterization. And it is this misunderstanding—that classical analysis "understands" by imposing its objective theory on the patient's material—that becomes the basis for Kohut's restriction of its applicability.

I shall present an alternative view of understanding in classical analysis in the second section of this chapter. Meanwhile, it is well to recognize that one cannot employ a diagnostic criterion (disorder of the self) that originates from a new set of theoretical postulates (self psychology) to restrict the usefulness of the paradigm one wishes to amend (classical psychoanalysis) without raising the specter of circular reasoning.

Kohut's characterization of classical analysis has propelled us into an unnecessarily polarized way of thinking, one that I have previously pointed out with regard to empathy (see Chapter 9). While it is central to question whether classical psychoanalysis can address the clinical concerns raised by self psychology, this issue cannot be properly considered as long as Kohut's characterization of classical analysis is accepted as accurate. In turning my attention to an exploration of the different systems of exegesis at work in self psychology and in classical analysis, I hope usefully to reorient the discussion.

Interpretation in Self Psychology

To arrive at the rules governing interpretation in self psychology, I shall, of necessity, restrict myself to written texts and attempt to infer the rules from the understanding offered the patient or the reader. In this way, I attempt to limit myself to data and avoid expressed intention. I choose to focus on a case from the *Casebook* (Goldberg 1978) because of the *Casebook's* quasi-official status, cross-referenced as it is to patients mentioned in Kohut's work, yet going beyond the work of one man to that of a school. In the case of Mrs. R., the patient dreamt early in the analysis that she was in a foreign country, possibly Mexico, crawling on hard ground strewn with emeralds and other precious stones. As she collected them, a godlike voice prohibited her from continuing (p. 311). Much later in the treatment, the following interpretation was offered to her:

> The gems were a representation of her brilliant, infantile self that had remained unavailable (repressed) to her everyday self-experience. The god had disapproved of her gathering up these emeralds of her self. But without these (nuclear self) gems, she was (later) the dead Victorian woman in a casket. . . . She had not been given enough of a sense of being loved, or of affirmation of the value of her self in her developing years by her self-absorbed mother or, later, by her more responsive but infantilizing and ultimately disappointing father. And, already vulnerable and prone to a depressive sense of loss, she lost the gems her experiences with him had given her, the gems which . . . for a moment at least she imagined to be hers. [pp. 350–351]

A footnote adds that the patient experienced her mother as "hardened, foreign soil."

What can be deduced from this account concerning the system of interpretation at work? Clearly, self psychology assumes a hidden content in its broadest sense; otherwise the work of interpretation itself would be unnecessary. There also seems to be a reference to hidden content in its specific dynamic sense, since the nuclear self is designated "repressed," and in a case I shall discuss below, exhibitionism is designated as "latent" (Kohut 1977, p. 203). Yet these apparent references to the topographic model are misleading. They do not imply the systems unconscious and preconscious. Rather, they are ways of describing something not obvious. They designate, generally, a disjunction between what I shall refer to as the signifier and the signified. These terms, introduced by de Saussure (1916), are clumsy but useful. Signifier refers to the visual or auditory symbol, signified to the meaning attached by convention to the symbol. The task of interpretation in self psychology is to explain the disjunction between the signified and the signifier and, as I shall later suggest, to restore a connection where formally there was a disjunction.

If we study the interpretation of the dream of Mrs. R., we can delineate certain connections between the signifier and the signified that are established by the interpretation: hard ground (signifier) = mother (signified); foreign soil = mother; precious stones = (repressed) brilliant, infantile self; emeralds = nuclear self; the god's voice = superegolike "No" with roots in mother's indifference to her core self. A particular pattern emerges: each major element in the dream, each signifier, substitutes for a historical person or an aspect or attitude of such a person (signified). The hard ground, the mother; the foreign soil, the mother; the voice, the result of the mother's indifference. That is, the only signified attributed to each signifier involves a historic reality. How are these equivalents arrived at? Through the application of a theory of development that is held to be immanent in the account of the dream.

A look at the relation of these elements to each other will clarify this point. There are actually two sets of relations described. The first is a partial description of the early or preanalytic inner state of the patient: the brilliant infantile self (gems) is unavailable to her everyday self-experience. The god disapproves of "her gathering up these emeralds of her self." Note that the description easily flows into a description of the dream so that the meaning of the god is enlarged upon in a footnote, almost as an afterthought.

The reason for this fluidity between a description of the inner state of the patient and the surface of the dream is that the two are virtually identical. While there are hidden signifieds for each element in the dream, *the relation between the signifieds is identical to the one delineated in the manifest content of the dream between signifiers.* Only the specific elements of the dream have a hidden content. Their relation to each other does not change. As far as the arrangement of the *elements is* concerned, there is no content other than what is manifest.

To draw an analogy: suppose that a map of imaginary country X represented the relation of specific cities, mountains, and rivers to each other, as maps generally do. Suppose further that real country Y had exactly the same rivers, mountains, and cities in exactly the same topographical relations. All one would have to do to identify X as Y would be to substitute place names, but *this supposes that one already knew Y to exist*.

On the basis of this specimen analysis at least, it would appear that self psychology assumes no hidden meaning concerning the relation *between* signifiers. In this respect, surface content needs only to be revealed by the proper identification of the hidden elements according to a belief already known (a constructed history of the patient).

Signifiers are related in another way as well. This second description involves history (Goldberg 1978):

> She had not been given enough of a sense of being loved . . . by her self-absorbed mother, or later, by her more responsive but infantilizing father . . . she lost the gems her experience with him had given her, the gems which in her dream for a moment . . . she imagined to be hers. [pp. 350–351]

This second delineation of a relation between elements in the dream has more movement. Rather than soil being only *equated* with mother, a narrative is offered in which Mrs. R. has *lost* something and temporarily imagines it to be hers again. In this second description, the signifier "gems" is given another hidden meaning, the experiences with the father. This attribution of meaning is not explicit; it is accomplished implicitly, through a metaphor. The inference to be drawn from the metaphor is that the repressed, nuclear self equals the sum of the good but unsustained contacts with the father. Signifier and signified are equated through metaphor. Then the new amalgamated structure of meaning is animated by a reconstructed series of historical events: "she lost the gems her experiences with him had given her." In this second explanation, manifest and hidden elements, signifier (gems) and signified (self-experience), are placed on one plane by a theory of development and are unified by a historical statement. In other words, the relation explicitly described by self-theory is always manifest and awaiting revelation. Only its elements are disguised.

The second description, however, is not a description of the relation of the (repressed) nuclear self to the sad remnants of the individual. Rather, it is an account of how the first relation came about. This second interpretation *accounts for the movement in the manifest content of the dream*. It does so by offering a theory of the etiology of the disturbance. The product is held to account for its own genesis. Self psychology, in other words, uses causes to account for behavior or for a perceived subjective state: "You feel this way because your mother did not give you enough of a sense of being loved." Classical psychoanalysis, as we shall see, does not.

To reiterate, self-psychological interpretations, not only the one considered here, but those generally found in the literature, seem to assume that self-theory informs and is present in the manifest content in two ways. The first concerns the constancy of the relation of the individual elements. That constancy is dictated by the theoretical description of the self. The second concerns the explanation of action in the manifest content of the dream. That action is held to depict a theory of development. Neither the relations among the elements nor the actions of the elements are assumed to have a hidden content. Only the elements per se are assumed to have a hidden content.

The case of Mr. X. confirms these observations (Kohut 1977). As Kohut describes the case, the analyst had been interpreting Mr. X.'s grandiosity as a defense against an oedipal defeat and concomitant depression. In his "overt grandiosity," however,

> the patient was no more than the agent of his mother's ambitions. What had remained disregarded was the patient's latent . . . grandiose-exhibitionistic self—an independent, boyish self that had

first yearned in vain for confirmation from the side of the mother
and had then attempted to gain strength by merging with an
idealizable, admired father. [p. 203]

Confirmatory evidence for this assertion is a daydream following
the analyst's summer vacation. In this daydream, the patient runs
out of gas on an expressway and tries to signal for help. Car after
car passes, and his anxiety mounts as he finds himself alone. Then
he dimly remembers long ago having stashed away an extra can
of gas in the trunk. He recovers the gas under a heap of odds and
ends, pours it into the tank, and drives off.

If we look at the relation of signifier to signified in the daydream, we get something like this: car = depleted remnants of the
self; cars that will not stop = indifference of mother; junk in the
car trunk = memories of devalued father; gas = (repressed) nuclear
self related to memories of a satisfying relationship with the father. Again, the manifest relation among elements reveals the
theory about the depleted self, while individual elements are relatively easily translated into historical figures conforming to a
theory of genesis.

The account of the manifest *action* of the dream, moreover, also
relies on a theory of the genesis of the disturbance: in the face of
the mother's disregard, X. turned to the father whom mother
devalued. Among the devalued dross exists a full can of gas, the
equivalent of the memories of the idealizable father. These memories comprise the repressed, nuclear self. Once recovered, X. imagines they made the self (car) function smoothly.

This method of interpretation is an extremely old one. Medieval allegories such as the *Roman de la Rose*, the sixteenth-century
epic poem, *The Faerie Queene* by Edmund Spenser (1596), and the
seventeenth-century *Pilgrim's Progress* by John Bunyan (1678)
are all informed by a common knowledge that readers will apply
this interpretive strategy when they read allegory. To take an
episode from Spenser's poem (Book II, Canto vii), for instance:

Sir Guyon, conducted by Mammon (who prized the riches of heaven over its virtues and ended in hell) comes upon Mammon's daughter, the seemingly wondrous Philotime. Philotime has a chain, the upper end of which is attached to highest heaven, the lower end to deepest hell. All her suitors, courtiers, and admirers crowd around trying to win her favor so that they can catch hold of the chain and climb toward heaven. "Those that were up themselves, kept others low,/Those that were low themselves held others hard,/Ne suffred them to ryse or greater grow,/But everyone did strive his fellow downe to throw" (11:33–36). As a favor to Guyon, Mammon offers the Knight the hand of his daughter, reminding Guyon that access to her will gain extraworldly bliss and advancement up the chain to heavenly immortality. Guyon declines on the grounds that he is mortal and therefore unworthy of the favor offered and that he is pledged to his own Lady by a love he has no power to break.

To discover the hidden meaning of this allegory, Spenser and his readers held in common an interpretive method similar to that of self psychology. First, the hidden meaning of each element has to be identified. Thus, Sir Guyon = Temperance; the chain = ambition; the behavior of the people on the chain = the evils of ambition; Philotime = false artifice, pride, and temptation. The truth that emerges as the elements are identified is already present, its elements barely disguised, in the manifest narrative: the virtue of temperance protects the soul from the temptations of sin. This hidden but readily discoverable belief may also be used to explain the action of the narrative by means of a narrative of genesis—this time literally. That narrative of genesis proceeds as follows: Man is, by reason of the disobedience of Eve and the subsequent weakness and acquiescence of Adam, mortal and corruptible. Man's immortal soul is therefore endangered by the corrupting influence of sin. Only the teaching of Christ and his disciples can protect man from this calamity. See how Guyon, guided by the ideal of Christian temperance, preserves the innocence and integrity of his soul.

The similarity between the interpretations of Christian allegory and those of self psychology emphasizes aspects in the rules of interpretation of the latter upon which I have already commented. To restate them:

1. Surface elements are translated into hidden elements according to the dictates of a theory of the self.
2. The relations among those elements as well as the actions of those elements are undisguised aspects of that theory. That is, self psychology treats the product to be interpreted, whether dream, daydream, or complaint, didactically. *The product to be interpreted always reveals the theory of the self.*
3. The hidden content that interpretation uncovers is always an aspect of the self or the narrative of its (deficient) genesis.

If the nature of the self-psychological interpretation is didactic, the system of exegesis by which meaning is arrived at depends on belief in the existence of another meaning of which the self is the content. Every self-psychological interpretation is thus a *restoration of meaning,* one that repairs the disjunction between signifier and signified. Ricoeur (1970) identifies such hermeneutics with traditional interpretations of the sacred. It is no accident that this activity of interpretation parallels the self psychologists' description of the healing process in the therapy. According to the theory of therapeutic action, the restoration of the self occurs because of the restoration of meaning: the analyst's empathic understanding provides what unempathic parents could not, thus paving the way for structure building.

We may recognize in this parallel between the restoration of the self and the restoration of meaning a tendency to concretize understanding, to transform it into substance. Indeed, this tendency is responsible for the confusion, in self psychology, between theoretical language and language in the clinical process (Gediman 1983, p. 65, see Chapter 8).

Interpretations of this nature do not require that the patient provide particular verbal connections (as opposed to accounts of manifest history) between the surface meaning and the meaning to be restored; self theory does not account for verbal transformations, for the transformation of dream thought into pictorial representation, for instance. Thus, associations to "self-state" dreams are irrelevant (Kohut 1977, pp. 109–110); rather, it is the theory of the self that provides these connections. Restoration of meaning depends on a prior belief on the part of the interpreter that there is a specific translation of elements to be made.

Self psychologists will undoubtedly contend that the missing evidence is supplied by the behavior of the patient in the transference. It is the presence of one or the other of the typical self-object transferences that furnishes the signal of the need to invoke self theory in the process of understanding the patient. Yet, it should be pointed out that *self psychology interprets the manifest transference behavior of the patient in the same way as it does the patient's verbal productions.* That is, specific constellations of manifest transference behavior—idealizing of the analyst or of the self, for instance—are held to be a sign of defective self-structure. They are used to confirm the invocation of self theory. But behavior, like verbal productions, must, in the context of a therapeutic situation, be *understood;* meaning emerges through a systematic application of a set of rules of understanding, however intuitive the subjective experience of comprehension may appear. If the same rules of interpretation apply to the transference behavior as apply to other of the patient's productions, then manifest transference behavior cannot be used to supply the evidence missing for other self-psychological interpretations. When, in contrast, manifest transference behavior is considered a compromise formation (Brenner 1982), an entirely different understanding of the same phenomena is possible.

If we bear in mind that the fundamental interpretive strategy of self psychology is didactic in nature and that its goal is a restoration of meaning, we are in a position to understand at least tentatively Kohut's attitude toward classical psychoanalytic interpretation. It is likely that he wove the same rules of understanding into the fabric of self psychology as he applied when using the classical paradigm, that is, he attempted to reveal classical theory-truth to the patient in order to restore meaning. If so, his reproaches that classical psychoanalysis allows theory to dictate interpretation reflect a misunderstanding of classical psychoanalysis rather than a defect inherent in classical psychoanalysis per se. Consider, for example, Kohut's report on his interpretive activity during the first analysis of Mr. Z. (Kohut 1979, italics added).

Most conspicuous during the first year of the analysis . . . [were] his demands that the psychoanalytic situation should reinstate the position of exclusive control, of being admired and catered to by a doting mother who—*a reconstruction with which I confronted the patient many times*—had . . . devoted her total attention to the patient. [p. 5]

As the patient's main resistances, I saw his defensive narcissism and the mechanism of denial. *I attempted to demonstrate to him that he had* . . . denied the fact that his father had indeed returned home . . . and that his pre-oedipal possession of his mother . . . was a delusion. [p. 6]

In my interpretative reconstructive attempts . . . I tried to discern and interpret to him the motivations for his clinging to pregenital drive aims. [pp. 6–7]

All in all, my approach to Mr. Z.'s psychopathology as it was mobilized in the analysis can be said to have been fully in line with the classical theories of analysis. [p. 7]

At any rate, *I* consistently, and with increasing firmness, *rejected the reactivation of his narcissistic attitudes, expectations and demands* during the last years of the analysis *by telling the patient that they were resistances against the confrontation of deeper and more intense fears connected with* . . . competition with men. [p. 8]

What is most striking about these passages is the impression one receives of the analyst insisting that he is in possession of a truth to be imparted to the patient *no matter what.* That the truth the analyst attempts to reveal resembles formulations familiar to classical psychoanalytic theory does not make this procedure a classical psychoanalysis. Indoctrination remains indoctrination regardless of the doctrine.

Indeed, Ostow (1979) has argued that the first analysis of Mr. Z. was not properly conducted, that well-known formulations were imposed inappropriately on material, and that manifest content was accepted at face value when evidence abounded to the contrary:

> Dr. Kohut chose to interpret the [patient's] anger as a response to his efforts to show the patient he was still craving, in the transference, his mother's single-minded admiration and commitment. It seems to me that the analyst might have been impressed by the contrast between the idyllic relationship the patient described, and the hostility he exhibited in the transference. This contrast alone suggests that the manifest account covered repressed hostility. [p. 531]

It would appear that the self-psychological characterization of classical psychoanalysis assumes that classical psychoanalysis employs the same system of hermeneutics as self psychology, one that I have described, following Ricoeur, as a *restoration* of meaning. The larger assumption is that this system of exegesis is the only one possible; an assumption on the part of self psychology that accounts for the original need to set up the series of dichotomous categories Richards describes (1981, p. 320). It was necessary in this schema to diagnose the patient before deciding which truth it was therapeutic for him to have restored. If the patient suffered from a disorder of the self, one theory and one truth were necessary. If the patient had a "cohesive self," another theory and another truth were necessary. Diagnosis in psychoanalysis is generally thought to evolve through the unfolding of the psychoanalytic process. The need to distinguish between pathologies and then match pathology to paradigm, necessitated by the original formulations of self psychology, emphasizes an attitude essentially contradictory to that process. Similarly, while self psychology relies on the clinical evidence of the developing transference as a guide, that transference itself is subject to the same hermeneutics as are all other patient productions. Given also that self psychology applies the same rules of understanding to the transference as to all other phenomena, the likelihood is that more and more pathology will be diagnosed as necessitating a restoration of meaning appropriate to self-disorders. It is therefore not surprising to discover Kohut (1984) in his last book attributing all pathology to self–object failure. This natural evolution in his thinking merely extends one truth at the expense of another; it does not represent a fundamental change in the assumption that truth must be restored to the patient.

Interpretation in Classical Psychoanalysis

The hermeneutic system of classical analysis need not be seen as a system that restores meaning. While it is true that theory about internal psychological processes represents a systematic organization of data one chooses either to accept or not, and that the reasons for adoption of a particular theory may be only more or less rooted in rational assessment, never fully rational, it does not follow that all psychoanalytic theory necessarily occupies the same position vis-à-vis the understanding of clinical material as does theory in self psychology. In fact, what separates interpretation in classical psychoanalysis from interpretation in self psychology is the possibility classical theory affords of a change in relations among the analyst-observer, the data to be interpreted, and the theory that helps organize the data. That this possibility is not always realized is not the fault of the theory, but evidence of the human frailty of its practitioners.

This discussion extends that of a previous work on the misappropriation of psychoanalytic theory in applied psychoanalysis and of the concomitant tendency to neglect the concept of psychoanalysis as process (see chapter 8). In that work, I emphasized certain relations between the word (signifier) and its possible meaning (signified).

One of those relations concerns the gap between the experience of physical desire and the word that speaks about that desire. Words lie partly in the objective world. To communicate with each other, we ultimately learn and adopt certain common linguistic conventions (de Saussure 1916). In contrast, the experience of affect or impulse is inner and subjective. Classical theory allows us to ask how this translation from subjective impulse to objective discourse is effected. It answers, with a series of rules, possible ways in which a transformation and translation may take place.

Classical theory and analysis tolerate, indeed exist in the paradox of subjective impression and the necessity of expressing that impression in words that have objective meaning. The patient is encouraged in his struggle to move from enacting to speaking (Freud 1914). The conceptualization of this human dilemma is not limited to conflict among the separate structural entities of ego, superego, and id. Before we even conceptualize a conflict among systems, we must think about the complex interplay between inner and outer worlds that is built into later structures and is exemplified by the constant need to translate the purely subjective into the communal. Yet while incorporating this inevitable human dilemma into its theoretical language (Grossman 1967, Grossman and Simon 1969), classical psychoanalytic theory also offers us a way of conceptualizing it. Drive derivatives arise from within, inchoately at first, but nevertheless imperatively. What

is desired and what one gets, achieves, or allows oneself to have
varies with circumstances and endowment, among other factors.
Suffice it to say that it is never entirely all that one wants. Verbal
communication arises gradually out of these affect states of frustration, incorporating and transforming them. The word, in a
sense, substitutes for the wish and is also the sign of its renuncia-
tion or frustration.

The translation of inner impulse into action or expression is
no simple one-to-one matter. The more unattainable the impulse,
the more the wish is expressed through substitutions. The more
substitutions impose themselves, the more subjectively unrecognizable the impulse is. Signifiers thus may attain a polyvalence of
unconscious meanings (and affects) that condensed, reverberate
in one repeated phrase. Concreteness is sometimes in the eye of
the beholder.

"I wish that had never happened," a patient laments. She refers
to a past intervention of the analyst that she experienced as painful criticism. In that sense, the patient's words are a complaint,
with a referent in the treatment relationship, and express the pain
of a narcissistic wound. In the present stage of the treatment, however, this phrase has other, more immediate meanings. For one,
the phrase functions as a resistance to further exploration. It says:
"I am so hurt, I am not able to go farther and it's your fault." More
important, as she associates further, she remembers the many
times she explored an abandoned estate with her father. Once they
went farther than they ever had before. It was exciting, but she
felt she was trespassing and, as they continued, became increasingly anxious. Then she remembers waking from a nightmare as
a child and running to her parents' bedroom. Her father returned
her to her own bed. Thus, the phrase also expresses that which is
apparently defended against. It says: "I want to be close to you,
but I try not to let us know about that because I know if I do feel
these yearnings for closeness, I will also feel sexual excitement.
Then I will remember my terror, and worse, I will remember the
humiliation of how I was cast aside as a child and of how I had to

stay alone in my own bed at night. I don't want to remember that. If I don't show these feelings and instead accuse you of hurting me, I can maintain my secret illusion that I am loved and favored and stay in this analysis forever." The classical analyst who listens only to resistance and the self psychologist who listens only to material relating to the empathic failure of a self-object are listening to theory, not to the patient. By making room in its theory for the polyvalence of words, classical psychoanalysis challenges us to listen to the patient, if we can.

Such listening includes not accepting the patient's theory at face value (Grossman 1982). Consider the following vignette. The patient, a recent law school graduate, discouraged, recalls her mother's criticisms of her: "She was right. There's nothing to be done. I'm just a rotten apple." This statement lends itself to a self-psychological interpretation, for it offers a representation of self theory. The patient refers to her own impoverished, "rotten" self. Its cause is not hard to find in the disparaging mother. Even the transference, manifestly idealizing, could be called on for evidence. Classical theory provides no comparable way of organizing manifest data into understanding. Instead, it prompts one to wonder why the patient is comparing herself to a rotten apple? "What comes to mind about a rotten apple?" Classical theory here *affords a way of opening up material for mutual exploration.* Associations lead to a neighboring farm of her Pacific Northwest childhood, where apples were put into a barrel to ferment. They seemed soft and rotten, but the mixture was, in fact, strong and potent—too strong for children, forbidden. We come then upon the theme of attraction to the forbidden, the wish to taste something mysterious, allowed only to adults. Classical theory about content, itself empirically derived from evidence in other analyses, suggests that these thoughts may he related to infantile sexual researches and wishes, but that possibility must await further associations. What is evident for the moment is the connection between self-reproach and the thought of tasting something potent and forbidden.

Classical theory puts us in the humbling position of not knowing anything about the patient's meaning from the manifest content, including the manifest content of the transference. It requires, instead, that we rely on both the patient's free associations, and nonverbal communications such as re-enactments. Thus, while the patient who saw herself as a rotten apple was expressing her conscious, internal, subjective state, neither analyst nor patient could know in advance the reason for that state.

The metaphor she used was a condensation of unconscious fantasy, memory, wish, and in its very indirectness, of the defense and the danger situation that gives rise to the defense. Classical theory gives us these general indications without any specifics toward understanding meaning. It throws us forever back on the patient's associations.

The reasons for this humble position vis-à-vis the patient and his material are prescribed by conflict theory. Because drives are seen as energy, they are seen to cause internal movement, wish, signal anxiety, and defense. The interaction of these components creates the phenomenon of substitution, of one desired object for another, more acceptable, which represents the first, and so on in a chain that ends in various compromise formations including sublimations, symptoms, and character traits. Not only do manifest elements have another content, mental energy directly and indirectly rearranges the relations between elements as well. *Relations between elements have manifest and latent forms.*

It follows that a manifest formal resemblance between a patient's dream and analytic theory of the kind we found self psychology making use of in interpretation does not imply the relevance of the theory. Where self psychology would likely understand a patient's statement that he was "fragmenting" as evidence for the in cohesiveness of the self, a classical interpreter would understand only that the patient was experiencing intense anxiety (Gediman 1983). That interpreter could not know what the anxiety is about, what wish instigates it, what danger the patient foresees, and what defensive measures, however ineffective, he calls upon. Fragmenting, in this example, is a word used to communicate an internal state. Classical analysis explores the reasons why the patient uses the word, and this exploration may include the fact that the word belongs to the analyst's theory. Through the word, analyst and analysand explore the reasons for which the state occurs.

Reasons are not the same as causes (Grossman 1967, 1982). When meaning is restored rather than explored, restoration inevitably involves the explanation of causes. Self-psychological interpretations move directly from the concept of a repressed, nuclear self to the genetic *causes* assumed to be responsible for that deficit (self-absorbed mother, weak father); classical theory, while taking into account the historical reality of the patient's past, asks the patient and analyst to explore the internal *reasons* for a given subjective state, e.g., "you feel rotten because your graduation has revived in you a childhood wish to taste something potent that only adults were allowed."

Because the classical interpreter cannot rely on surface content for clues leading directly both to theory and to a revelation of the truth—that is, because surface content is essentially mysterious—empathy and introspection are not enough. He must also observe the patient's free associations, noting patterns, pauses, and changes of subject, so that he may slowly discern patterns of relations between elements and sometimes correlate those patterns with a real event that may act as a stimulus: the juxtaposition of self-reproach, the thought of the forbidden fruit, and the graduation, for instance. To be sure, actions and other nonverbal communication must sometimes be translated into associations before this stage is reached.

Classical interpretations do not seek to restore truth to the patient. They do not mend the disjunction between signified and signifier, between gems and the self. Instead, amid the investigation of reasons for actions, thoughts, fantasies, and affects, the classical analyst discovers with the patient the latter's own system of exegesis that he employs without conscious awareness to interpret the data of internal and external perception. Thus, when you thought of doing something only adults are allowed to do, you perceived yourself as incorrigibly bad.

Classical theory permits different relations among the interpreter, his data, and theory than does self psychology. Because drives provide movement that rearranges the entire configuration of the surface, not just the appearance of individual elements, the interpreter must rely on the patient's associations. Any given element may stand for another by virtue of temporal and spatial contiguity as well as of resemblance. Any affect may defend against another. Classical theory allows us to understand how and why this may occur. It does not tell us what specifically to find. Classical theory gives us the principles by which meaning becomes disguised and distorted. It tells us that there will be an interaction of wishes, anxiety, and defense. It may even suggest a likely area of wish (e.g., oral or phallic), the kind of danger situation generally imagined, the kind of defensive patterns possibly employed. It does not, however, tell us which wishes toward which people or things, which danger situations, which defenses, or which current situations stimulate them. It gives us rules for discerning patients' reasons. It does not give us the reasons themselves.

The different relations among clinical data, interpretation, and theory that exist in self psychology and classical analysis may be clearly seen in their interpretive approach to rectal and bowel symptoms. In the case of Mr. I.:

> The problem of separation from the self-object indeed entailed the question of whether his own independent psychic structure would now be strong and stable enough. Mr. I. also seemed concerned whether he would ultimately be able to incorporate the analyst's approving, optimistic, and confident interest in him. All this led to hypochondriacal bowel preoccupations, along with an exacerbation of bowel and rectal symptoms of more than ten years' duration. His attempts at self-regulation of his separation experiences were thus still partially sexualized in the hyperstimulation of his

bowels, and his imagery depicting the process of structure formation through his internalizations was still in crude oral or anal
terms. [Goldberg 1978, p. 87]

The forces contributing to the symptom are not inherently of
interest to the self psychologist. There seems to be no interest in
the elements of the symptom or of how that particular symptom
rather than another came to be. Instead, the explanation of self
psychology tends toward the general. Understanding moves directly from the manifest symptom to theory: the concepts of separation and tension regulation.

In contrast, let us turn to a case treated by Stoller (1973).
Mrs. G. suffered from rectal bleeding as well as the hallucination-
delusion that her brains were rotten and that flies were buzzing
in her head. (Although the treatment was a very intensive psychotherapy, classical psychoanalytic theory was employed in its
understanding.) Exploration of the first symptom led to the recovery of a repressed traumatic memory, an anal rape, and repressed guilt over its initial encouragement. The semen, seen as
worms, became associated with rot and rotting—so, too, the buzzing flies. But why the brain? "I guess because my mother always
told me my brains were in my ass" (p. 131).

In classical analysis, theory guides exploration, not explanation. If a symptom is understood as a compromise formation, it is
necessary to investigate its individual parts in order to alleviate
it. The interpretation then moves away from theoretical gener-
alities to the blood and sinews and accidental happenings of a
patient's life. The rectal bleeding and the delusion of a rotten brain
are connected, not vaguely, but by the specific fact that the mother's
disparaging words rearranged anatomy.

Interpretations in self psychology move from the patient's specific material to theoretical generalizations that tend to repeat the
theory of self psychology. They restore meaning to the patient
by translating the signifier according to a specific theoretical belief. In classical analysis, interpretations move toward the fabric

of an individual's life. By discovering with the patient his heretofore unconscious system of exegesis, classical psychoanalysis does
not restore meaning to the patient so much as it gives the patient
the freedom to modify the way he himself has interpreted data.

Discussion

As I have tried to demonstrate, the two systems approach clinical
material in entirely different ways. Not only do they employ different rules of understanding but their assumptions about the
proper function of imparting understanding to the patient also
differ. Self psychology interprets causes and relies on a system of
interpretation resembling that of allegory; classical psychoanalysis
investigates reasons and tries to discover the patient's unconscious
system of interpretation. Self psychology refinds its own theory
in the relations between disguised elements in the manifest content of patients' productions; classical psychoanalysis considers
manifest content as something mysterious that needs to be opened
up by the patient's association to individual elements to be understood. Self psychology reiterates theory in its interpretations;
classical psychoanalytic interpretations move away from theoretical generalizations toward specific fantasy/memory constellations. Finally, theory in self psychology organizes directly the
content of interpretations; theory in classical psychoanalysis organizes a technique of exploration and furnishes general sequences
(e.g., wish, anxiety, defense) according to which the data can be
understood.

This view of classical analysis differs from Kohut's characterization. If it is accepted, it follows that there can be no question
of one theory for one type of patient and another for another.
Differential diagnosis of this nature is extremely subtle and must
involve some degree of interpretation, especially of transference
phenomena. Otherwise, we would be faced with the unsolvable
question of which system of understanding to utilize to arrive at

a diagnosis. Also, to ask which theory is appropriate for a particular patient assumes another question: Which truth should this patient have restored? Such a question is antithetical to exegesis in classical analysis.

That these two theories utilize different systems of interpretation is particularly relevant for psychoanalytic education. Experienced psychoanalysts attracted to the psychology of the self and finding its perspectives helpful to a greater or lesser degree have been thoroughly exposed to classical tenets and treatment. It is not unusual to hear a self-psychological interpretation from such a practitioner that is similar to a classical interpretation and addresses phenomena ordinarily considered drive-related, such as passivity. Nor are such practitioners likely to diagnose every manifestation of narcissism as related to developmental arrest and be unaware of the possibility that it serves other psychic functions. Since there are more things in the consulting room than are dreamt of in our theory, the verbatim records of analyses conducted by classically trained self psychologists would provide wonderful data for studying the relation of practice to theory, particularly the question of the degree to which the integration of the prior classical training influences clinical perception.

Unlike self psychologists originally trained in classical theory and technique, however, candidates at institutes where the self-psychological paradigm is favorably regarded and introduced early into the curriculum are being asked to integrate two entirely different and in many senses opposite ways of understanding data at once. Surely, what is involved in learning to practice psychoanalysis is a way of listening and integrating data, that is, a system of exegesis. Moreover, the new paradigm presents itself as an alternate way of organizing clinical data, and one initially easier to understand. Because of this ease, its wholehearted adoption may mask an inhibition that the necessity to master the very difficult task of integrating clinical data with the dynamic formulations of classical theory would challenge and lay bare.

Whether such a conflict is or is not at issue, the possibility now exists for the emergence of a generation of practitioners who have adopted self psychology as their primary focus and have a very shallow or minimal understanding of intersystemic and intrasystemic conflict and the way such conflict manifests itself in the clinical situation. Furthermore, these new practitioners are the very ones likely to misunderstand the nature of exegesis in classical analysis. The effect of such confusion on psychoanalytic theory and practice needs to be assessed.

One potential consequence concerns the capacity for self-analysis. An exegetic system that refinds theory and substitutes the explanation of causes for the exploration of the reasons for action and affect can only continue to reiterate the same causes. The restored meaning functions a little like a soothing reassurance, to be repeated at times of distress. If, on the other hand, interpretations in classical analysis uncover the idiosyncratic system of exegesis of the analysand and allow him the freedom to modify that system, then interpretations function in a way that parallels the theory: they provide rules for discovering future reasons without providing the reasons themselves. Classical analytic interpretations build a capacity for self-analysis.

Self psychology is said to have grown out of dissatisfaction with the results of classical analysis. That so many have accepted at face value Kohut's characterization of classical analysis suggests that the nature of its system of exegesis has been imperfectly understood. Perhaps it is often imperfectly practiced, as well. If that is so, then the opportunity to identify these misunderstandings and attempt to clarify the potential of exegesis in classical analysis is welcome.

Self psychology has asked important questions about the relations among theory, interpretation, and the clinical data that support them. Its solution, however, is to return to an older, pre-Freudian method of exegesis, that of allegory. To assert that by returning to allegory self psychology has tapped a system with more potential for resolving these dilemmas than that of classical analysis, is, at best, a dubious proposition.

8 Psychoanalysis, Psychoanalysis Appropriated, Psychoanalysis Applied

While psychoanalysts have been frequently accused of reduction in their attempts to interpret art, they have been slow to investigate a reverse phenomenon: the reduction of psychoanalysis. This second reduction often occurs when psychoanalytic interpretations are appropriated by other disciplines. In its most easily recognizable form, any sword may a phallus be and any woman a mother, but it may appear in other, less obvious guises as well. The fact of this reduction suggests that something central to psychoanalysis is easily lost in its application. It follows that to identify what is lost may make it possible to approach applications of psychoanalysis in a different way.

In what, then, might this reduction consist? I shall approach this question by describing an opposition that I shall exaggerate for the sake of clarity. The opposition I exaggerate is that between the different requirements in hearing and thinking about language expressing theory and language in the clinical process. I shall propose that in much applied psychoanalysis there is a tendency to interchange assumptions appropriate to reading and explaining psychoanalytic theory with those appropriate to listening to the patient in the clinical process. The chief element in the reduction of psychoanalysis when it is applied is the weight given to assumptions characteristic of theory specifically, and to a stance of theoretical certainty to the detriment of clinical exploration more generally.

Since my exploration of this issue will be somewhat unconventional, some clarification of my method of exposition is in order. The first section of this chapter discusses the different assumptions about language in psychoanalysis itself and the different kinds of interpretation to which they can lead. The second section exemplifies these different assumptions through an analogy: a contrast in strategies of interpretation implied by two poems, one from the seventeenth century, the other from the nineteenth century. The poems are not studied as artistic objects. It is the kind of interpretation they illustrate which is important. The third section examines these different assumptions and tendencies to interpretation at work within one text by exploring the tension between method and statement in Freud's study of Leonardo da Vinci. The fourth section addresses the problem of method and statement in applied psychoanalysis more generally. The final section makes a speculative leap to treat Freud's *Leonardo* as a text to be interpreted.

It will be characteristic of this exposition that the relationship between literary text and psychoanalysis is not constant. That is, psychoanalysis is not always applied to literature; instead, literature is sometimes used only to illuminate a contrast within psychoanalysis so that the relationship between literature and psychoanalysis shifts from section to section, or even within one section. I hope that this approach will draw attention to the many ways the two subjects can intertwine and mutually illumine each other without the reduction of either.

Assumptions About Language Used to Explain Theory and Language in the Clinical Process

The processes involved in understanding theory, on the one hand, and in listening to clinical data, on the other, differ in nature. To some extent, that difference is reflected in the language (i.e., characteristic combinations of words and syntax) used about or in each activity. What I shall for shorthand call "the language of psychoanalytic theory" and "the language of the clinical process" come to represent the differences in process and quality of conceptualization required by each activity. While I emphasize the extremes of this difference for the sake of my argument about the appropriation of psychoanalysis, it is important to note that different uses of words always lie on a continuum. Not every theoretical concept in psychoanalysis is without ambiguity (see Chapter 9), nor is every word in the clinical process heavily laden with multiple meanings. Nevertheless, at one end of the continuum, theoretical language in psychoanalysis reflects the fact that it is often an attempt to generalize and conceptualize clinical data and thus sometimes an attempt to represent, in secondary-process language, elusive early wishes, fantasies, memories, and their psychic consequences (Skura 1981). At the other end, the language of the clinical process involves a mutual search for words that can replace re-enactments and approach these conflict-laden fantasy-memory constellations that are the source of present suffering.

Thus, the role of the word in the clinical process tends to be different from that of the word used to elaborate theory. In the clinical process, the content of words as it is subjectively perceived by both analyst and patient, changes. Words, groups of words, narratives, deepen with affect and changing perspective within the dyad. In this mutual effort to represent and consciously understand the patient's subjective experience, the patient's words are not presumed, a priori, by the analyst, to mean a specific thing: words are rather defined and redefined by mutual exploration. As a result, there is a specific assumption about the relation of manifest to latent content. The analyst refuses prematurely to assign a specific latent meaning to the individual patient's words; he consciously adopts a stance of uncertainty toward them. Their meaning, he knows, will change; it is mutable, overdetermined.

In the case of theoretical language, the relationship of observed data to its abstraction is extremely complex and merits a study in itself (Pontalis 1977, pp. 104–111). If, instead, I rely upon a venerable and limited characterization, it is because this formulation appears, at least, sufficient for my present and limited purpose: to contrast the function of words in the clinical situation and in theoretical formulation as that contrast refers to misapplications of psychoanalysis. A fuller exploration of the relationship between clinical data and its organization into theoretical language must await a future study. While such a study may modify the formulations presented here, it will not significantly change what I have to say about the appropriation of psychoanalysis. According, then, to Waelder's (1962) formulation, no matter how close to or how far from the clinical situation, theoretical conclusions are verbal propositions that generalize phenomena originally discovered in psychoanalytic explorations of individual utterance. Theory turns the clinical discovery of unconscious content into generalized truth and, in so doing, tentatively identifies the latent content of many patients' words. Even if we make allowances for overgeneralization, it is possible to say that the purpose of some theory is to fix latent content in a general way and that this endeavor is in contrast to the clinical openness that assumes fluidity of meaning. Of course, not all theory attempts to fix latent content in this way. Some theoretical utterances are concerned with describing the clinical process, for instance. Yet even when this is the case, the *form* of the theoretical language differs from the form of language in the clinical process: theoretical language retains its secondary-process, bound nature. Further, our listening or reading is determined by its function as theory. When we hear it, we assume it means what it says. By contrast, the words of each clinical session offer an occasion for the exploration and discovery of new relationships between their manifest and latent meanings. It is largely the difference in our attitudes occasioned by the various contextual functions of words—functions and attitudes that become somewhat formalized in styles of discourse—that I wish to stress.

When the analyst's neutral, exploratory attitude toward the patient's language is interfered with, for whatever reason, it is often replaced by an attitude more appropriate to the reading of theory. Deadlock then replaces the psychoanalytic process. Grossman and Stewart (1977) describe two women whose analyses ended in stalemate after the interpretation of penis envy. Second analyses revealed in each case that penis envy had become a metaphor delusionally organizing conflicts over rage and abandonment. Here, the first analysts' fixing the meaning of the patients' words precluded mutual exploration of further latent content and was paralleled by the patients' use of the inexact interpretation as an organizing, defensive metaphor. One might say that an attitude of certainty characteristic of theoretical language interfered with the analysts' listening. I wish to emphasize, however, that although the attitude is appropriate to the reading and writing of theory, it should not be equated with theory. Theory does not create clinical deadlocks, although analysts who cannot remain open to latent content but instead substitute theoretical certainty may. Thus my phrase, "the certainty characteristic of theoretical language" refers to an attitude in the analyst, not to a contaminating quality of theory.

Nor do I wish to propose, as have some (e.g., Ornstein 1979), that the clinician lay theory aside in the process of listening to the patient. For one thing, there are certain theoretical assumptions that cannot be put aside, for they are implicit in the act of listening to the patient and, indeed, of exploring latent content with him. For another, theoretical language, comprising as it does an aggregate of individual explorations, stands as a provisional, potential organizer. Objective principles of organizing are necessary whether these principles are held to be recovered in the objective understanding that follows free association (Arlow 1963, Beres and Arlow 1974), or whether these principles are deemed to provide the framework for the process of free association only. Indeed, the tension in psychoanalysis, here reflected in the differing degrees of certainty posited by the psychoanalytic language of theory and that of process, is another aspect of the general and characteristic tension in psychoanalysis between subjective and objective viewpoints (Grossman 1982).

These differing assumptions about language are both necessary to psychoanalysis, for the body of theory grows from the practice, becoming more subtle and sophisticated, a better instrument for organizing patients' productions. There is thus a mutual interdependence between the relatively certain attitude required by the language of theory, and the relatively uncertain attitude toward the patient's meaning necessary to the clinical process. When each nourishes the other, a productive, dynamic balance exists. Stasis threatens when the attitude of uncertainty toward the patient's words is pre-empted too early by the certainty more characteristic of the attitude toward theory.

Although stalemates may happen if the reverse occurs, I emphasize the danger of too much certainty because I believe it particularly characteristic of unsatisfactory efforts to apply psychoanalysis. At their most disappointing, these efforts conceptualize psychoanalysis as a series of theoretical propositions to be demonstrated by a text. The most extreme instances of this tendency occur when knowledge about psychoanalysis seems to have been acquired exclusivly through the reading of theory and is devoid of an experiential dimension. For to approach a text and "apply" a knowledge of psychoanalysis that is purely theoretical, as many experts in other fields do of necessity, is to "listen" and organize with a language very different from the one used by the clinician. The language with which the latter organizes and listens incorporates—one hopes—not only the abstract representation of experience typical of and appropriate to theory but also the experiential element represented by the theory as well. That is, to listen to a text with the benefit of the theoretical language of psychoanalysis alone is to listen to a text with the benefit of a very different analytic instrument—to use Isakower's phrase—from that of the clinician trained not only by the reading of theory but by supervised clinical work and a personal analysis as well.

To summarize some of the differences between the language of theory and that of the process: (1) Two different assumptions about the word are involved. In the former, the relationship between manifest and latent content tends to be generalized and fixed. Even when that is not the case, the language of theory is presumed to mean what it says. In the latter, the relationship between manifest and latent content is not assumed to be fixed; words are assumed to be multivalent and mutable. (2) Theory represents, relatively abstractly, aspects of affective experience. In the clinical process, affective experience is reactivated and joined to the words appropriate to it. (3) There is a mutually enriching interdependence between the language of theory and that of the clinical process. The product of that interdependence is part of the knowledge of psychoanalysis acquired by each analyst. (4) When the clinician listens, he listens with an instrument honed by both his knowledge of theory and his understanding of affective experience. When knowledge of psychoanalysis is acquired solely through the reading of theory, the listening instrument is a completely different one.

This last difference is particularly important. Two different kinds of interpretation follow from it. The first of these is the optimal clinical interpretation emerging from the form and content of the patient's utterance and organized around affectively understood theoretical concepts, a blend of personal experience, evidence, and the experience of others. Because it neglects the multivalent and mutable quality of language, the second of these applies a kind of listening appropriate to the reading of theory. It then attempts to confirm what dogma asserts by simple-minded equations, for example, between theory and the surface content of whatever text is under scrutiny.

The Analogy of Literature:
Two Implied Methods of Interpretation in Poetry

Since literature constitutes a different attempt to represent unconscious and conscious phenomena through language, it is instructive to turn to it for another perspective on two different
attitudes toward words, one where meaning is thought of as certain and fixed, the other where it is considered mutable, uncertain, unfixed.

I begin with a seventeenth-century poem by Andrew Marvell
that implies an attitude toward its language—at least on a first
reading—that I designate as theoretical or certain. While I shall
treat this attitude as outside the psychoanalytic sphere, it has an
important historical and aesthetic place. Ricoeur (1970) would undoubtedly classify it as representative of what was traditionally
considered as the sacred. I shall contrast this poem with one by
the French symbolist Stephane Mallarmé, whose poetry defies a
"certain" reading, exemplifying an attitude toward language in
which we may recognize the absence of certainty. In describing
these poems, I do not attempt to treat them as poems. Nor is the
psychoanalytic understanding of either assayed. My use of them
will be restricted to what they exemplify about interpretation.[1]

The Word as Certain: On a Drop of Dew

Marvell's (1681) poem, "On a Drop of Dew," divides into two parts.
In the first, the poem describes a drop of dew fallen from the heaven
to earth. The drop of dew is an exile. Shunning the temporal world,
its "Mansion new," it "round in itself incloses." It is "its own Tear."
It trembles, fearful of becoming impure, until it is pitied and exhaled back again to the "clear Region" of its birth. In the second
stanza, this drop of dew is likened to the soul that does, in its "pure

---

1. See Appendix for text of the poems.

and circling thoughts, express the greater Heaven in an Heaven less." The drop of dew, like the soul, remains a transient on earth, "but on a point below."

The poem is based on an analogy. Moreover, in its analogical structure, the poem contains clear referents to a larger fixed system of beliefs about the world, a system particularly hospitable to the proliferations of analogy. In this larger system, the drop of dew takes its place as a microcosm that embodies in shimmering crystalline perfection the macrocosm of the supralunary regions. The earth is thought to be surrounded by nine to eleven concentric spheres. Those above the sphere of the moon are full of light and made of ether, the matter of the soul and of spirit. They are eternal. Among them are found those incorporeal beings, the higher orders of angels. The spheres resound in the heavenly harmony of an angelic chorus, testimony of the symmetry and perfection of their creator.

Below the sphere of the moon are the non-ethereal spheres where the air becomes progressively dirtier and thicker until at the very center one finds the earth. These are the regions of matter and thus of decay and mortality. As the drop of dew takes on a body and becomes its own tear yet yearns to divest itself—to evaporate—so is Man a being similarly divided. In part his nature is spiritual and ethereal, in part animal and thus corporeal. If he has a soul and therefore possesses the pure light of reason, he is also a physical presence with physical appetites. As such, he both bridges the animal and spiritual worlds and is continuously, by his very dual nature, in conflict. The physicality of man raises a further series of analogies. Man is in physical harmony when his humors—which correspond in the microcosm of the human body to the elements in the macrocosm of the universe—are in balance. Illness of the body or mind is thus a disorder, a break in the cosmic order. Illness is also corruption, of the flesh in death or of the soul in sin. But the system of analogies also moves outward here, from the microcosm of the human body in corruption to the macrocosms of the disorder, illness, or corruption of the political body, of nature, and finally of the cosmic order described earlier (Tillyard 1943).

The point I wish to emphasize is that Marvell's poem *contains its own publicly available interpretation.* It draws on a conscious and preconscious system of shared beliefs, analogical in form and thus perfectly suited to intertwining, metaphorical exchanges and echoes. Its self-interpretation is based upon overt similarities between form and meaning. Consider, for instance, which physical properties of the drop of dew merit comparison with which metaphysical properties of the soul: the dew drop's translucence, its retention of its own form, its trembling, its capacity to change its outward form and become vapor. All these suggest a lack of corporeality, a reluctance to exist in the physical world, an imperviousness to contamination. These analogies are supported by an unquestioning belief in the sinful corruption of physical matter on the one hand, and by the innocence of that which is without matter on the other.

The Word as Uncertain: L'Après-Midi d'un Faune

To move from a poem such as this one to one of Mallarmé's is to move not only from the seventeenth century to the nineteenth century, but also from a text with a well-ordered, articulated system of beliefs to a text that, while poised, exquisitely crafted, and painfully beautiful, is also disturbingly obscure.

Perhaps because he consciously sought, as he writes in *"La Musique et les Letters"* (Mallarmé 1894, p. 648), "those motifs which compose a logic with our very fibre."[2] Mallarmé's poetry evokes experience physically felt, experience in which the body re-emerges as the locus of metaphor, thought, and poetry itself.

---

2. All translations of Mallarmé are attempts at the impossible. With the exception of Fowlie's translation printed in the appendix to this chapter, the attempts in this article are mine, and are, of necessity, approximate.

This enterprise is easier to observe in his earlier, less obscure poetry than in his later work where a coherent surface narrative has entirely disappeared. "The Afternoon of a Faun," for instance, alludes to the myth of Pan and Syrinx (Mallarmé 1865). In the myth, Pan the satyr pursues the nymph Syrinx who implores the Virgin Goddess Diana for help. Diana turns Syrinx and her sisters into reeds. Pan then takes possession of the reeds by making them into pipes and playing his music on them. Out of this rich material, Mallarmé fashions a poem in which three main levels of meaning simultaneously interweave like musical themes. Awakening, alone, from a deep sleep the faun speaks (1) of his sexual desire for two nymphs he has startled, pursued, and just failed to possess; and/or (2) of his wish to return to a dream of two nymphs desired and almost possessed; and/or (3) of his wish to create music that will (re)create and replace the vision dreamed or desired. Around this fictional representation is the presence of the poem and the reality of its creation, a frame that makes the subject matter of desire and creation immediate and multidimensional— a matter of reading experience. This is a poem that exemplifies the process of wish and various attempts at fulfillment, including the hallucinatory. In representing the sexual desire of the faun, the poet re-creates a realm of experience where the seeking of satisfaction through the body, through fantasy, and through the creative act are all evoked at once.

As readers of Mallarmé's elusive language, we experience viscerally this desire, the faun's attempts to satisfy it, and its frustration. Referring to the noon landscape into which he has awakened, the faun notes

> no water murmurs not poured from my flute onto the wood bathed with chords.

Since the lost vision (of the nymphs) is at best only memory, the nymphs and their landscape simultaneously represent the faun's desire *and* are its object. Similarly, liquid song fills a landscape otherwise parched. What Mallarmé's synesthetic language ineffably conveys is a sense of solitude in desire combined with the physical sensation of thirst. Later, the faun's notes will be an arid rain, *"une pluie aride,"* and the creative enterprise will make of ordinary erotic dream *"une sonore, vaine, et monotone ligne"* (a sonorous, vain, and monotone/monotonous line). It is important to note, here as elsewhere, that the musical beauty of the line— lost in translation—belies the ambivalent attitude toward esthetic transformation. Because it is born out of the frustration of a wish, artistic creation always signifies loss.

This continual contrast between form—the musical beauty of the language—and content—the impossibility of being other than alone in desire—is one of the most fundamental ingredients in the experience of reading Mallarmé. The opening line of the poem immediately announces the polyphonic nature of this reading to be required:

> These nymphs, I want [them] to perpetuate them.
>
> [*Ces nymphes, je les veux perpétuer.*]

The position of the objective pronoun (*les*-them) is somewhat unusual. One would ordinarily write less poetically, *je veux les perpétuer*. Its position emphasizes the faun's desire—I want them (*je les veux*)—before one even reads the infinitive *perpétuer*. One must then read polyphonically, *je les veux/je les veux perpétuer* (I want them/I want to perpetuate them) so that the word "perpetuate" itself becomes multifaceted. Perpetuation will be accomplished at different levels within the poem with daydream, penis, and pipe; without, by pen. But Mallarmé defies reduction because there is a simultaneity of level of evocation. Another way of describing this characteristic quality is by saying that the signifier is not fixed, but moves regressively and progressively so that the water that murmurs simultaneously evokes the onanistic and the creative act.

In making us aware of the movement of the signifier from the body itself to the thing representation and back again, Mallarmé accomplishes two things. First, whereas Marvell's poetry refers us to the similarity between specific objects and an accompanying, externalized communal system of beliefs, Mallarmé's poetry asks us instead to re-experience something internal: *the gap between the physical experience of desire and the word that speaks about physical desire.* Second, as a result, Mallarmé changes the nature of manifest content in a radical way. He increases its opacity while decreasing the clarity of the representation of reality. He turns daydream into dream:

> The contemplation of objects, the image on wing of reveries, evoked by them are song. . . . To name something is to suppress three-quarters of the pleasure of the poem. . . . To suggest it, that is the dream." [Mallarmé 1891, p. 869]

To translate into the theoretical language of psychoanalysis, Mallarmé exemplifies the fact that multiple meanings and compromise formation are at the heart of the secondary process. To suggest rather than to name is to disturb the polished surface and free its component parts for reverberation in its audience.

Two Implied Interpretative Strategies: The Word as Certain and Uncertain

These two poems offer two different attitudes toward the word and by doing so offer polar models of interpretation more generally. Marvell's poem is constructed on a certainty about the divine world and the permanence of its referents; Mallarmé's poem is fashioned about an inner experience of a chasm between a wish for something and the representation of that wish, a chasm filled at different times, in different ways, by signifiers ultimately signifying only the original absence. In the first, there is a sense that the universe is permanent and that that permanence extends to the word; in the second, there is a sense of a gap and of an infinite variety of signifiers that fill and by filling at the same time represent that gap. The first system of interpretation asks us to identify and describe the network of references to the prevailing worldview; interpretation reaffirms the belief—here the eternal presence of God in the word. The second asks us to take note of the interplay of signifiers that bridge the gap between communication about desire and its physical presence in the body: interpretation acknowledges the role of substitution and, ultimately, the fact of frustration.

In its emphasis on the gap between a wish and its expression in words, the second system resembles the exploration of a clinical psychoanalysis, a process that may be described as an investigation of the interplay of substitutions that interpose themselves between a fundamental transference wish and its expression (Lacan 1956). Mallarmé's poem both makes us conscious of this type of unverbalized longing and opens up consciousness to an interplay of references to that longing through the use of sometimes minute details of language itself—the unusual placement of the objective pronoun in the opening line of the "Faun," for instance: *"Je les veux perpétuer."* Mallarmé, whether intentionally or not, focuses our concentration on the role that the contiguity and similarity of individual words within the poem plays in meaning rather than on the identity of large analogical patterns linking an object described in the poem and an abstract belief, as in Marvell.

It remained, of course, for a younger Viennese contemporary of Mallarmé to systematize in a work on dreams the kind of interpretative procedure Mallarmé's poetry suggests (Freud 1900). Dream interpretation, however, seeks to make the individual aware of his private, otherwise unintelligible mode of representation: Mallarmé makes this process refer to collective modes of representation.[3]

---

3. Unlike the interpretative work of a clinical analysis, the literary interpretation to which I refer concerns surfaces. The radical change exemplified in Mallarmé's poem is a change in manifest meaning and form. We must not make the mistake of assuming that the change from the seventeenth century to the nineteenth century is also one from manifest to latent content. Rather, the surface of the poem ceases to repre-

One may characterize these two approaches to interpretation according to the role each assigns to the word: in the first, the signifier is fixed; in the second, it is always a substitute for something unattainable and a variable one at that. Moreover, these two approaches to the word, and therefore to interpretation, designate polarities that characterize the way psychoanalysis can be used. If the signifier is considered fixed, theory about the psychoanalytic process will be disregarded and theory about unconscious content will be used as dogma that establishes certainty by reiteration; if the signifier is considered mutable, then all psychoanalytic theory will be the basis of a process of investigation that requires uncertainty for a much longer period. That is, assumptions about language similar to the certainty characteristic of and appropriate to the language of theory can be applied, or assumptions about language similar to the uncertainty characteristic of language in the clinical process can be applied. While I am here primarily concerned with the way psychoanalysis is applied to literature and art, my remarks are also relevant to the way it is applied clinically, in less intense therapeutic modalities, for instance.

The way Marvell interprets his own imagery may be (somewhat unfairly to Marvell) used to represent the way other disciplines sometimes appropriate psychoanalysis and misapply it. When psychoanalysis is appropriated, theory about content becomes dogma. Let us take a hypothetical, but by no means atypical, example: One might interpret Marvell's poem by saying that

---

sent aspects of everyday reality—even metaphysical aspects—and instead seeks to evoke and represent inner states.

If these are two different surfaces, the fact that these two poems imply different methods of interpretation does not exclude psychoanalytic insight from the first, nor suggest that the linking of penis to pen and pipe constitutes more than a description of manifest meaning in the second. It would be possible to approach a poem by Mallarmé by attempting to decipher his private means of representation as well.

it is about "separation" from the mother (tear), ensuing feelings of helplessness or experiences of bodily instability (trembling), and a wish to return to a merged state. Such an interpretation is based on overt surface resemblances between psychoanalytic theory and poetic imagery. It is not the culmination of exploration; rather, it is an act of *substitution*, equivalent to the kind of interpretation Marvell's poem implies where the drop of dew is replaced by the soul.

In contrast, an approach to the text that uses psychoanalysis as a method of investigation might begin by noting the imagery in which the transformation of substance is combined with increasing eagerness of movement away from, upward, and finally toward. The drop of dew, "Trembling lest it grow impure," is exhaled back again by the sun, while the soul, "loose and easie hence to go/. . . girt and ready to ascend/ Moving but on a point below . . . all about does upwards bend," is compared to Manna's sacred Dew, "White, and intire, though congeal'd and chill/ . . . [which] does, dissolving, run/Into the Glories of th' Almighty Sun." Such an approach would note the relationship of the warm sun to the trembling, evaporating, running substance. It would note the shift of action from the sun that exhales the dew, to the dew that dissolves and runs toward the sun. It would notice the form of the analogies in the poem, where the language makes less and less clear what is being compared to what, so that as the poem progresses the things compared seem to be running together and losing their substance in the same way as do the objects referred to in the poem. It would begin to ponder which clinical analogies might be relevant—what unconscious fantasies and other unconscious process (for example, defensive ones) might begin to account for the particular choice of figurative language, shifts in form, and shifts in affect. It could draw, however, no immediate conclusions but would prefer more evidence, particularly evidence that might give this material a context.

This latter method approaches the text as a very dense compromise formation (see Chapter 11). Like the dream, each element is overdetermined and extends its referents in many directions. Unlike the dream, however, the text is an artifact consciously constructed for an audience. Although this collective aspect limits, for all practical purposes, the endless multiplicity of references to those relevant to communal experience, much as the current state of the transference in an analysis defines the territory for exploration, communal experience of the text is not unidimensional but multilayered. What reverberates in the reader are all the collective fantasies and relevant private associations and fantasies evoked by the surface and by the various components of which the surface is the compromise (see Chapter 10).

The way stations in this communication are words, but words understood as signifiers. If Mallarmé had but one lesson to recall for us, it would be that words constantly shift their function and meaning. A poem is a daydream, fantasy, melody; a note is semen, rain, sound, line, not alternately, but simultaneously.[4]

Because it is based on the mutability of the signifier, the second interpretative method does not seek to establish broad analogies on the basis of surface similarities. It recognizes instead the density of the surface and must be attuned to the interplay of references that density opens up in the reader–interpreter. It pays attention to the shifting *function* of signifiers and thus to tiny details—the misplaced pronoun in the opening line of the "Faun," for instance, to contiguity, similarity, and contradiction. If it is to proceed beyond the surface text to the creative processes of the artist or the latent fantasy material evoked in the reader, it will require additional evidence.

------

4. It would be inaccurate, however, to contend that Mallarmé creates primary process. Although it is true that his style shares formal properties with those of primary process, we need to distinguish between the representation of the process and the process itself (Reed 1983).

Method and Statement in Freud's *Leonardo*[5]

The two strategies toward interpretation under discussion in their extreme forms involve, first, a tendency to fix the signifier by attributing one certain meaning to it (often, but not always close to the manifest content of theory) and, second, a tendency to approach the signifier as a condensation of (endless) multiple meanings. Obviously, these strategies are relative and in clinical practice appear in some combination. For example, certain unconscious meanings are involved in the neurotic structure to be analyzed, some are not, and the analyst only interprets those dynamically active in the given conflict. There are other times, during countertransference interference, for instance, when the tendency to fix meaning seems clearly to conflict with the psychoanalytic exploratory process, excluding and foreclosing important unconscious elements.

Freud's study of Leonardo da Vinci is instructive because of the presence of both strategies simultaneously and of the impact each has had on commentators. To be sure, in concentrating on the Mona Lisa's smile, we shall be concerned with a visual not a verbal signifier, but it is still illuminating to see how the impetus to explore meanings and open up the signifier to an interplay of references simultaneously coexists with a tendency to fix the meaning of the signifier in a more reductive way. Although this second tendency should not be taken as definitive, surprisingly often it is, so that Freud's contribution to the methodology of applied psychoanalysis is often overlooked. It is the method I emphasize in the summary that follows.

---

5. I am indebted to all the members of the Interdisciplinary Colloquium on Psychoanalysis and Literature at the New York Psychoanalytic Institute for the work on *Leonardo* and particularly to Drs. Arlene Heyman, Donald Kaplan, Francis Baudry, James Spencer, Jr., and Alan Bass for several of the ideas that follow.

Method

Freud does not seek to fathom Leonardo's artistic creations per se. Rather, he locates a set of puzzling contradictions in Leonardo's behavior and examines the art as one part of his search for a solution. How, he asks, can one explain the fact that Leonardo's passion for scientific research overtook his artistic endeavors? How explain the increasing slowness and hesitation with which Leonardo worked, his tendency to leave his paintings unfinished, and his indifference to their future fate? How further reconcile the contradictions in his character signaled by his "quiet peaceableness," his refusal to eat meat, and his freeing of birds sold at market for food, on the one hand, and his inventions of war and his sketching the final agonies of convicted criminals, on the other? Again, how explain his surrounding himself for apprentices with youths of ideal beauty and uncertain talent? And what does one make of Leonardo's apparent repudiation of sexuality, the lack of passion in personal relations?

Clearly, the instinct for research reinforced by other sexual currents takes over as sublimatory activity. Everything—including painting—comes to be regarded as a puzzle to be investigated: hence Leonardo's slowness and hesitancy before a canvas. But why should the drive to know be so strong in him? Freud's solution, including as it does his well-known error, is to call our attention to a childhood memory of Leonardo's in which a vulture beats its tail inside the child's mouth, to identify the memory as an adult homosexual fellatio fantasy transposed to infancy, and to identify the vulture with the phallic mother of infantile sexual theory. Freud proposes that Leonardo lived alone with his peasant mother for the first three and one-half years of his life and then joined his stepmother and father. The young child who broods on the mystery of where babies come from in a home with no father to inhibit his researches or to be taken into account in the process is the precursor of the adult researcher especially preoccupied with the flight of birds. Freud himself takes a long flight into archaeology and mythography to suggest that the androgynous mother goddess Mut, represented in Egyptian hieroglyphs by a vulture, is the prototype of the phallic mother represented in Leonardo's vulture memory. Freud next applies himself to the problem of why the experience of being alone with the mother leads to a homosexual orientation and suggests from clinical experience an unconscious fixation to the mnemonic image of the mother and a narcissistic identification. A homosexual of this type loves boys the way his mother loved him. Turning to biographical evidence, Freud points to Leonardo's tender care of his apprentices and adduces from entries in Leonardo's notebooks traces of distorted affect in the detailed accounts of expenditures on these apprentices and on a funeral assumed to be for Leonardo's mother. Next Freud returns to the vulture fantasy and suggests that this also refers to the memory of the mother's kisses on his mouth. This leads Freud to the Mona Lisa's smile. Seeing this smile on the lips of the model awoke in Leonardo the memory of his mother's smile. Once this memory was aroused, Leonardo could not free himself from it. It reappears, less uncannily, in all later paintings, particularly in the St. Anne painting with its two women of almost identical ages. Only Leonardo, Freud tells us, could have painted this painting. With its two mothers, it contains the synthesis of the history of his childhood. Finally, Freud notices a perseveration in Leonardo's notebook entry about his father's death, evidence of a distorted expression of mourning. This hidden emotion allows Freud to conclude that Leonardo, identified with his father, abandons his works just as his father left him in infancy. Further, this early absence of the father made Leonardo able to do away with the need for authority, strengthened the instinct for research, and made him skeptical of the divine authority he was in the vanguard of his age in overturning.

Unlike those who are dogmatic in their applications of psychoanalysis to biography, Freud does not try to substitute one large pattern for another, nor does he attempt to replace the narrative of Leonardo's life with a "secret" depth-psychological narrative.

He does not treat Leonardo's art as a symptom, or say that he painted these pictures because his father abandoned him and his mother overstimulated him. Instead. Freud *defines a problem pieced together from smaller facts and contradictions.* Why does the artist devote hours to scientific research and abandon his art? Why does a man free birds so that they will not be slain for food, yet design cruel engines of war? Why does this man leave detailed records of a few isolated expenditures, yet lead a life removed from passion? When no obvious encompassing solution to these contradictions presents itself, the lack of an answer leads Freud to consider unconscious motivations. Always, the driving force is that there is a contradiction to resolve: "what calls for an explanation is not Leonardo's behaviour [in giving clothes to his apprentices], but the fact that he left these pieces of evidence [the notations in the notebook of his expenditures] behind him" (Freud 1910, p. 103). That is, Freud does not use an applied psychoanalytic interpretation as a gratuitous reinterpretation of a life or a work or an act: he would not say that the drop of dew is the soul; rather, he might hypothesize that the drop of dew and the soul both stand in for some other, unnamed desire, and wonder why, for instance, the element of wetness was part of the comparison. Psychoanalytic explanations attempt to resolve otherwise incomprehensible contradictions *between* acts or words.

Statement

In the Leonardo paper, Freud sets himself the problem of explaining the artist's contradictory behavior. To do so, he introduces biographical evidence and identifies a fantasy. If the contradictory behavior, culminating in the inability to finish a painting, brings Leonardo into the consulting room, the fantasy becomes the key that, when analyzed, will unlock the mystery. This fantasy then offers us a signifier to interpret: the memory of the "vulture." And the vulture signifier is quickly associated with a second one that appears in the artist's painting: the Gioconda's haunting smile.

The opportunity thus exists to treat this signifier in the manner of theoretical language—to assign it *a* meaning, or to free its overdetermined meanings to reverberate within it, in the manner of the clinical process. What Freud apparently does is to construct a historical reality: the small Leonardo living alone with his peasant mother for the first three and one-half years without the presence of his father; the subsequent nostalgia for the smile of the mother. Freud appears to attribute a fixed, certain meaning to the signifier: this smile means that this series of historical events occurred.

This apparent attribution of a fixed meaning to the signifier is made the focal point of a well-known criticism of Freud's paper by the art critic Meyer Schapiro (1956). Schapiro assumes that the real history constructed by Freud is a necessary ingredient in the interpretation of the fantasy as a fellatio fantasy involving the phallic mother. When he therefore offers evidence that calls in question the validity of the historical construction, he throws out the interpretation of the fantasy as well.

In taking literally Freud's reconstruction of history, Schapiro ends up misunderstanding Freud's *method*. For example, he points out Freud's error of translation: the Italian word *nibbio* denotes the kite, not the vulture, as the German translation from which Freud partly worked had it, and Schapiro argues that Freud's error invalidates some of the collateral evidence he introduces to support the fantasy of the phallic mother, especially the vulture symbol, the Egyptian hieroglyph for the word, mother. While Schapiro's contention of fact is correct, it does not necessarily follow that the error invalidates the psychoanalytic interpretation of the fantasy.

Further, the fact that the bird is a kite leads Schapiro to challenge every element in the interpretation of the "vulture" memory. According to Schapiro, the kite, with its forked flexible tail, is the bird from which Leonardo could best study flight. In fact, Leonardo mentions it several times on the opposite side of the sheet where the memory is recorded. "If, in Leonardo's fantasy," writes Schapiro, "the kite beat his tail in the child's mouth, one may see there an allusion to the characteristic movement of the tail against the wind and the currents of air of which the breath is a counterpart." Moreover, Schapiro explains the fact that the tail is in the child's mouth on the basis of an established literary convention. According to Cicero, ants filled the infant Midas's mouth with grains of wheat as he slept, a fact that led to the prediction of Midas's adult wealth. Bees were said to have settled on young Plato's lips as well, a sign that as an adult he would be gifted with sweetness of speech. Leonardo's fantasy can thus be classed as an "omen of future achievement" and, Schapiro continues, that achievement probably refers to his wish to fly—literally.

In ascribing one certain significance to each detail of the fantasy, Schapiro, more so than Freud, illustrates the danger of certainty in the service of foreclosing interpretation, for despite Schapiro's contentions, cultural and historical conventions do not necessarily constitute *alternative* explanations to conscious choices. That tales of bees in children's mouths existed does not exclude the possibility that these tales—or Leonardo's fantasy—represent sexual fantasies. As is well known, the ego will make use of indifferent material to further the aims of the id, even as the ego uses the same material adaptively. Yet Schapiro proceeds as if the concept of multiple function (Waelder 1930) did not exist, offering alternative explanations for individual elements in the puzzle *without offering an alternative explanation that takes into account the series of contradictions Freud delineates* and that solves the whole. In fact, he seems strikingly unaware of the relationship between the series of contradictions and Freud's explanatory hypothesis.

Unwittingly, Schapiro takes to an extreme Freud's apparent reduction of the signifier to one certain meaning and in doing so demonstrates that when the mutability and multiplicity of the signifier are lost sight of, psychoanalytic understanding itself is misunderstood.

Freud's construction is almost certainly not historically correct, but historical error, while undesirable, does not invalidate the presence of the phallic mother fantasies that are also part of Freud's interpretation. Taken in this sense, Freud's method of investigation could culminate in an opening up of the Gioconda's smile to the unconscious reverberations behind its creation that echo within us as we look at it. As Paul Ricoeur (1970) has beautifully written:

> This memory only exists as a symbolizable absence that lies deep beneath Mona Lisa's smile. Lost like a memory, the mother's smile is an empty place within reality; it is the point where all traces become lost, where the abolished confines one to fantasy. It is not therefore a thing that is better known and that would explain the riddle of the work of art; it is an intended absence which, far from dissipating the riddle, increases it. [p. 173]

Most important of all, the method accounts for unconscious content without seeing the surface as camouflage or disguise. It sees the surface, instead, as a compromise formation (Brenner 1982).

Method: The Problem of Maintaining Uncertainty in Applied Psychoanalysis

While Freud sets up his investigation of Leonardo in terms that resemble a clinical analysis, the problem only *resembles* a clinical investigation. The paradoxical uncertainty I have described as a necessary part of the clinician's stance—that necessity of waiting while the psychoanalytic dialogue unfolds and the latent meaning of words emerges with the transferential intensification of drive derivatives—will not lead to the unfolding of the clinical process because in applied psychoanalysis there is no clinical process.

The mutually interdependent relationship between theory and clinical investigation tends also to be fundamentally altered. The temptation is to find appropriate theoretical explanations to fit the facts, rather than to foster discovery of more data that may or may not incidentally also modify theoretical explanation.

Because a stance of uncertainty does not lead to an unfolding process and a stance of certainty does not preclude one, the temptation to make clever, sure-sounding pronouncements is intensified. The more this temptation to certainty motivates interpretation, the more psychoanalytic theory is treated as if it were a dogma, assumptions about language appropriate to theory are applied to the text, and the more interpretation consists of wholes substituted for other wholes: the drop of dew is the soul. Thus one sees interpretations in which theoretical formulations are substituted for manifest literary patterns, or in which theoretical formulations replace biographical narratives that have replaced manifest literary patterns, or in which a secret biography replaces a fictional narrative. To offer one biographical example, it is commonplace to find an assertion such as this: in having Mr. Murdstone send David Copperfield to London to work in a factory, Dickens is repeating a trauma of late childhood caused for him by his father's debts. But what does it mean psychodynamically that an author reproduces a childhood experience in a narrative? If a patient reported that he had depicted a painful childhood experience in a novel, the analyst would not immediately assume an explanation of the repetition of trauma, not even of an earlier trauma represented by a later one. The more careful approach would be to recognize that the hypothetical novelist/patient uses experience from his life to represent several unknown drive derivatives and defenses against them (etc.). The latter alternative, however, confronts the interpreter with considerably more ignorance than certain knowledge. It does not assign one signifier, "this trauma," to the latent content of one manifest event. Instead, it raises innumerable questions. It is possible, for instance, that the biographical experience functions at the time the work is written to ward off some other painful affect or wish.

It is largely by means of method that a clinical attitude in applied psychoanalysis can be preserved, and it is here that we need to rely on that aspect of psychoanalytic theory that holds that the signifier is multivalent in order to maintain a clinical stance of uncertainty toward language in a nonclinical setting. If we lend a typical clinical skepticism toward the manifest content of words or toward the scrutiny of the manifest content of whatever evidence we deem suitable, whether it be historical (Reed 1976), artistic, or other, we will be forced to ask questions of other questions before we jump in with answers. And when we do, finally, draw speculative conclusions, the nature of our clinical skepticism will ensure that those conclusions are based on a clinical level of inference.

There is, however, a preliminary step necessary to foster the exercise of clinical uncertainty, and that is to set up the investigation as an analogue to a clinical investigation. I do not mean to imply that the artist *cum* patient is the sole subject qualified for scrutiny. On the contrary, the artist is only a figure; he does not, per se, present us with contradictions or other signs of psychic conflict inexplicable except in terms of unconscious motivation. *And contradictions that require unconscious motivation for resolution,* following Freud's approach to Leonardo da Vinci, *are precisely what we require* to set up an investigation analogous to a clinical one. To be sure, evidence of conflict is easier to delineate when the subject of our scrutiny is the artist directly and we may call on biographical, historical, and autobiographical material. From this point of view, however, artistic productions are merely another source of evidence.

Since they constitute the motive for our interest, however, would it be possible to begin an applied psychoanalytic investigation with the work itself? In observing the literary text out of the context of biography and history, how might one locate the required contradictions? One answer resides in considering the relationship of content to form. Indeed, it seems to me that a psychoanalytic interpretation that focuses on a text should account for and reconcile manifest content and manifest form.

In this endeavor, it is well to remember that form may be the manifest content of a latent organizing fantasy in the author that structures a whole series of references within the work. I have attempted such a reconciliation of form and content in Diderot's *Jacques le Fataliste* where I have shown that the formal pattern of interruption is connected via a primal scene fantasy to an entire series of seemingly unrelated stories within the novel (see Chapter 10).

The reconciliation of form and content requires an explanation that accounts for both the manifest formal elements in the text and the manifest content of the text. To account for both, one needs to move beneath the surface to a statement about the author's unconscious fantasy. To move beneath the surface, judicious recourse to known clinical data used as analogy is necessary. Thus the manifest formal pattern of interruption observable in the novel I investigated was reported as a manifest form in certain relevant clinical situations concerning the primal scene (Arlow 1980). Other formal aspects of the novel, as well as the contents of the apparently indifferent stories, resembled well-known primal scene derivatives. But it was the fact of conjunction—that manifest form and content both resembled manifest clinical data concerning identical latent content—that allowed me to consider the clinical analogy useful. I do not contend that such a conclusion is specific enough to be psychoanalytically very satisfactory. I think, rather, it is not. I do suggest that the attempt to maintain a clinical method points us in the right direction. It enables us to maintain a stance of uncertainty for longer.

In the same article, I also suggested that valuable evidence may be gleaned from observing the shape and character of the general critical response to a given text. To locate the points at which critics are least content to allow contradictions to develop and most impetuous in jumping in with "certain" or foreclosing interpretations may indicate, at the very least, where the contradictions reside that may fruitfully offer themselves to analytic scrutiny. Moreover, the form of the critical response, what is avoided and what insistently emphasized, may conceivably furnish additional evidence of derivatives of and defenses against unconscious fantasies that organize the text.

This method extends the concept of parallelism (Arlow 1963, Ekstein and Wallerstein 1958, Gediman and Wolkenfeld 1980, Sachs and Shapiro 1976). In it, uncertainty subsumes certainty, for by extending the concept of parallelism, I make use of both interpretative methods here investigated. The interpretation of the first type, that which is certain and forecloses, becomes evidence that leads toward an interpretation of the second type.

But form not only involves large units, a novel rather than a drama, or a consistent pattern of interruption rather than a more fluid construction; it also comprises small details, the placement of a pronoun or the choice of a metaphor. Following the lesson of Mallarmé and Freud, I would now add that contradictions fruitful for psychoanalytic exploration may perhaps be most consistently identified through a careful study of the language of a text, most particularly through the study of the multiple and occasionally contradictory surface meanings of specific words. What I am proposing is, in the first instance, a *description* of the range of meanings and connotations with which certain nodal words reverberate within a text. Such a description would constitute a map detailing manifest "outcroppings" of latent fantasies similar to, but conceivably more extensive than the outcroppings that Arlow (1979a) mentions in connection with metaphor. The map would delineate a network of contradictions to resolve: Why does this signifier signify x here but y here? The more detailed that map, the more material for judicious clinical analogy would be available and the more possible it would be for method to approximate the clinical process.

A Speculation About Freud's Emphasis On History

As an example of one direction in which a clinical approach might take us, I propose to consider briefly and speculatively a different but equally intriguing contradiction that has emerged from the examination of Freud's *Leonardo*: Why does Freud assign a history to the signifier? Freud, after all, is the man who, in the depths of despair over the discovery that his patients' stories of seduction were not true historical events, realized that they were no less true as psychical events. Why then claim that the vulture fantasy conceals the historical reality of the child's experience rather than a fantasy-wish constellation?[6]

A recent study by Bass (1985) provides us with a good deal of evidence as well as a possible answer. The paper is also noteworthy because of its applied psychoanalytic method. Bass treats Freud's vulture/kite error as a symptomatic act. In other words, Freud's substitution of the word vulture for kite is viewed as the formal element to be reconciled with the manifest content of Freud's study. Thorough scholarship into Freud's correspondence with Fliess, Jung, and Abraham allows Bass to demonstrate that Freud was working on the *Leonardo* study at the same time that he was discovering the structure of fetishism in his clinical work. Freud's error is a parapraxis intimately connected with this discovery, Bass suggests. For the discovery of the secret of fetishism is the discovery of the importance of phallic mother fantasies. The continuation of the mistranslation of *nibbio* enabled Freud to present all the phallic mother material from Egyptian mythology that otherwise would not have been admissible collateral evidence. That evidence substantiated *Freud's* clinical discovery, not the interpretation of Leonardo's fantasy.

Throughout Freud's *Leonardo* study, there is ample additional evidence of Freud's identification with the Renaissance artist, primarily as with one who is an intrepid investigator struggling against a society with a superstitious view of the universe. Sensitized as he was by his identification with Leonardo, it is not unreasonable to hypothesize a re-enactment: the mysterious smile

6. Freud (1918) discusses the fantasy/memory controversy at length in his case history of the Wolf Man, but the type of memory he there defends, the memory of the primal scene, is very different from the global reconstruction of three and a half years in the *Leonardo* study.

of the Gioconda, that "empty place within reality" (Ricoeur 1970), may have evoked in Freud the same phallic mother fantasies he attributed, through history, to the artist. If so, then the vulture/ kite error may be seen as an instance of the parallelism phenom- enon—a substitution of the vulture representing the Egyptian goddess Mut and her phallic associations for the kite. Moreover, the emphasis on history at the expense of fantasy may then be a second instance of parallelism—an insistence on the reality of that which is not, the mother's phallus. Needless to say, I offer this speculation tentatively, for further investigation.

Conclusion

I have examined two sets of assumptions toward language, both of which have value for psychoanalysis. In one set the signifier is fixed and easily identified; it is a set of assumptions appropriate to and characteristic of the language of theory. In the other, the signifier is multivalent. This set of assumptions is characteristic of the language of the clinical process. Further, I have noted two polarities of interpretation, each corresponding to one set of as- sumptions toward language.

The difference between an interpretation that identifies one certain meaning for the signifier—whether that meaning be his- torical, theoretical, or other—and one that understands the signifier as multivalent has profound implications. One might describe the difference metaphorically in terms of a dichotomy between History and Fantasy. Those who advocate History (and I am not including Freud, who always ascribes a fantasy to im- portant historical events, so much as his commentator) under- standably desire a certainty about the world: this has occurred, this means x and not y. Those who entertain Fantasy understand the signifier as part of a long chain of signifiers substituting for, but never replacing, an original, unrequited wish. It is a choice that accepts the tact of frustration.

Because we are human, complete acceptance of frustration is fortunately impossible; otherwise there would be no activity of substitution at all. Psychoanalytic theory, whether it advocates more reified concepts or more dynamic ones, whether or not it holds for the multivalence of the signifier, is, after all, our mythology (Grossman 1982). Both tendencies toward interpretation appear in Freud's text because it is not possible for psychoanalysis to resolve the tension between certainty and uncertainty in any absolute way. Nevertheless, it is easy to see why the second interpretative procedure, involving as it does more delay and frustration, would always be imperiled by the desire for the security of the first, especially when, in applied psychoanalysis, there is no patient to remind us to listen to him. With the absence of the process and thus of the promise of a gradual unfolding, applied psychoanalysis is, if anything, more frustrating than clinical work, not less. Properly attempted, it should neither constitute a glib reaffirmation of dogma nor be the occasion for a holiday from a clinical stance. In order to avoid the reduction of psychoanalysis, we need first to remind ourselves of the importance of the psychoanalytic process to the act of interpretation.

Appendix

On a Drop of Dew

See how the Orient Dew,
Shed from the Bosom of the Morn
  Into the blowing Roses,
Yet careless of its Mansion new;
For the clear Region where 'twas born
  Round in its self incloses:
  And in its little Globes Extent,
Frames as it can its native Element.
  How it the purple flow'r does slight,
    Scarce touching where it lyes,
  But gazing back upon the Skies,
    Shines with a mournful Light;
      Like its own Tear,
Because so long divided from the Sphear.
  Restless it roules and unsecure,
    Trembling lest it grow impure;
  Till the warm Sun pitty it's Pain,
And to the Skies exhale it back again.
  So the Soul, that Drop, that Ray
Of the clear Fountain of Eternal Day,
Could it within the humane flow'r be seen,
  Remembering still its former height,
  Shuns the sweat leaves and blossoms green;
  And, recollecting its own Light,
Does, in its pure and circling thoughts, express
The greater Heaven in an Heaven less.
  In how coy a Figure wound,
  Every way it turns away:
  So the World excluding round,

Yet receiving in the Day.
Dark beneath, but bright above:
Here disdaining, there in Love,
How loose and easie hence to go:
How girt and ready to ascend.
Moving but on a point below,
It all about does upwards bend.
Such did the Manna's sacred Dew bestil;
White, and intire, though congeal'd and chill.
Congeal'd on Earth: but does, dissolving, run
Into the Glories of th' Almighty Sun.

Excerpt from L'apres-midi d'un Faune

Églogue
LE FAUNE
Ces nymphes, je les veux perpétuer.

                    Si clair,
Leur incarnat léger, qu'il voltige dans l'air
Assoupi de sommeils touffus.

                    Aimai-je un rêve?
Mon doute, amas de nuit ancienne, s'achève
En maint rameau subtil, qui, demeuré les vrais
Bois mêmes, prouve, hélas! que bien seul je m'offrais
Pour triomphe la faute idéale de roses.
Réfléchissons . . .

               ou si les femmes dont tu gloses
Figurent un souhait de tes sens fabuleux!
Faune, l'illusion s'échappe des yeux bleus
Et froids, comme une source en pleurs, de la plus chaste:
Mais, l'autre tout soupirs, dis-tu qu'elle contraste
Comme brise du jour chaude dans ta toison?
Que non! par l'immobile et lasse pâmoison
Suffoquant de chaleurs le matin frais s'il lutte,

Ne murmure point d'eau que ne verse ma flûte
Au bosquet arrosé d'accords; et le seul vent
Hors des deux tuyaux prompt à s'exhaler avant
Qu'il disperse le son dans une pluie aride,
C'est, a l'horizon pas remué d'une ride,
Le visible et serein souffle artificiel
De l'inspiration, qui regagne le ciel.

O bords siciliens d'un calme marécage
Qu'à l'envi de soleils ma vanité saccage,
Tacite sous les fleurs d'étincelles, CONTEZ
"Que je coupais ici les creux rosaux domptés
• *Par le talent; quand, sur l'or glauque de lointaines*
• *Verdures dédiant leur vigne à des fontaines,*
• *Ondoie une blancheur animale au repos:*
• *Et qu'au prélude lent où naissent les pipeaux*
• *Ce vol de cygnes, non! de naïades se sauve*
• *Ou plonge . . ."*

Translation of the excerpt[7]

I want to perpetuate these nymphs.
                    So clear,
Their light rose color, that it floats into the air
Heavy with the sleep of the woods.
                    Do I love a dream?
My doubt, accretion of the aging night, ends
On their branches, which, remaining the real
Woods prove, alas, that alone I offered to myself
As a triumph the ideal fault of roses.

---

7. This translation, by Walter Fowlie, is reprinted, with the permission of the publisher, from Mr. Fowlie's book, *Mallarmé* (Chicago: University of Chicago Press, 1953).

Let me reflect . . .

        or whether the women whom you explain
Figure a desire of your fabulous senses:
Faun, the illusion escapes from the blue cold
Eyes, like a spring weeping, of the more chaste girl;
But, the other one all sighs, would you say that she contrasts
Like the warm breath of day in your fleece?
But no! in the motionless and tired faint
Suffocating with heat, the cool morning, if it struggles,
Does not murmur with any water which my flute doesn't pour
Over the wood sprinkled with chords: and only the wind
Out of the two pipes to exhale before
Dispersing the sound in an arid rain.
It is, on the horizon, not disturbed by a line,
The visible and serene artificial breath
Of inspiration returning to the sky.

O Sicilian edges of a calm swamp
Which to the envy of suns my vanity destroys,
Tacit under flowers of sparks, TELL
'That here I cut empty reeds conquered
'By talent; when, on the green gold of distant
'Verdure dedicating its vines to fountains,
'Floats an animal whiteness at rest:
'And that at the slow prelude where the pipes are born
'That flight of swans, no! of nymphs escapes
Or plunges . . .'

9 The Antithetical Meaning of the Term "Empathy"

"Empathy" entered the English language as a translation for the German *Einfühlung*, a word used in the late nineteenth century to describe esthetic perception. Though the German word was first applied to esthetics by Friedrich Vischer in 1873 (Wind 1963, pp. 150–151), the concept of *Einfühlung* is identified with Theodor Lipps, who systematized it. Independently of Vischer and Lipps, the English critic and novelist Violet Paget (Vernon Lee) elaborated a similar theory, one subsequently enriched by her discovery of the German work (Wellek 1966). Paget first alludes to *Einfühlung* in a lecture given in 1895, where she translates it as "sympathy" (1909, pp. 239–240). By 1913, however, "sympathy" has become "empathy" and is defined as "a tendency to merge the activities of the perceiving subject with the qualities of the perceived object" (p. 63).

Since its original aesthetic invocation, the word has entered psychoanalytic discourse, attracting to itself a history of particular citation, context, and connotation. It has become, among other things, the carrier of scientific status and the container of technical controversy. Highly charged, it has been woven into the fabric of what might be called the "common symbolic universe" (Leavy 1973, p. 323) of psychoanalysis in such a way that an unusual degree of conflict and confusion surrounds the word and is matched by an equally unusual amount of inconsistency and contradiction characterizing its use. While some measure of ambiguity is characteristic of and indeed necessary for psychoanalytic language (Grossman and Simon 1969), there is currently a quality of controversy surrounding "empathy" that is unusually strong and that risks removing the term from useful dialogue.

The study that follows examines the use of the term "empathy" in the psychoanalytic literature with two interrelated goals in mind. One is to explore the "common symbolic universe" of psychoanalysis insofar as the term "empathy" is concerned in order to clarify and make explicit at least some of its varied meanings, resonances, and connotations. The other is to investigate those reasons for the controversy surrounding the term that may pertain to meanings evoked by the word itself. This position differs in *perspective*, though not necessarily in substance, from one that would hold the controversy merely to reflect larger theoretical battles in the psychoanalytic community. It emphasizes the word as the carrier of the concept because it focuses on empathy not as a clinical experience, but as a technical word that describes an aspect of clinical experience and that appears in psychoanalytic literature for purposes of communication.

Methodological Considerations

My perspective derives in part from the traditions of literary criticism. Critics frequently investigate the connotations and meanings of words in context, especially as these words resonate in a particular community of readers, be the community historical, specialized, or circumstantial (Culler 1980, Wimsatt 1963). Those critics who believe that the relationship within the word or sign between the signifier and signified is arbitrary and conventional (Saussure 1916) quite purposefully search out verbal and formal conventions that are not explicitly recognized (Said 1972). Yet the assumption of verbal conventions also permeates a much broader spectrum of criticism (Mukařovský 1977), including the older tradition of etymological research.

Conventions, both verbal and formal, grow out of repeated individual experience; hence beneath the literary perspective of my study of empathy resides a set of assumptions about psychoanalytic discourse based on psychoanalysis itself. First, verbal conventions, like all human endeavors, are compromise formations. They are synchronizations of the data of external perception and internal fantasy (Arlow 1969a,b). Second, these conventions are communal and are based in part on shared unconscious fantasy (Arlow 1961, 1981) and in part on communality of clinical experience and training. Third, a technical term in psychoanalysis—especially one close to clinical experience—functions as a stimulus for the re-experiencing of the commonly held fantasies and beliefs related to it. These fantasies and beliefs are "re-enacted" in each new written use of the term. Fourth, in addition to the commonly held fantasies, beliefs, and experience, the technical term also contains for its user and evokes in its audience private, idiosyncratic associations, fantasies, and memories that create variations in understanding. Some of this private meaning may eventually become part of the communal meaning of the term.

Arlow (1969a,b) has used the term "synchronization" to describe the meshing of the data of external stimuli and internal fantasy in individual conscious perception. If all conscious perception represents such a synchronization, it follows that acts involving conscious perception must similarly include a synchronization of the data of external stimuli and internal fantasy. For the writer of expository prose, who must not only perceive but express creative perceptions—whether theoretical, clinical, or narrative—in the conventional language of an assumed audience, synchronizations of conscious perception and unconscious fantasy are multiple. To divide and name these synchronizations somewhat arbitrarily: those involved in the perception of which mode of explanation is necessary for a given audience; those involved in distinguishing words of primary personal valence from those with communal resonance; and finally those involved in the actual coding of the perception into communally understandable sequence and grammar. It might be added that such an effort is always one of translation (Leavy 1973), and thus always an approximation. Nevertheless, the inevitable ambiguities and uncertainties, provided they do not overwhelm the content, facilitate clarification and illumination because they facilitate questions. That is, it is the very fact of synchronization that makes of a piece of expository prose the beginning of a dialogue—a system not closed but open to another person's subjective inquiry.[1] What I am describing is not, of course, foreign to the analytic process itself, where there also exists the constant interplay of conscious perception and unconscious fantasy through language.

To the extent that the writer of expository prose—here a writer on psychoanalysis—writes for a particular audience whose conventions and beliefs he (or she) shares, it is important to remember that those conventions and beliefs themselves are the end products of synchronizations of conscious and unconscious perception. In the case of specialized language, there is a tradition signified by the term "ego," for instance, familiar to students of psychoanalysis, which includes among other elements Freud's structural use (1923), the work of Anna Freud on defense (1936), the work of Hartmann on adaptation and autonomy (1939), and the work of certain developmental researchers (e.g., Mahler, Pine, and Bergman 1975, Spitz 1965), to name only some contributors to the current communal meaning of the term. Individual understanding of such a term is influenced by both idiosyncratic and

---

1. That intersubjective dialogue fails to materialize if the assumption of a closed system is held by the writer and/or the reader. Then attack replaces inquiry.

communal factors. That is, the way the individual perceives and remembers this body of work and relates it to clinical and personal experience may be, on the one hand, highly personal, since the laws of psychic determinism that govern all perception and memory operate here as well. On the other hand, in communal discourse, the degree of variance is limited by the need for and fact of communication. Too idiosyncratic or distorted or divergent a use of a particular term will not be admitted by the community. Instead, a schism may develop. Communal terminology, then, must be flexible enough to accommodate individual differences and firm enough to withstand too much divergence. One has only to consult the dictionary compiled by Laplanche and Pontalis (1967), which traces the historical development of psychoanalytic concepts and in doing so re-emphasizes meanings, to realize the existence of the necessary "play" in psychoanalytic terminology. Psychoanalytic discourse ordinarily accommodates individual differences in understanding the body of communal literature and provides a constant enough frame so that individual differences do not become too wide. This ambiguity in technical language, born of synchronization, is not a failing. Rather, it is a fact of human existence, leading to dialogue, discovery, and creation.

Where communal discourse limits idiosyncratic uses of a term, it does not limit the sharing of concepts and beliefs. Such sharing may extend to unconscious fantasy (Freud 1908, Sachs 1942). Arlow, in particular, has elaborated on the concept of communal fantasy in several communications, most recently as it involves psychoanalytic theories of pathogenesis (1961, 1981), and Abend has written of the relationship between theories and fantasies of cure (1979). Fantasies are shared—ever more specifically as the common ground of the community becomes more specific—by virtue of common biological and physiological factors, which the fact of participation in the human condition imposes; by virtue of common cultural heritage and similar educational experiences; by virtue of common sharing of goals and assumptions, theories, and work. Such shared phenomena contribute to the connotations surrounding a term and silently enrich it, providing a depth of ambiguity for exploration, evocation, and discovery. This depth, of course, also presents an opportunity for confusion and inconsistent usage, but this last should merely alert us to the potential for integration.

Those experiences, beliefs, associations, and fantasies that silently contribute to collective understanding contribute because they are continually experienced by individuals. Psychoanalysts experience empathy in life and within the clinical situation both as analysands and analysts, and they bring this experience in its conscious and unconscious components to their writing of the word. Although the most personal and idiosyncratic aspects of the unconscious components may not be shared by professional readers, those aspects closest to common experience will be. The written technical word, then, becomes the vehicle of affective experiences, beliefs, associations, and fantasies. Because of the extensive similarity of experience represented by a sharing of theory and work, the word itself has an evocative potential. But evocation of the less conscious meanings of the word is also affected by the manifest *form* of the writing. That is, signals for the unconscious beliefs and fantasies appear in the style, ellipses, parapraxes, and figurative language of the written text.

Thus, as part of my exploration of the unrecognized meanings evoked by the term "empathy," I return to literary criticism and its technique of close examination of texts (Auerbach 1942–1945, Spitzer 1948, Wimsatt 1963) to take note of inconsistent uses of the term, ellipses, and the larger context in which the term frequently appears. From the standpoint of the evocation of unconscious fantasy particularly, most significant is the examination of the figurative language in which the term is embedded, for it is metaphorical discourse that joins and condenses unconscious with conscious communication (Arlow 1979).

This experiencing, writing, reading, re-experiencing, and writing may be seen as a process akin to that which occurs when literary critics write about a particular text. There, I have previously hypothesized (see Chapter 10), critics re-enact in their criticism aspects of an unconscious fantasy of the author that organizes the text, clues to which are embedded in the surface of the work. In psychoanalytic discourse, each writer may similarly re-enact a range of conscious and unconscious meanings attached to the technical word in the way he writes about and uses the term.

Because personal experience looms so large in the comprehension of psychoanalytic writing, the technical term must not become petrified or rigid. It must not only evoke previously recognized shared meanings but must also allow the integration of communally relevant personal insight. We may conceive of the useful and living technical word as a signifier of relatively constant individual conscious, preconscious, and unconscious conventional associations as long as we also understand that those associations have the potential of multiplying, becoming integrated with the earlier associations, and therefore altering the communal connotation of the term.

The Use of "Empathy" in Psychoanalytic Discourse

Most authors writing on empathy include an explicit, usually descriptive, definition of the phenomenon. The trouble begins with their divergent definitions. In an effort to wrest order from chaos, Buie has formulated a cognitively coherent composite: "Empathy occurs in an interpersonal setting between persons who remain aware of their separateness, yet in essence it is an intrapsychic phenomenon based on the human capacity to know another person's inner experience from moment to moment" (1981, p. 282; cf. Kernberg 1979, p 76). Since I have chosen to investigate the confusion and creative ambiguity that Buie attempts to remedy, I cite several other definitions to stress their diversity:

1. Empathy has been called in one sentence both knowledge and communication: "The form of knowledge that we call empathy is also a form of affective communication" (Modell 1979, p. 70).

2. It may be presented simultaneously as a capacity, a process, and an expression: "'Empathy' is the capacity of the subject instinctively and intuitively to feel as the object does. It is a process of the ego, more specifically, an emotional ego expression. As to its functioning: the subject temporarily gives up his own ego for that of the object" (Olden 1953, p. 113).

3. It may be designated an ability: "I define empathy as the ability to sample others' affects, and through this sampling to perceive them and be able to respond in resonance to them" (Easser 1974, p. 563).

4. It may be described both as a mode of (prolonged) data gathering and as a vehicle for discerning complex mental states in single acts of recognition:

> Empathy is the mode by which one gathers psychological data about other people and . . . imagines their inner experience even though it is not open to direct observation. Through empathy we aim at discerning, in one single act of recognition, complex psychological configurations which we could either define only through the laborious presentation of a host of details or which it may even be beyond our ability to define. [Kohut 1966, p 262]

5. It may be defined as an experience, "the inner experience of sharing in and comprehending the momentary psychological state of another person" (Schafer 1959, p. 346).

6. It may be described as "a very special method of perceiving" (Greenson 1960, p. 147).

7. Finally, empathy may be categorized as a means of communication and of nonrational understanding:

> Empathy is a means of communication and of understanding another's mental processes and mental contents that is very different from our usual rational means of observation and inference . . . empathy alone can help us grasp that part of [another person's] mental content, his feelings and needs which are largely unconscious. In this method of empathic comprehension we use ourselves, however briefly, as resonating instruments that share and reflect our subject's emotions and needs. [Karush 1979, p. 63]

It is difficult to conceptualize something that is predicated at once as a form of knowledge, a form of communication, a capacity, a process, an ego expression, a mode of data gathering, an ability, an experience, a means of understanding, and a mode of perceiving. To take but one example: if empathy is a capacity, the word must refer to an individual's equipment. How, then, can it also be a process? True, one can have the capacity to engage in a process, but the definitions quoted do not make that precise distinction. In any case would the capacity or the process be empathic? If we assume that these authors are all discussing the same clinical phenomenon, we may legitimately wonder whether the confusion at the level of description occurs in part because of a difficulty with "translation." In other words, confusion may be the result of a lack of verbal integration of various aspects of the internal perception of the clinical experience. At the very least, this plethora of description suggests a diversity in the subjective experience of empathy and ensuing conscious attitudes toward it.

Clearly, the language used suggests both active and passive versions of the experience, either or both of which may be stressed by an individual writer. In the active, one encounters verbs such as "gather," "discern," "grasp" (usually the unconscious meaning);

in the passive, "respond in resonance," "use ourselves . . . as resonating instruments," "gives up his own ego for that of the object."
In one of the clearest studies, Beres and Arlow (1974) elaborate
on the passive aspect of the experience. According to them, a fantasy may appear in the mind of the analyst, unbidden, an association to and commentary on the patient's material. "A measure
of the analyst's empathic capacity lies in his ability to be stimulated by the patient's unconscious fantasy when the analyst is
not yet aware of the existence or the nature of the patient's unconscious fantasy" (p. 45). The active part of the experience,
for these authors, follows empathy: "The therapeutic situation
requires that empathy and intuition go on to interpretation
and insight" (p. 47). That is, passive receptivity becomes active
cognition, understanding, and ultimately interpretation. Thus,
the two aspects of empathy are reasonably encompassed. The
experience of empathy is a passive one, which must then be used
actively.

Perhaps because of this quality of sudden insight in which all
at once "the confusing, incomprehensible elements make sense"
(A. Reich 1951), the experience also takes on an air of "uncanny
communication" (Modell 1979, p. 70). Empathy then becomes
connected, fearfully and generally through negation, to the unscientific and occult. Burlingham (1935) considers, then rejects,
an explanation of telepathy (see also Modell 1979, p. 70). Along
similar lines, Beres and Arlow take pains to insist on the possibility of rational explanation: "This part of our experience . . . is one
we tend to regard and mistakenly believe to be beyond the realm
of scientific analysis" (1974, p. 27). Kohut, too, chooses to defend
himself against fears that his emphasis on empathy is a "move
toward nonscientific forms of psychotherapy and . . . a replacement
of the scientific mode of thought by a . . . mystical approach" (1977,
p. 304). Buie notes that "some analysts . . . endow empathy with
special powers for apprehending another person's thoughts and
feelings," and counters that his study is "based on the assumption
that no mystical or physical phenomena beyond the scope of cur-

rent scientific investigation are involved" (1981, pp. 283–284). "Empathy," writes Beres on a definitive note, "is not a mystical experience" (1968, p. 368).

It is worth noting that mystical aspects of empathy tend to be associated with a somewhat mythological version of early mother–infant interactions. When Kohut endows empathy with the status of a primary human capacity, when he considers it an irreducible capacity, he refers to this early dyad: "Primary *empathy* with the mother prepares us for the recognition that . . . the basic inner experiences of people remain similar to our own . . . the capacity for empathy belongs, therefore, to the innate equipment of the human psyche" (1966, p. 262). Loewald, too, writing of the parallel loosening of the subject–object split in both analyst and analysand, states, "Communication with the other person then tends to approximate the kind of deep mutual empathy which we see in the mother-child relationship" (1970, p. 52). Similarly, Olden believes "the phenomenon of empathy to be as deep and early as the first days and weeks of life, when there was no outside world, no 'I,' when the complete oneness with the mother provided only the subjective experience of comfort or discomfort" (1953, p. 114). What is at issue here is not the merit of a genetic explanation, but the association of empathy to mothering *and* to the mystical phenomenon of oneness.

In the psychoanalytic literature, empathy makes its appearance against the background of a debate not only on rationality versus mysticism but also on art versus science. The passive experience of unconscious fantasy or its attending affects is reminiscent of the audience's response to art (Beres 1962), as well as the artist's experience of his own creative states (Kris 1952). It is thus not surprising that empathy should have long been associated with creativity: "empathy is a creative act . . . and its communication will be creative" (Schafer 1959, p. 360).

But creativity's connection to the irrational and unscientific frequently lends this association a negative sign. The new emphasis on empathy "reveals a wish for extrication from science and closer alliance to art," writes Shapiro (1981, pp. 428–429), adding, "if psychoanalysis were to accept empathy as its tool . . . we would then risk relinquishing our place among the sciences altogether." If, for Shapiro, there is too much art, for Leavy, there is too much science:

> Even with the concept of empathy we do not entirely depart from our attempt at *objectivity* about psychic processes, an objectivity that seems to be necessary for the scientific respectability of psychoanalysis. We maintain the ideal too of observation of natural phenomena with the use of a standardized, calibrated instrument itself neither modifying data nor being modified by them. [1973, p. 320]

The scientific model, Leavy seems to suggest, creates an illusory figure, that of the fully analyzed, ever-neutral analyst who observes and grasps the data of the unconscious and who surely is as much a mythological construct as the completely responsive mother of dyadic oneness.

In alluding to alliances with art and science, both Shapiro and Leavy refer to the position that holds empathy to be the signifier of the scientific status of psychoanalysis. Here, empathy is taken as the equivalent of the physical observation and measurement that characterize the "hard" sciences. This position is generally attributable to Kohut (1957), who has been its most articulate spokesman, but it is articulated by others as well. Waelder, in an article concerned with the scientific method and psychoanalysis, writes, "We have one source of knowledge about psychic events that is completely lacking in matters of the physical world, viz., *introspection* and its equivalent in the observation of other human beings, which . . . I propose to call *empathy*" (1962, p. 628). What is important here is the fact that empathy, associated as it is with ideas of mysticism and irrationality, has conferred upon it—almost by reaction formation—the role of guardian of the very scientific status it seems to threaten.

A certain structure of opposites emerges from our exploration thus far. First, there are the active and passive versions of the clinical experience of empathy—the former associated with grasping meaning, understanding, and interpreting; the latter with resonating, sudden illumination, losing the self. Second, there are the rational and mystical sides to the concept of empathy—the first associated with concepts such as perceptual scanning, organization of derivatives, and inference; the second, usually rejected, with telepathy and the uncanny. Third, there is an opposition between science and art, in which the dispassionate observation of data that leads to uncontaminated understanding contrasts with the creative resynthesis of data. Recognizing that in practice these oppositions are combined in various ways and quantities, we may still note the dichotomy between, on the one hand, an active mode involving scientific observation, which grasps unconscious meaning and finds rational explanations for apparently mysterious data, and, on the other, a passive mode, which involves losing the self, mystery, merger, oneness, ineffable experience, and creative participation. The first of these we may tentatively and generally represent by the mythological figure of the dispassionate, rational scientist of "calibrated" ego; the second, again tentatively and generally, by the mythological figure of the perfectly attuned, resonating, responsive mother. I might add that although the former myth may be a more readily acceptable characterization to analysts, the latter may be no less strongly desired. It tends to go unchallenged, not in characterizations of analysts, but in discussions of early infancy (Arlow 1981). These fantasy figures and the dichotomies they represent, then, incarnate the antithetical meanings and tensions involved in the single term "empathy."

More specific data for these antithetical meanings may be observed in the sometimes unwitting meaning implied by the way the term appears in the sentence. The imagery is especially striking for the active mode, where empathy takes on a distinctively phallic cast. Greenson claims that "the motive for empathy is to achieve an understanding of the patient" (1960, p. 418). Here empathy refers to a purposeful action, for that is what the word "motive" implies. This action is commonly conceived to be carried out by an apparatus. Freud (1921, p. 110n) uses the word "mechanism,"[2] Annie Reich (1966, p. 351) and others use "tool," whereas Shapiro (1974, p. 5) refers to an "instrument." Moreover, this tool or instrument is not something everyone is privileged to possess: "one either has it or one hasn't" (Greenson 1960, p. 148; see also Modell 1979). It can have "distortions" and "flaws" (Shapiro 1974, p. 5) or "disturbances" (Greenson 1960, p. 149), yet when it is working well it becomes an instrument of intrusion. Then, empathy "enables the analyst to employ introspection on an object which although external has for a moment become internal. He performs thus . . . in order to lay hold of a thought belonging to someone else" (Fliess 1953, p. 280). The imagery here suggests that the tool is one of incision, with the end result the seizure of something belonging to another person.

The conception of empathy as an instrument of intrusion is not limited to Fliess. Olden writes that empathy "has the capacity . . . to trespass the objects' screens of defenses, behind which the real feelings may hide" (1953, p. 115). Intrusion here is coupled with "trespass," that is, entry into forbidden territory, again at the service of discovering a hidden reality. The metaphor of invading an enclosed territory—this time by looking—may also be found in Kohut: "Empathy seems here to be able to evade interference and to complete a rapid scrutiny before other modes of observation can assert their ascendancy" (1966, p. 263).

Side by side with this view of empathy as a tool of intrusion is its antithesis: a view of empathy as an atmosphere, medium, or

---

2. *Mechanismus* in the original German could also be translated as "system." Although the English in Freud's footnote is faithfully translated, I am reliably informed that this sentence makes much better sense in German than it does in English. Could it be that the substitution of "empathy" for *Einfühlung* subtly changes the meaning?

surround reminiscent of maternal nurturing and oneness. (Often, it should be stressed, both views appear in the same work.) Empathy "embraces," "initiates and promotes growth in the subject, the object, and the relationship between them" (Schafer 1959, pp. 350, 344). It is an "indwelling" and "takes the form of conveying in words . . . something that shows that the analyst knows and understands the patient's deepest anxieties, and . . . functions as a symbolic 'holding'" (Modell 1979, pp. 71, 72). Or, in another instance, empathy involves the "unity of observer and observed," and the observer's "protracted empathic immersion into the observed" (Kohut 1977, p. 302).

Thus, to the dichotomies previously noted, we may add the antithesis, penetration versus creation of a surrounding environment, and speculate that these dichotomies may, in general, refer to fantasies of male penetration and female nurturing. In any event, these communal fantasies become the contributors to the antithetical meanings held in dynamic tension by the word "empathy." They account for the confusing and contradictory uses previously noted. Thus, ellipses and mixed metaphors are not the sign of sloppiness or infelicity, but the results of attempts to reconcile these opposite meanings of the term.

Sometimes efforts to reconcile these opposite meanings lead to primary-process-like illogicalities at the level of secondary-process discourse. Indeed, the idea that the word "empathy" contains antithetical meanings explains some particularly puzzling uses. There is, for instance, empathy as a "tool" with "altruistic aims" (Shapiro 1974, p. 4), a formulation that, taken concretely, invents a peculiar device. There is, too, the notion of "empathic grasping" (Ornstein 1979, p. 100), which again is hard to envision at the literal level.

Next to these illogical combinations, we may place Kohut's (1977) description of the process involved in epoch-making discovery, a description found in a passage immediately preceding a long discussion of empathy. Although Kohut is discussing creative insight generally, rather than clinical insight specifically, the jux-

taposition and related subject matter make this quotation relevant
to our exploration. He states: "On this basic level of experience
... there is no clear separation between observer and observed ...
thought and action are still one. ... We seem to witness the parthenogenesis of an idea of enormous power" (p. 301). If we apply
this image to empathy, we note that the antithetical meanings
discerned in our exploration thus far reappear and are reconciled
through a metaphor of parthenogenesis in which insight is the
result of a union within the individual of the male who penetrates
and the female who conceives. Such a reconciliation, however,
takes place on a metaphorical, not on a theoretical, level.

In other creative reconciliations of the antithetical meanings
of empathy, the opposite meanings may be explicitly and unam-
biguously recognized. Beres and Arlow (1974) do so while restricting empathy to its receptive aspect. Schafer writes that "the recognition and protection of the object's separateness involve some
combination of motherly care, fatherly workmanship and com-
mand, fraternal allegiance, filial reparation, and sensuous intimacy
of an intrusive and receptive nature" (1959, p. 354). Loewald, in
an article in which he speaks of the lack of antithesis between
science and art, refers to the analyst's "empathic objectivity":

> It is neither insight in the abstract, nor any special display of a
> benevolent or warm attitude on the part of the analyst. What seems
> to be of essential importance is insight or self-understanding as
> conveyed, as mediated by the analyst's empathic understanding,
> objectively stated in articulate and open language. ... Interpreta-
> tions of this kind explicate for the patient what he then discovers
> to have always known somehow." [1975, p. 287]

Discussion

Noncontroversial secondary-process discourse requires a relatively constant conventional relationship between signifier and

signified. The signifier "empathy" as it defines itself in psycho-analytic discourse, however, refers simultaneously to two opposite kinds of clinical action: intrusion and reception. Freud (1910a) wrote about a different, but somewhat related, phenomenon when he described the antithetical meaning of primal words in a communication on the work of the Egyptologist Abel. Freud was concerned here with the issue of ontogeny recapitulating phylogeny and with words like *sacer* and *altus*, which differ in nature from "empathy." For, like "charity" and other words lending themselves to allegory, "empathy" requires an action for definition. Nevertheless, its antithetical meanings suggest something in common with Freud's observations. Freud connected the phenomenon of the antithetical meaning of primal words to his earlier observation that the dream work often represents unconscious wishes by their opposites. It may be that that characteristic of the dream work—and indeed of unconscious functioning in general—plays a part in the debate we are discussing.

In the controversy surrounding the term "empathy," we may observe that when the use of the term does not acknowledge its two meanings, or limits its definition while recognizing the existence of its antithetical component, but instead emphasizes only one component, then that consciously intended meaning of empathy tends at some level to evoke its opposite. Certainly, it is a regular feature of the literature for the spokesman for scientific "grasping" to acknowledge the need for empathy or tact and for the spokesman for maternal holding to reaffirm analytic objectivity, and to deny the accusation of curing through love. Since some combination of these modes is a necessary part of each analyst's work character and of each analytic treatment, the reason for this continual process of counterimplication may be that *the meaning most faithful to the analyst's experience of the clinical process (of which empathy is a central part) involves a synthesis of opposites.* By synthesis, I do not intend to imply a blending of opposites into something unrecognizable. Rather, I mean that the term "empathy" has come to signify both active and passive components of the analyst's work experience and that these two components need to be explicitly acknowledged and recognized to prevent equivocation, misunderstanding, and ambiguity.

Recently, however, the antithetical meanings of empathy have become increasingly separated by divergent emphases on its use in the clinical setting. Even though this difference may not, in fact, be quite as wide as it is perceived to be, the emotional intensity stirred up leads to a perception of polarity, which to all practical purposes creates the reality of vast differences. As this difference is perceived, there are, on the one hand, those clinicians who believe that the proper use of empathy involves an effort to stay subjectively attuned to the patient at all times, to comprehend the "feelings and thoughts from the vantage point of the patient's own inner experience as contrasted with the vantage point of an external observer" (Ornstein 1979, p. 99). This position eschews inferential thinking while listening to the patient's material (Ornstein 1979). On the other hand, there are those clinicians who hold that empathizing precludes analyzing (Shapiro 1981). The theoretical realities as well as merits of these positions aside, the *perception* of antithetical positions involves the term in a polarization that impoverishes. Where the proclivity is toward maternal holding, an interpretation of latent content takes on the pejorative connotation of intrusion; where the proclivity is toward rational understanding, not to uncover latent content suggests another negative: a failure of performance. In both cases, the perception of polarity leads to the loss of useful flexibility in the term and threatens an eventual loss of clinical flexibility.

The possibility of a synthesis of the antithetical meanings of empathy, however, assumes theoretical agreement on the issue of manifest and latent content. Implicit in the position of those who believe that one always hears evidence of unconscious wishes, conflicts, and fantasies in a patient's associations is that empathic understanding involves comprehension of the unconscious content; for them, empathy will always involve some degree of intrusion, that is, of consciously knowing more than the patient consciously knows. To the extent, however, that certain productions are not considered derivatives of unconscious wishes or defenses against them, but rather productions with no dynamic latent content—descriptions of self-states for instance (Kohut 1977, pp. 109–110)—empathy cannot by definition involve the same sort of intrusive understanding of latent content. That is, where no dynamic latent content is assumed, the antithetical alternative inherent in the term "empathy" ceases to exist.

If, as I have suggested, a use of the term that reflects a synthesis of its antithetical components most accurately reflects the clinical experience of empathy, then what occurs when this antithetical alternative is ruled out by theoretical assumption? What we may then perceive is a movement away from the possibility of a creative synthesis. Instead, that antithetical tension is re-created at the level of theory in the controversy over whether to accord primacy to the drives or to the self. Empathy, then, with each antithetical meaning representing a different theoretical position, loses its value as a creative clinical concept and becomes a signifier of conflict alone.

10 Toward a Methodology for Applying Psychoanalysis to Literature[1]

Introduction

Methodological Problems

The methodological problems of applying psychoanalytic knowledge to works of literature are legion. Historically, psychoanalysts have sought the pathology of the author beneath the text so that the author assumed the position of patient, and his work together with his biography became by analogy the clinical evidence. This approach has been so attacked that it is worthwhile reminding ourselves that when the analytic knowledge is thorough, its application subtle, the conclusions based on a clinical level of inference, and the work of art regarded for its formal as well as for its thematic content, the results can be both illuminating and

1. I am indebted to the work of the Interdisciplinary Colloquium on Psychoanalysis and Literature, the New York Psychoanalytic Institute, and to Drs. Francis Baudry, William Grossman, and James Spencer, Jr., for specific substantive suggestions.

satisfying. Nevertheless, this approach dissolves the work of art a priori into an explanation for something beyond itself. Further, it contradicts that important tradition in literary criticism that considers the text itself paramount and looks to criticism to increase the conscious appreciation of literary complexity. Literary critics who wished to concentrate upon the text but also to take into account psychoanalytic knowledge have instead tried to trace psychoanalytic patterns discernible from the manifest content. To be sure, there is a psychoanalytic tradition here too, one as old as the naming of the Oedipus complex; in naming the Oedipus complex, however, Freud was delineating a model. Critics who interpret a text by naming the manifest patterns are assuming a reification of concepts foreign to the spirit of psychoanalysis. Unfortunately, the opposite procedure, a foray into latent content with only the text as evidence, justifiably invites the charge of wild analysis.

More recently, Norman Holland (1975a,b) has attempted to escape the dilemma by de-emphasizing the text in favor of the reader's reactions to it. Arguing against the belief "that the reality and meaning of the external world exist alone, independent of the perceiving self" (1975b, p. 809), and for a formulation of matching defensive fantasies, he insists that the real reader and the meaning he makes are inseparable.

While the shift of emphasis away from the autocratic concept of correct readings has been helpful, the idea of a highly subjective reader–text dyad should not replace inquiry into the collective experience of art, nor should it allow us to dismiss the idea that the work has an emotive power of its own that deserves investigation. For surely what distinguishes art in general is its power to move, to transfix, to enthrall its audience. And its audience is a group, not an individual. If, then, applications of psychoanalysis to literature have ironically tended to transform the text into something other than itself, the problem facing us is to find a way for psychoanalysis to fathom the unique quality of the work of literature.

A Methodological Hypothesis

Despite his rather polemical use of literature, Freud was also acutely aware of the writer's "innermost secret" (Freud 1907), that ability to transform unconscious fantasies into communally pleasurable works (Freud 1908). In studying the literarity of the text, I think it useful to return to this formulation, at least to the extent of reconsidering the interrelationship among fantasy, artistic form, and the effect of the work on the community of readers.

Arlow (1969a,b) has suggested that conscious perception is the result of a complicated process of synchronization between external stimuli and internal fantasy. On the one hand, unconscious fantasy may determine the perception and integration of reality; on the other, external stimuli may trigger the emergence of unconscious fantasy. As a simple example of the latter, the perception of oneself in a small enclosure may evoke intrauterine fantasies. What is important here is the relationship between the details perceived and the fantasy, for it is the fantasy, with its interwoven memories, that lends the experience of being in the enclosed space a particular affective weight.

I posit that the literary work represents a similar, though more complex, synchronization of external stimuli and internal fantasy, with the added necessity that both elements to the synchronization also be communicated. Accordingly, where strong affects exist, I assume that clues to a fantasy are imbedded in the surface detail of the work, in its form and its metaphors, even in the placement of its silences, so that the surface of the work elicits the same fantasy in its readers as organizes it. That is, on some level, the reader shares the organizing fantasy of the work.

These shared fantasies may be universal in nature, the product of common biological endowment and participation in the human condition. Or, on a somewhat less general plane, there may be communal fantasies of relatively fixed nature facilitated by common developmental experiences and cultural heritage (Arlow 1969a, Sachs 1942). It is also conceivable that still less general fantasies may be evoked and shared, but that is the subject of another discussion.

Leaving aside for the moment the temptation of reductionism, such a formulation may appear to raise more problems than it solves. It does not rid us of the nagging methodological problem of arriving at latent content without clinical evidence, and it presents us in addition with the difficulty of trying to discover and confirm shared fantasy. Some might suggest exclusive reliance on the critic's countertransference-like reactions to the text. But such an approach provides nothing beyond one critic's responses and is open to charges of subjectivity, especially by the nonanalytically oriented. The same objection may be raised to that clinical intuition that is in reality a combination of experience, knowledge of the unconscious, and an ability to identify analogies to clinical situations. At the very least, additional evidence to supplement this clinical "feel" would be helpful.

Although I do not share the theoretical position of the French, some of their work has suggested to me an avenue by which to obtain supplemental evidence. Recent articles by Felman have elaborated the critical possibilities of Jacques Lacan's approach to Poe (Felman 1977, 1980, Lacan 1966). In a brilliant paper on James, Felman (1977) points out the curiously constant way in which critics seem to repeat something in the text by their squabbles about the text. To pursue the implication of her observation, I suggest the following hypothesis: the kind of questions critics ask and avoid asking about a text, the kind of answers they offer or wish to receive, the language (especially metaphors) they use to describe the text, their interactions around a text, provide valuable clues to its latent but powerfully emotive content. Thus, I suggest that critics may re-enact a fantasy that they do not consciously perceive, but that is nevertheless an integral part of the text's esthetic power. To be sure, there will be idiosyncratic individual responses. Where there exists a uniformity in response, though not necessarily in the manifest content or form of that response, I posit the working of a shared fantasy.

This approach carries with it some built-in limitations. First, to suggest that a particular fantasy operates between the critics' reading and the text is not to describe an author's personal conflicts. On the basis of this approach we cannot distinguish between the creative use of unconscious fantasy and an author's individual pathology, nor does this approach afford us sufficient evidence for statements concerning the latter. Second, the common fantasies identified need not represent the only fantasies informing either the work or the critics' response. To suggest that they do would violate the principle of multiple function (Waelder 1930) as well as neglect the whole dimension of personal psychology beyond my scope. Finally, it will ultimately be necessary to tease out the dynamics inherent in the critical position per se from responses specifically related to a particular work. While the critical position may, I believe, intensify certain responses, particularly competitive ones, I am assuming here that it does not distort them.

The Example of Diderot's
Jacques le Fataliste et son Maître

I wish now to investigate this hypothesis by examining the critical literature on *Jacques le Fataliste et son Maître*, a novel by the eighteenth-century French philosopher and encyclopedist, Denis Diderot. This curious challenge to fictional convention has no easily recounted plot. It is seemingly written to lay bare and ridicule all of the laboriously amassed technique for promoting novelistic illusion built up by the eighteenth century. Unlike *Don Quijote* and its imitators, however, this play with illusion is less charming than aggressive. The work has two sets of main characters. The first set, two characters who appear only as voices in dialogue and narrative, are the fictional author and his reader. The former has absolute control over the fiction. He introduces events, narrates occurrences, withholds details or changes them in midstream, interrupts his characters, anticipates and mocks his readers' assumptions, flaunts his power to shape events, and generally behaves in an arbitrary and high-handed manner. The latter is a pesky child who interrupts, questions, and demands answers.

The novel begins with the following words and without any punctuation to distinguish the dialogue from narration:

> How did they meet? By chance, like everyone.
> What were their names? What does it matter to you?
> Where did they come from? From the nearest spot.
> Where were they going? Does anyone know where he's going?
> What were they saying? The master said nothing, and Jacques said that his captain said that everything either good or bad that happens down here has been written up there.[2]

The second set of characters, the valet, Jacques, and his unnamed master, belong to a different mimetic level. They speak "on stage." That is, their dialogue is preceded by their names as though the novel were a playscript. Jacques and his master both take part in fictional events and narrate events that have happened to them or to others. They also become the audience for the narratives of other characters they encounter. At times the various mimetic levels become quite tangled. At others, there is a virtual shouting match between the author who suddenly decides to tell a story and the reader who wishes to hear what happens to the main characters. Sometimes a story is interrupted successively within the fiction by an event and within the narrative frame by the author. It is no wonder that one critic has described the novel as an "insurmountable and irreducible disorder" (Roelens 1973, p. 128).

Part of the dialogue between master and servant involves the philosophic issue of whether the individual controls his life or whether, as Jacques claims his captain has taught him, life is predetermined "up there" on a Great Scroll in such a way as to make the individual indifferent to action or knowledge. But the glue that

---

2. This and all subsequent quotations from French works are my translations.

holds together the novel's diverse and fragmented episodes is Jacques' attempt to recount the story of his falling in love. Overtly borrowed from Sterne's *Tristram Shandy*, the narration of this story is constantly and tantalizingly interrupted. Finally, the novel form, too, is definitively undermined when the author is replaced by an editor, a manuscript, and three possible manuscript endings, none of which is endorsed.

The Evidence of the Critics

Because of *Jacques'* tangled textual history and unusual literary qualities, most of the literary criticism concerning it has appeared over the last thirty years. Like other criticism written during this span, it reflects the changing fashions of critical history. The older work is more concerned with philosophic and historical content, the newer with form and narrative technique. Despite these differences, however, universal trends emerge. For one, critics seem so bewildered and belittled by the willful obscurity of this text that they are driven to explain, interpret, or speak in place of Diderot. J. Robert Loy (1950), for example, after writing pages setting out Diderot's philosophy, ends:

> Every effort presupposes a series of cause factors in which to speak of a first cause or an isolated cause is nonsense. The insistence is on the effect and what it brings in the way of new possibilities. *All this . . . is what Diderot is trying to say.* [p. 130, italics added]

While he avoids asking why Diderot might be incapable of speaking for himself, Loy discusses a related set of critical concerns. Is Diderot espousing individual freedom or arguing that it is impossible? If the former, then he is arguing against Spinoza. Is that his intention? What is Spinoza's position and Diderot's understanding of it? Does *Jacques* mark a change in that position or a covert affirmation of it?

Thus the text engenders concern with the authority of the interpreter: who speaks definitively for Spinoza, who for Diderot's understanding of Spinoza, who for Diderot himself, and who is to say what is written "up there"?

One common critical solution to this predicament is a recourse to philosophical authority. Here Spinoza's thought is first defined; then Diderot's position on his predecessor at a given time is established through examination of other writings. Although neither of these procedures is immune from controversy, critics then attempt to use Diderot's assumed position on Spinoza as a cipher, a key that unlocks his enigmatic text. Yet, if the text is so obscure that it requires a cipher, why do critics prefer speaking for the author to exploring the text's ambiguity?

This question is important because critics have not asked it. Instead of exploring the question of authority, *critics have assumed authority*. They have acted rather than observed. The text seems to encourage them to replace the authority of the author with their own.

Ironically, critics are especially ready to speak authoritatively for Diderot on the subject of freedom. Loy contends that Diderot believes in both determinism and the possibility of human freedom, but Francis Pruner (1970) believes the novel to be a self-protectively concealed defense of Spinoza, hence, a secret argument against human freedom. In the same vein, Coulet (1967) agrees that *Jacques* argues against human liberty, while Aram Vartanian (1974) asserts that *Jacques* represents a "vindication of the principle of freedom" (p. 326).

Despite the disagreement over its meaning, critics are equally sure that Diderot seeks either to ridicule a particular doctrine, to persuade the reader of its merits, to reconcile its antithetical tensions, or to point out that these tensions are irreconcilable (Ehrard 1970, Fellows 1968, Kohler 1970, Sherman 1976). What is more, critics cannot agree on whether Diderot is exemplifying the possibility of moral choice or foreclosing it. Nola M. Leov (1965) writes of Diderot's "ethic of comprehension" (p. 46), while I. H. Smith (1962) insists that the novel represents "a bankrupting of ethics" (p. 29). Despite the plethora of conflicting opinions, one does not have the sense of scholarly dialogue. Indeed, the urge to interpret authoritatively seems to preclude the kind of learning that emerges from dialogue.

But authority in this context involves more than the authority of interpretation. Jacques Wagner (1977) begins a critical article on *Jacques* in these words:

> The wolf is accommodating. He lodges in his mouth those who wish to destroy him. And how escape from this warm and comfortable tongue? How speak otherwise, how write otherwise, how read otherwise, that is, better? [p. 23]

The metaphor of the wolf holding in its mouth those who wish to destroy him describes a struggle against a superior and compelling force. To struggle against it, to gain distance for interpretation, to move outside of tradition (which is, after all, what Diderot also attempts) is equated with a wish to destroy. Yet what does destroying entail? To speak, read, and write better. That is, the text stimulates the critic to become involved in a struggle not only for authority but also for authorship. Interestingly, this struggle duplicates the ongoing competition between the novel's fictional author and reader over how to write and that between Jacques and his master over who should tell stories.

But critics not only act out a struggle, they perceive the novel in terms of one as well. For many, that struggle is between free will and determinism. For others, the conflict is perceived in terms of class strife and approaching revolution (Butor 1966, Kohler 1970, Laufer 1963). Still another critic, exploring linguistic relationships, insists that the tension arises from the opposition between the pronouns "he" and "I" (Kavanaugh 1973).

Regardless of whether the terms they use are philosophical, sociopolitical, or linguistic, commentators who describe meaning envision the novel as a conflict between two forces. Moreover, these critics frequently describe the conflict as a scene, repeating a tendency in the novel itself to present characters on stage. Thus free will becomes the individual with his wish for freedom and need for morality, while an oppressive class structure becomes by metonymy the master. Furthermore, some critics perceive one force dominating this scene of struggle: fatalism, ethics, the servant, for instance, while others stress the tense interrelation of the two partners to the conflict.

The *form* of the novel also inspires metaphors of struggle. Critics understand the novel as a revolt against the conventions of fiction (Cohen 1976, Thomas 1974); however, this revolt against convention ends in perpetual entanglement because Diderot is obliged to use the very rules he attacks (Mauzi 1964, Werner 1975). As Werner (1975) writes:

> *Jacques le Fataliste* is a work of fiction about the prospects of fiction, a literary text whose 'subject matter' is the negation of its own content: a narrative meant to demonstrate the comical lameness of narrative. [p.13]

By implication, then, *Jacques* is not only about a struggle. Through its form it *embodies* a struggle. And this dynamic struggle, manifested by its form, becomes the novel's content.

Significantly, this dynamic struggle is associated with ideas of creation, of birth, and of coupling. Ira Wade (1968) writes of Diderot's characteristic depiction of the "rhythm of becoming" (p. 4). Thomas Kavanaugh (1973) adds, "[T]he only story told by the text is that of its coming to be, its coming to 'mean'. The work is a chronicle of its own creation" (p. 35). Lecointre and Le Galliot (1971), meanwhile, envision a union beneath the novel's surface, an unchanging "model of the double which joins meaning" (p. 25).

But creation is perceived to coexist with destruction. If the work chronicles its coming to be, then that coming to be never quite occurs. As Lecointre and Le Galliot also observe:

> This novel resembles Penelope's weaving: as soon as it takes shape it simulates its self-destruction. It progresses only to come back constantly to its starting point. It is without a becoming. [p. 30]

The novel thus binds creation to destruction. Not surprisingly, *Jacques* inspires metaphors associated with struggles that no one wins. It is called a "deadlock" (Werner 1975, p. 36) and an "impasse" (Cohen 1976, p. 19).

Another critical theme is that the text conceals a dangerous secret beneath its surface. For Lester Crocker (1961) a nihilistic truth lurks in the depths of the text, a truth from which the author protects the public (p. 98). And Pruner (1970) believes this truth to be dangerous enough to condemn Diderot to death (p. 14). This danger is seen to reside in something hidden beneath the surface, a sub-version. Van Laere (1973) writes of a second register, "where what is shown recalls the evanescences of a symbolic or hermetic order" (p. 100).

It follows that the text is conceived as a riddle, puzzle, or enigma in which the surface hides a secret beneath it. Of course, the metaphor of meaning lying beneath is a common one, but its use by critics of *Jacques le Fataliste* seems to describe the novel concretely rather than to characterize a general literary mode of signifying.

Yet, though this idea of a secret beneath a chaotic surface obsesses critics, the search for what is hidden is not an attempt to uncover the assumed danger; it is rather an attempt to make the surface predictable by finding a symmetrical system that will contain unruly narrative proliferation.

While these efforts are often incredibly ingenious (Chesnau 1968, Loy 1950, Mauzi 1964), the real question remains: What in the text propels this effort to divide, classify, contain, and predict? Critics are bewildered by the surface of this text, by its interruptions and digressions, its proliferating stories, its annoying narrative apostrophes, its blatantly arbitrary plot sequence, its refusal to divulge a meaning. In fact, the *real* enigma is not *beneath* the surface; it resides in the manifest disorder *of* the surface. This surface both excludes critics from knowing and increases their desire to know. Although they therefore wish to solve the enigma, critics curiously turn away from the surface content of the work where it resides. As part of this turning away, they do not seem to see, and almost never discuss, a number of graphically depicted sexual scenes that comprise an important part of the surface. I shall describe these scenes when I discuss the text itself.

Significantly, some critics both avoid the surface and attempt to solve the enigma by searching for the secret of the text's generation. Kavanaugh (1973) seeks to identify "a language totally internal to the work and which, like a hidden motor force, activates all surface movements" (p. 34).

Lecointre's and Le Galliot's (1971) avowed goal of discovering the "model of the double which joins meaning" (p. 25) also falls into this category. In looking for deep and mysterious linguistic structures, critics again retreat from the surface, only this time they also re-create it. "From whence, from what secret spring, does this creation issue?" they ask in their search for a "hidden motor force." In so asking, they repeat questions of origin asked about the protagonists in the first paragraph of the novel: "How did they meet? . . . where did they come from? . . ." The attempt to control an uneasiness over manifest content and form by locating the secret of its generation apparently involves the critic in the re-enactment of aspects of that unpredictable surface that seem to make him uneasy.

Besides bewilderment, the novel stirs up frustration, anger, and humiliation in its readers. When Vartanian (1974) writes of his discomfort, he attributes it to being kept in the dark. "The reader of Diderot's labyrinthine [novel] . . . finds himself groping about in a world where events, seen alternatively as belonging to a necessary order and as unfolding with a capricious freedom, never lose their equivocal character" (p. 325). One might extend this to say that the critic is paralyzed. How can he interpret when he does not understand events? (see also Roelens 1973, p 130.)

Such a position is humiliating. Rarely acknowledging humiliation, critics instead resent the author, without even differentiating between Diderot and his fictional creation. The polite Gabriejla Vidan (1967) refers to "the almost obnoxious assurance with which Diderot manipulates the plot" (p. 72), while Ehrard (1970) sees the novel's disorder as "insolent" (p. 145). Mauzi (1964) goes further. He describes a pattern of teasing: one of Diderot's favorite pastimes in *Jacques* is to "neutralize the concession he seems to make, to refuse and hide all while giving the impression of giving and showing" (p. 99). That is, the reader is humiliated because he is led to expect to see something and then does not see it. Instead, the author appears to be responsible for an absence. By giving the impression that he will give and show only to withhold and conceal, the author forces the reader to anticipate a presence and then to come face to face with a lack.

The implication of this pattern of taking away is profound. Just at the moment when the desire—for an answer, for a completion—in anticipation of an answer or completion becomes most intense, that completion is withheld so that the only revelation is of the desire itself. This continual and humiliating revelation of desire is what lends the novel's enigmatic surface its power. What, after all, is an enigma if not a situation in which a form of satisfaction is withheld? To want to know is to wish to possess knowledge. To encounter an enigma, therefore, is not to possess the object of one's desires. Each critic's insistence upon giving answers may perhaps best be understood as a way of avoiding the humiliation of coming face to face with an absence that stands for the frustration of his desires. Interpretation becomes the critic's attempt to substitute something for nothing. It is an effort to ward off humiliation and defeat.

To summarize the critics' reactions: critics perceive the text as an enigma. They feel humiliated by the text's obscurity and excluded from its meaning. They want to know its secret, yet they ignore its surface. In so doing, they avoid looking at that part of its surface that includes graphic sexual scenes. At the same time they search its hidden depths to discover the secret of its generation of meaning. Critics also perceive the text as embodying a struggle. The struggle is associated both with the act of creation and with destruction. Critics describe the author who creates the novel before their eyes as sadistic, as humiliating, and as taking something away. Finally, the text stimulates a wish in the critic to replace this author both as interpreter and as creator.

The critics' feelings of exclusion and bewilderment, their refusal to see and wish to know, the element of struggle, the association of struggle with creation and destruction, the preoccupation with the secret of generation, the wish to replace the author, the perception of the author as sadistic and humiliating and as taking something away—all these factors suggest to me that the fantasy evoked in critics by *Jacques le Fataliste* is one of the primal scene.

The Evidence of the Text

While an examination of the critics does not leave us the space for the full discussion the text itself must receive, many formal and thematic elements in the work suggest that primal scene fantasies inform it as well. There is an explicit depiction of sexual activity in the novel, part of that surface that critics avoid. Among the relevant scenes are several in which intercourse is either overheard or witnessed. As Jacques lies suffering in bed from a knee wound, he hears the arguments and lovemaking of the peasant couple who have taken him in and in whose hands his fate rests. Jacques also tells his master of a sexual assignation in the barn of one Dame Suzon. Jacques and Suzon are interrupted by the vicar who has arrived for the same purpose as Jacques. The two men struggle and Jacques, thrusting a pitchfork between his rival's legs, throws him up into the hayloft from where the priest is forced to watch the resumption and completion of Jacques' activities. Although Jacques then escapes, Suzon's husband appears, summoned by the vicar's enraged cries of "thief." The peasant whirls the priest on the pitchfork around the barn and threatens to parade him in this fashion through town.

As a counterpart to Jacques' unfinished love story, the master tells his own. It ends with the following episode: his best friend, in reality a first-class rogue, guiltily confesses to sleeping with the woman the master has been unsuccessfully and ruinously pursuing. In conformity with the master's wishes for vengeance, the so-called friend arranges that the master secretly replace him in the lady's bed. As the master begins to describe his exquisite pleasure, he is interrupted by Jacques. The text makes clear that Jacques is thereby revenging himself for the many times he himself has been interrupted. When, several incidents later, the master picks up his narrative, it is to describe how his lovemaking itself has been intruded upon by the entrance into the bedroom of the young lady's entire family accompanied by the police. The master is held financially responsible for the child born seven months later.

These last two incidents, especially, include important common elements: the humiliation of a rival and of a love object; revenge on the rival and the love object; the making public of intercourse and its interruption. Individual versions of these common elements are elaborated in any number of other incidents, whether overtly sexual or not. In fact, interruption is clearly the dominant formal element in the entire novel. The author interrupts narratives and events, the reader interrupts the author, the master interrupts Jacques, Jacques interrupts the master, a duel interrupts the journey's end, a change in convention interrupts the fictional illusion—our list could go on almost indefinitely.

Interruption also appears as a manifest element in primal scene fantasies. Arlow (1961b) has described a typical dream in which the dreamer is interrupted and his act of defecating—a regressive representation of the primal scene—is turned into a more or less public spectacle. Here, the fact of being interrupted represents the wish to be the one indulging in the interrupted parental activity. The same author has recently connected repetitive re-enactments of the primal scene with the individual's wish to avenge himself upon the betraying parents. Although interrupting and witnessing couples engaged in lovemaking is one common form of vengeance, Arlow (1980) believes that the more significant vengeful repetitions are those in which the individual causes others to interrupt and be witness to his activities. "The unconscious import of this behavior is to make the betraying parents experience the sense of humiliation, exclusion, and betrayal" (p. 523).

The complex narrative structure of *Jacques* allows room for the play of both kinds of interruption: interrupting others and the "vengeful repetitions" that place someone else in the painful and humiliating position of interrupter. The narrator, whether fictional author, character within the fiction, or character contained within the narrative of a fictional character, re-creates dialogue in such a vivid way that the reader sees the telling and the told. That is, the reader participates in the watching and in the creation of the tale. No sooner is the reader enmeshed in this doubly gratifying fictional illusion than it is wantonly ruptured, the narrator prevented from finishing, the reader from watching and knowing. The reader is interrupted and witnesses the interruption. Moreover, the existence of a fictional reader within the text to whom the author attributes reactions and questions and to whom he addresses comments also forces the real reader into the role of reader that Diderot writes for him. This role frequently involves interrupting. The character of this fictional reader is, in fact, similar to that of the imperious child in one of the novel's interrupted stories who awakens in the middle of the night and demands that everyone in the castle be awakened, brought into a room, and arranged in a circle around him. All he can offer by way of explanation is the rhythmical cry, "I want it, I want it."

Identification of primal scene fantasies in *Jacques* allows us to connect the formal element of interrupting not only with the manifest content of sexual episodes but also with the manifest content of episodes of an apparently indifferent character such as this one. Further, it permits us to account for and take cognizance of something the critics have largely ignored: the degree of narcissistic rage informing the entire work. This rage emerges in acts of vindictiveness, betrayal, and revenge; in the humiliation of others; in the way the author undermines the fictional illusion; in the purposeful opaqueness in which he shrouds narrative events.

That is, it accounts not only for a good deal of the content but also for the form of the novel, a form that may be described as a vengeful re-enactment. It is the real reader, and the critic who represents him, who is cast as humiliated witness and who refuses, like the child in the story, to accept the role passively.

It is thus possible to contend that the critic of *Jacques*, bewildered, humiliated, left in the dark wanting to know yet refusing to see the sexual content before his eyes, re-enacts the role of voyeur in the primal scene. Further, in doing so he shares the organizing fantasy of the work. The study of the critical response to *Jacques* tends, therefore, to support my original hypothesis that critics, in writing about the text, re-enact a fantasy latent in the text and that is the carrier of the text's affective power.

Discussion

The theoretical justification for re-enactment is found in Freud's (1914) "Remembering, Repeating and Working Through." If the patient re-enacts in the transference what he cannot remember, one can perhaps envision the critic re-enacting in his writing about a text elements of its latent content that he unknowingly apprehends. The circumstances of the two situations are, however, different enough to make us uneasy with such a leap.

An intermediate step between possible occurrence and conceivable theoretical justification would seem to be required. One such step may be found in the clinical phenomenon of parallelism. By parallelism I refer to the well-known but relatively infrequently discussed re-enactments in supervision by the supervisee of current aspects of his patient's affect, behavior, or conflicts of which he is not consciously aware (Arlow 1963, Ekstein and Wallerstein 1958, Gediman and Wolkenfeld 1980, Sachs and Shapiro 1976, Searles 1955). These enactments are sometimes well focused and dramatic. Arlow (1963) describes a supervisee who did not grasp the meaning of his patient's intrusion into another patient's session. The supervisee then burst into his supervisor's consulting room after an analytic hour had begun to retrieve an article left behind. Searles's (1955) examples are more indirect and tend to involve the duplication of unrecognized affect.

But startling or subtle, re-enactments occur with experienced analysts as well as with novices (Gediman and Wolkenfeld 1980) and are not necessarily evidence of countertransference difficulties. Indeed, Searles stresses their informational value.

Although they generally base their explanation on Freud's remembering and repeating formulation, several authors have also attempted to account for observed parallelism phenomena more specifically. One explanation: transient identifications shared by patient and therapist. These may be based on shared unconscious conflicts, anxieties, defenses, id wishes, ideals, or values (Arlow 1963), or shared narcissistic vulnerabilities (Gediman and Wolkenfeld 1980). Identificatory re-enactments involve shifting levels of ego functioning such as occur in the change from objective understanding to empathy. Occurring both in listening to the patient and in reporting the material in supervision, these shifts reflect a similar oscillation in psychoanalysis proper between free association and self-observation (Arlow 1963). Re-enactment may thus be understood as a product of empathy untempered by conscious understanding. And empathy, as Beres and Arlow (1974) point out, is achieved through the transient sharing of fantasy.

While there may be other analogies, the parallelism phenomenon provides one useful clinical analogy for my hypothesis that critics re-enact aspects of unconsciously apprehended shared fantasies that are part of the esthetic fabric of the literary work. Since analogies are tools of explanation, not of deductive logic, it does not follow that similarity of structure is synonymous with the identity of constituent parts of that structure. That is, the text is not equivalent to a patient, nor the critic to a therapist. Rather, my analogy pertains to an intersubjective constellation: the *interrelationship* among (1) the patient and his material, (2) the therapist and his reporting of that material, and (3) the supervisor may be usefully compared to the *interrelationship,* among (1) the author and his text, (2) the critic and his writing about the text, and (3) the critic's audience.

As part of these similar intersubjective structures, both critic and (supervised) therapist share certain assumptions, vulnerabilities, modes of understanding, and fantasies. Both believe that the meaning of the material they scrutinize extends beyond its readily apparent aspects. Both undoubtedly entertain or have entertained in some form fantasies of rescue whether of author, meaning, work, or individual. Both find themselves in positions where they are expected—by themselves or others—to be omniscient. Both expose themselves to criticism, correction, and disagreement, and to a situation in which competition is inherent. Both are part of multidirectional structures, since the critic's interpretation of a work will influence the subsequent readings of that text for his audience. Both deal with highly evocative and affective material for the understanding of which both rely on intuition as well as on logic, on imagination as well as on knowledge. Both apprehend through a partial ego regression to visual imagery (Balter et al. 1980).

Moreover, just as the structure of the supervisory situation places the therapist in a situation similar to the patient's in therapy, thereby facilitating transient identification, so the critic writing about a text places himself in a situation similar to that of the original author of the text. The critic repeats the author's act of writing. Further, he repeats the act of writing for an audience with all the sharing of narcissistic vulnerabilities that having an audience implies. Although the critic chooses his own subject matter, his choice is a particular text, the product of an author whose act of writing he duplicates. This situation not only implies a congruity of subject matter but also suggests a sharing of some aspect of unconscious content.

To be sure, this intersubjective parallel requires further elaboration. I invoke it here primarily to suggest that it is possible to find an analogy in clinical practice for the phenomenon of the critics' re-enactment of fantasies latent in the literary text that I have just described.

It is important to stress, however, that identification of latent shared fantasies is only the beginning of the necessary critical work. One of the tasks that now awaits us is the study of the interplay between latent fantasy and existing art. Such a study of artistic transformation may begin to answer the mysteries of the literary work: how it achieves its complex and powerful emotive effects, how it transfers and conveys the necessary defenses and sublimations, and how it enables us to integrate and transcend the infantile fantasies at its core. What is more, such an orientation will allow us to use psychoanalysis to enhance our understanding of a text without turning the object of our scrutiny into something other than itself.

The identification of latent shared fantasies is thus only a first step in a longer process. It is, however, a useful first step. Analysis of the critics' response provides us with textually derived evidence to help toward that identification. Alone, that response is, of course, insufficient. Taken in conjunction with the text itself, I believe it illuminating.

Summary

In order to consider the affective power of the literary work itself, rather than turning that work into a symptom or its author into a patient, this article has proposed the following hypothesis: the text evokes an unconscious fantasy in the reader; critics who respond to the text empathically but without conscious understanding re-enact aspects of that organizing fantasy in the way they write their criticism.

A study of the literary critical response to Diderot's *Jacques le Fataliste et son Maître* reveals that critics feel excluded and bewildered by the text, wish to decipher its enigmatic secret, refuse to "see" explicit and manifest sexual content, associate the novel with a struggle and that struggle with creation and destruction, and wish to replace the author as creator. All these factors suggest that critics re-enact the role of voyeur in the primal scene.

Specifically sexual episodes, episodes containing indifferent material, and devices including the novel's major formal element of interruption reveal the existence of primal scene derivatives as organizing factors of the novel. Previously overlooked, the role of narcissistic rage emerges so that the form of *Jacques* as a whole may be understood as a vengeful re-enactment.

Finally, the article explores similarities between two inter-subjective constellations: text–critic–critic's audience and patient–therapist supervisor. Parallelism, the phenomenon in which the therapist re-enacts aspects of his patient's conflicts in supervision, is offered as a phenomenon clinically analogous to that of the critic's re-enactment.

11 On the Discipline of Applied Psychoanalysis

The ambiguity in the use of the term *discipline* is intentional. One possible meaning of discipline is a subject worthy of study or practice. Applied psychoanalysis can be proposed as such a field of study for the following reasons.

First, if applied psychoanalysis is seen as a field of inquiry, then the question of what can constitute its object of attention will necessarily emerge. This question becomes clearer if we compare and contrast the endeavor of applied psychoanalysis with that of psychoanalytic psychotherapy. In sharing with applied psychoanalysis the problem of drawing inferences about unconscious content from limited data, psychotherapy also shares with applied psychoanalysis certain problems of method. Psychotherapy differs from the analysis of culture, on the other hand, by virtue of the fact that it shares with psychoanalysis a common object of attention: the individual. This similarity of object is no small advantage, for psychoanalytic theory includes a particular view of what man or at least his mental apparatus is and how to work with it. The question of how to see the cultural object analogously is not at all clear.

A second reason for considering applied psychoanalysis as a discipline in itself is to allow us to observe the field from outside. From this vantage point we can study the transformation of psychoanalysis in the process of its application. Heretofore, the interest has tended to be in the other direction—what psychoanalysis "does" to art—yet the study of the transformation of psychoanalysis is an interesting one. Some strange things happen to psychoanalytic concepts when they meet the exigencies of an analytic examination of the cultural product.

Perhaps the most common of these occurrences is what I have called the appropriation of psychoanalysis by other disciplines (see Chapter 8). One form of appropriation is using an allegorical reading of manifest content to refind theoretical postulates. A more subtle and less discernible procedure involves the use of theoretical terms in contexts that expand them until they are not really psychoanalytic concepts at all. For example, fantasy is first used in the technical sense and then used so broadly that it becomes synonymous with theme. Not only does the technical word lose its psychoanalytic specificity but also a critical discourse purports to be psychoanalytic, even implies dynamic considerations, when in fact it is purely a description of what is available on the surface. A third and allied difficulty occurs in the process of utilizing the concept of dynamic conflict. If the critical aim is the interpretation of the text itself or of other comparable cultural objects, we encounter an "interpretation" that assumes dynamic conflict applied to a verbal or plastic medium in which conflict can only be represented.

Although this problem is rarely acknowledged, it frequently leads to covert but nonetheless questionable assumptions. Operating unnoticed in many interpretations of texts, even those with sophisticated, literary-critical apparatuses, is the equation of art=living and breathing being. Another solution is to reify dynamic theory and then to assume that the cultural object constitutes a model of the mind. I call these very representative solutions the Promethean and Medusan alternatives. The first infuses the cultural product with breath and starts blood pulsing in its veins; the second turns the mind to stone.

In advancing a discipline of applied psychoanalysis, I am suggesting that these covert assumptions be seen as interesting data. They emphasize a problem that sometimes seems insurmountable, but certainly cannot be ignored: How is one to preserve the integrity of the literary artifact and also honor the fact that psychoanalytic understanding of surface content is dependent on an understanding of unconscious wishes and defenses against them and that meaning and conflict are inextricably related and not mutually exclusive?

If such a goal is not entirely attainable, we should at least know what we are sacrificing from each discipline. And it is here that the meaning of discipline coincides with its more common meaning of rigor. I propose that we apply ourselves *with* discipline to the enterprise of applied psychoanalysis. Moreover, the place to start is not with considerations of method, as most of us have tried to do, but with considerations of analogy. That is, before we can apply psychoanalysis to the cultural object, we need to describe that object in terms that make it available for psychoanalytic inquiry.

Any description of the cultural object, however, imposes limits upon what psychoanalysis can attempt. Since psychoanalysis is concerned with psychic conflict, it is concerned with the interplay of drive derivatives and defense. Neither drive derivatives nor defenses lurk between the pages of a book or dwell in the accretions of paint on a canvas. They have a source. In interpreting a text we must ascribe them to some agency, either to the mind of the author, or to the mind of the audience for art or to both. (Incidentally, we cannot assume in dealing with the latter that we automatically deal with the former, or vice versa, so that a statement about conflict in the author of the work does not necessarily imply that this conflict has been communicated to an audience.)

To illustrate the limits imposed by a particular description only, I shall stay with the first alternative: that in interpreting a work psychoanalytically we are referring to the mind of its creator. One immediate consequence is that the statement, "This play is about oedipal conflict," might not be considered a psychoanalytic statement about a play. Instead, the statement might exemplify what I like to call *applied literature*: an endeavor that attempts to use the play to teach a psychoanalytic concept. If taken psychoanalytically, the statement would imply some unspecified oedipal fantasy/wish/conflict in the author that influences the form and/or content of the play.

But if anything we say about the work refers to the mind of the author, what happens to the original object of our attention, the art work itself? How it is conceptualized will influence the kind of statement that can be made about it. The cultural product could be considered the result of an act—of writing or painting, for instance. In this case, we might consider the act of writing or painting as analogous to a piece of acting out. (Granted, the accuracy of the analogy is questionable and will depend on the definition of acting out, however, it will do for purposes of illustration.) Interpretation, by which I mean here a description of psychoanalytic understanding, would focus on the meaning of the act of writing, and the form and content of the work would be used to further the understanding of the act. This focus could be broadened and writing studied as a *process* as well.

Alternatively, the art object itself could be seen as analogous to a symptom, a *product* of psychic conflict in the artist. Interpretation then might concern itself with enumerating the components of that conflict in whatever terms—structural, dynamic, or genetic—best lent themselves to the enumeration.

From a clinical point of view, these differences may only be differences of emphasis. From the point of view of what can and cannot be said about the cultural object, however, the differences are greater. Neither approach is likely to tell us much about why Proust's first novel, *Jean Santeuil*, which foreshadows *A la Recherche* and has some of the latter's content, is so remarkably pedestrian and dull while the latter is a masterpiece. The first approach may be able to say something about the changing significance of the act of writing for Proust or a change in the balance of the compromise of which writing is a part. The second may tell us something similar about the conflict of which the novels are seen as a product.

These examples describe the text by seeing it as analogous to very specific clinical entities. The result is a similarly narrow range of things that one can say about the text. A slightly different approach might involve drawing an analogy between the text and a more general theoretical concept. Several concepts that involve combinations of different elements suggest themselves; for example, Waelder (1936) on multiple function, Arlow (1969) on the synchronization involved in perception, and Brenner (1982) on compromise formation. Here, too, the way the components are categorized and their interrelations characterized will control what we can and cannot say about the cultural product. If we use Waelder's formulation, for example, we will find ourselves focusing on the work as an expression of the ego's coordination of eight specific inner needs and outer exigencies. It would point us toward a type of enumeration different from Brenner's in emphasis as well as in category. I shall leave to your imagination an exploration of the different effects that each of these formulations would have on a definition of a text, except to raise one exemplary issue.

Consider for a moment Milton's "Lycidas," frequently called the greatest conventional poem in the English language. It is a poem written for an occasion, the death of a college friend of the poet who was also a poet and minister. It is written entirely within the classical framework of the pastoral elegy: its location, nature; its persona, shepherds; its mythical references, nymphs and muses common to classical and Renaissance Arcadian literature (Kermode 1952).

However we decide to describe the text, we ought to have an element in the definition that takes explicitly into account the poet's use of convention. If we ignored convention, we could, for example, advance elaborate speculations about Milton's choice of a shepherd as mourner and speaker. Let us assume that these speculations revolved around homosexuality. Homosexual wishes of whatever specific form could be aspects of a particular communally held fantasy expressed through the pastoral convention. Certainly, the phenomenon of communally held fantasies is a familiar aspect of myth; however, even if the speculations were true with respect to unconscious communal elements in the convention, indeed, even if homosexual wishes formed part of the poet's motivation for writing the elegy, these speculations might say very little about Milton's choice of *shepherds*, a choice as appropriate in the circumstances as wearing shoes to go outside. To explore the poem in relation to the mind of the poet, we need to explore the way Milton *uses the convention.*

We might then become aware that Milton's extra-rigorous following of convention is connected to a marked self-consciousness about his exercise of the poet's craft. As every student learns, the poem's last line, "Tomorrow to fresh woods and pastures new," summarizes one major, if oblique, theme in the poem, the poet's progress in his development as poet. That development goes from the pastoral, a poetic form of a poet's youth, to the epic, the major challenge of maturity and worth. In vigorously following convention and emphasizing its role in a poet's development, the young Milton publicly measures his progress on and declares his ambition to proceed along the path successfully trodden by Virgil and Spenser. To convey the magnitude of Milton's public declaration of ambition, made through a self-conscious use of convention, one must suppose that among one's early publications was a paper on aphasia, at the end of which one indicated an intention to write a book on dream interpretation and then one definitively revising metapsychology.

One of the drawbacks to describing the text as a compromise formation or other combination of multiple elements is the tendency it imposes on the interpreter to break down the text into parts. That problem may, however, be one of perspective. We can look at a compromise formation, for instance, from the point of view of its elements or, once they are enumerated, from the point of view of the complex integration achieved. This second perspective leaves us room to ponder whether the whole is greater or different from its parts and, if it is different whether and how this difference can be described psychoanalytically. This issue is a very important one to include in the deliberations of the discipline of applied psychoanalysis.

If we believe that the whole would indeed be greater than the parts allowed by our psychoanalytic description of the text, that belief may reflect not only a sense that the description is inadequate but also that it is inadequate in a specific way. By referring only to the particular psychology of author, we have eliminated that which distinguishes a work of art, its communicative function. Unlike a symptom or character trait, a work of art is consciously intended for an audience. It has public as well as private meanings.

Accordingly, the analogy I find most useful in attempting to apply psychoanalysis to literature is that of the words of text to the words of the patient. I shall not dwell on the obvious differences between free association and purposive creation, but instead on the capacity of language to incorporate the private and the communal simultaneously.

First the private. Because words are chosen, use of a particular word is often the result of contending forces seeking expression. As early as the *Project for a Scientific Psychology,* Freud (1950 [1895]) described the "hysterical symbol" as the substitution of an indifferent idea A for an affect-laden idea B, which is repressed. The result is an excessively intense charge displaced from idea B onto idea A. In the Dora case (Freud 1901), the idea is explicitly verbal, a train of thought called "reinforced" or "supervalent." A similarity between two unconscious elements, whether they be thing presentations or word presentations also leads to the creation of a composite. The work of condensation and displacement thus endow apparently indifferent words with a force that comes from private, latent meaning.

Consider the word jewel-case (Schmuckkästchen) in Dora's first dream, "a term commonly used to describe female genitals that are immaculate and intact . . . and . . . on the other hand, an innocent word . . . admirably calculated both to betray and conceal the sexual thoughts that lie behind the dream" (Freud 1901, p 91). Freud continues:

> This element replaced all mention of Dora's infantile jealousy, of the drops (that is, of sexual wetness), of being dirtied by the discharge, and on the other hand, of her present thoughts connected with the temptation . . . and which depicted the sexual situation (like desirable and menacing) that lay before her. The element of jewel-case was more than any other a product of condensation and displacement, and a compromise between contrary mental currents (Freud 1901, pp. 91–92).

I return to Freud's early formulations because in them one frequently finds such a close relation between the patient's words and Freud's theoretical explanation. At the mention of supervalent ideas, one can hear Dora's voice rising as she complains about Frau K. and her father. It is not a big step from there to the idea of a quantitative increase in energy. Nor is it necessary to consider affect as separate from verbalization. Rather, the question is: To which words does the affect belong?

Words are a common element between a text and the psychoanalytic situation. To focus on the language of a text allows us to bring applied psychoanalysis closer to everyday clinical experience.

But as we become aware when we concentrate on words, part of that everyday clinical experience involves the communal or public aspect of words as well, so that the analogy of the words of the text to those of the patient carries us further. A brief clinical vignette will illustrate both aspects:

> A patient tearfully reported having felt miserable since she had been driving, seen an object on the road, and tried, not entirely successfully, to "straddle" it. When asked her associations to

the word "straddle," she stopped crying and reported, in a surprised manner, embarrassing sexual memories of a homosexual affair she no longer permitted herself. One line of associations led to guilt over phallic and masculine strivings, another to the intense peace and satisfaction she had enjoyed with her lover and now intensely longed for. This led to thoughts about the abrupt and mysterious disappearance of her mother when the patient was 6. The mother was disapproved of by the father and never spoken of nor seen again. Next came the new thought that maybe her mother had been a homosexual.

In the clinical situation, the thoughts, memories, and feelings condensed in the word "straddle" are gradually uncovered and explored. Once that occurs, various psychodynamic formulations become possible. That side of the clinical work concerns the private, otherwise inaccessible meaning of the term. But in this example, at least, the patient's use of the word "straddle" is evocative even without associations. If her words were a text and no associations were available, we could still say that her use of straddle suggests an identity between the car and the driver, for instance. Moreover, straddle evokes a masculine position with sexual connotations, as in straddling a horse and thoughts of having a foot in two camps, as in straddling a fence. All this is in the communal domain, implicit either in the connotations of the term or in the way the word is used in the sentence.

The words comprising a literary text are similarly composite. On the one hand, they carry, condensed, their unconscious private historical and affective meaning for the author; on the other they use the communal connotations available in our common language to convey complex meanings and feeling to the audience. The most promising task for applied psychoanalysis insofar as it is concerned with literary texts is not to say *what* a text means at all. Rather it is to study *how* these two domains, the public and the private, intersect in the words of the text to produce its various meanings and convey its varied affects.

Regardless of how we describe the object of attention for applied psychoanalysis, we should be clear about that description before we turn our attention to other aspects of method and certainly before we begin any endeavor in applied psychoanalysis. Otherwise, we shall contribute not to disciplined applied psychoanalysis, but to another category that, if not previously named, is certainly not without countless examples: wild applied psychoanalysis.

12 Dr. Greenacre and Captain Gulliver

"Convention, as Paul Valéry redefined it, . . . is a mysterious difference between impression and expression"   (Levin 1966, p. 60).

The psychoanalyst's listening and the critic's reading would seem, to those familiar with both, analogous endeavors (Levin 1966). Each task ideally requires the practitioner to lend himself to the experience of a "text," to empathize naively, yet understand with control of the theories and conventions of his discipline. If he or she descends too far into subjective reaction without a counterbalancing sense of why his text so propels him, if he only notices what confirms theory and loses his capacity for surprise, his effectiveness diminishes; he has lost an invaluable and freeing neutrality. Given such analogous endeavors, as well as the analyst's sensitivity to the imagery and affect of his patients, it is all the more disappointing to find the psychoanalyst's discussion of literature so apparently insensitive to the form, texture, tone, and context of the work.

It is inaccurate, however, to dismiss the question with an assertion that the skills of listening have been left in the consulting room. The significant fact is that most analysts bring to a text conventions of reading that differ radically from those of the lit-

CLINICAL UNDERSTANDING

erary critic, even the modern psychoanalytic one. If we accept a
definition of the poem, and by extension of the literary work, "as
an utterance that has meaning only with respect to a system of
conventions which the reader has assimilated" (Culler 1975,
p. 116), such differences in the conventions of reading become
crucial and worthy of exploration.

Phyllis Greenacre's classic work on Swift, the first part of her
study, *Swift and Carroll: A Psychoanalytic Study of Two Lives* (1955),
is particularly suited to illustrate the profoundly different conventions a psychoanalyst may bring to the reading of literature.
Working mainly with the evidence of *Gulliver's Travels*, bolstered
by occasional selections from other writings, and by biographical
data, she reconstructs probable occurrences of the writer's infancy,
suggests the pattern and genetic causes of his psychosexual development, explains psychodynamically the reasons for the unusual
relationships of his adulthood, particularly those with the women
he called Stella and Vanessa, and describes the latent fetishistic
erotic life of this most demanding man. What emerges is the
pathography of a posthumous child, neglected by his mother and
kidnapped at the crucial age of 1 by his nurse. Greenacre believes
that the nurse toilet trained the child severely at the same time
that she taught him to read so that the written word inevitably
became linked in his mind with excretory functions. She further
assumes that the nurse was pathological, that she became over-
invested in her charge, and lived in a too constant, close proximity to him, causing the child to identify too strongly with her,
a factor that would significantly influence his later development.
Blocked and compliant in the institution-like atmosphere of his
uncle's family, at boarding school, and later at college, Swift grew
up to be, in Greenacre's professional judgment, a man of uncertain gender identity. For her, his taking of clerical robes possibly
confirms latent transvestitic tendencies. Since she believes that
severe castration anxiety caused Swift's marked regression from
phallic to anal libidinal organization, she interprets his attempts
to convert the women to whom he became attached into asexual,

fetishistic-like objects as attempts to defend himself against castration anxiety, phallic sexuality, and feminine identification.

Greenacre finds this pathology manifest in *Gulliver's Travels.* Castration anxiety appears in the frequent fear of the hero for his eyes in Lilliput, a transvestitic identification with the female phallus in the episode involving the maids of honor in Brobdingnag, homosexual fellatio wishes in the kidnapping by the monkey. The monkey also represents the bad aspect of the famous nurse, the good being Glumdalclitch, the young giant girl who cares for Gulliver. Another splitting of good from bad occurs in the division between Houyhnhnms and Yahoos and re-enacts the conflict in gender identity, the Yahoos representing the dirty female aspect of Swift's character. In all, *"The Travels* appear [sic] as the acting out of Lemuel's masturbatory fantasies, which . . . are closely interwoven with anal preoccupations . . . rather than genital ones" (Greenacre 1955, p. 115).

Since Greenacre assumes that *Gulliver's Travels* reflects the author's conflicts as well as furnishing traces of their genesis, her conventions of reading involve a leap from the fictional to the real: "it occurred to me that . . . *Gulliver's Travels* and *Alice's Adventures in Wonderland* presented . . . exactly those sensations of which my [fetishistic] patients complained" (p. 11), she writes in her introduction, moving rapidly from a literary theme to the specific physical sensations of changing body size experienced by her patients (Greenacre 1953). The very lack of analogy makes us aware of the unspoken assumption beneath her leap: that the theme of changing body size in the work might indicate a pathology similar to that of her patients in the author of the work and thus have influenced "the production of these remarkable fantasies" (Greenacre 1955, p. 11).

Yet the term "fantasies" for Greenacre is not synonymous with literature. Instead, the term rapidly takes on a clinical meaning. Because the productions of the prolific writer are deemed the equal of the patient's "dreams and free associations" (p. 13), Gulliver comes to be considered the central figure of Swift's fantasies. For the psychoanalyst, Gulliver and Swift then become, as Lemuel and Jonathan, two aspects of the same real figure: "Lemuel went a step further than his creator in that he was a married man" (p. 114). In the resulting confusion, the literary text loses its fictional autonomy. Greenacre's second chapter consists largely of a selective recounting of *The Tales* in the past tense, as though the action had really occurred and Gulliver had really existed. Gulliver has become part of the patient Swift, detachable from his text, material for a case presentation. Ironically, the conventions that equate fiction with fantasy and consider Gulliver part of Swift create a new fiction, Gulliver-Swift the patient, a fiction that obliterates the very text to which the literary critic listens. No wonder that the analyst cannot attend to its tone or form.

While Greenacre affords us substantial insights into Swift's psychological conflicts, these conventions of reading that dissolve the text into evidence of psychological or historical reality seem to lead her to some questionable conclusions. The sequence of Books I and II and the table scene in Brobdingnag (II,i), for instance, become signifiers of an asserted chronology of real events involving Swift's stay with the nurse who is supposed to have kidnapped him. "What would appear to be back of this remarkable passage [in which the gigantic infant almost devours Gulliver] is that the nurse became pregnant after her return to England and in due time had a child whose suckling upset the infant Jonathan" (p. 112). The fictional text is simply transmuted into historical fact.

Moreover, while the psychoanalyst expects confusions of fantasy and history from his patients, Greenacre seems surprisingly to have suspended clinical skepticism. Ehrenpreis (1962) has subsequently pointed out that Swift, the mediocre student at Trinity College—a bit of history Greenacre accepts—is largely a myth of Swift's own making, a myth-making that would seem better grist for Greenacre's mill than the myth itself. Most particularly central to her deductions and constructions is the familiar story of Swift's kidnapping already alluded to, yet evidence for it beyond Swift's own firm belief is questionable; further, the received version of the incident comes from Swift's autobiography, written when he was 70 years old and error prone (Ehrenpreis 1962). This episode, too, might more profitably have been considered fantasy rather than the basis for historical reconstructions.

Apparently, conventions of reading that dissolve the fictionality of the literary work are complemented by procedures that allow first, a hasty reconstruction of reality from the fiction, and second, an uncritical acceptance of what may in fact be only historical fantasy. It is as if, once the author is accepted as patient, the need to make his infancy historically real is irresistible. The conventions by which the psychoanalyst understands a text may thus result not only in its dissolution, but, in this instance, in the construction of a new fiction masquerading as history.

Were Greenacre's endeavor to be considered purely pathography, as she herself would have it, the probability of this second fiction would be the only proper focus for discussion. Yet the confusion between Gulliver and Swift necessarily leads her to make interpretations that have been mistaken for psychoanalytic literary criticism (Voigt 1962)—the monkey as fellatio fantasy is a case in point. Since confusion between the clinical approach to literature and the interpretive act of the psychoanalytic critic has, in fact, been widespread and has led to misunderstanding and unmerited castigation in many cases, an account of the different conventions of reading and interpretation that the ideal psychoanalytic critic brings to a text is also of interest.

While the psychoanalyst listens to the words of a real patient, the critic listens only to his reading of a structure of words. The tone he hears, the discrepancies he intuits, he hears because he is sensitive to language, familiar with literary convention, and unencumbered by irrational expectations. The text is as essential to him as is the patient to the psychoanalyst. It is his true subject. This simple-minded distinction is crucial to differing concepts of interpretation. Interpretation in the therapeutic setting is, broadly, a translation into consciousness of the content of the (descriptively) unconscious, whether that content constitutes resistance, wish, defense, or the attempt to repeat the past in the present. If an interpretation is correct and well timed, it will, for the therapist, be confirmed by the insight it permits the patient into himself. Ultimately the mutual action of interpretation and insight results in dynamic and structural changes that alleviate neurotic suffering (Lowenstein 1957). The therapeutic interpretation then has but one audience, the patient, and but one function, to foster internal change.

When a psychoanalyst discusses a patient in clinical terms, he utilizes interpretations that might or might not be made to the patient in practice; that is, interpretation becomes clinical understanding or even diagnosis. Since psychoanalysts frequently discuss characters or authors as though they were patients, interpretation in this broader sense is easily and mistakenly confused with its literary cousin. Given the privacy of the therapeutic situation, however, clinical understanding is typically communicated to others who have neither heard nor seen the patient. The communication of such understanding about him serves instruction or the construction of theory, not the personal insight of the listeners. Literary interpretation is, on the other hand, a statement about something accessible, a re-creation of an often familiar text that delineates new patterns and explores their signifying functions. A literary interpretation may be said to make conscious a "latent content" that the work produces in the interpreter. Thus its validation is not the change in the patient but the degree to which the text supports the interpretation in the judgment of other competent readers (Culler 1975). This definition holds true whether or not the critic interprets psychoanalytically. What changes in the latter case is the specific complexity and polyvalency with which the critic assumes the work to resonate.

The critic, whether of psychoanalytic persuasion or not, does not, when *interpreting*, pursue clinical truth. Instead he communicates the apperceptions evoked in him by a text by translating them into perceptions about the text that may then be shared.

What prevents the plying of his trade from being a purely solipsistic exercise is the need to convey to other readers that what is original in his interpretation is not grounded in fantasy but in the reading of a common text. A new reading, when appropriately communicated, then works for the community of competent readers like well-timed clinical interpretations for the patient: it opens up aspects of the work hitherto unnoticed and may lead to a richer, more complex, perhaps new understanding of that work.

Unfortunately the "literary interpretations" of some psychoanalytic critics, with their rapid drawing of clinical conclusions, at times sound suspiciously like the psychoanalyst's diagnosis. Such confusion arises from a failure to distinguish between the respective endeavors, for a critic who understands that his *reading* is paramount will not stress clinical conclusions, but will delineate the patterns he sees, the reasons for the tone he adduces; in short he will re-create the delicate, beautiful, and complex unity of structure he perceives in the work. It is not, for instance, what Madame Bovary's child means to Flaubert that is important to the critic, but how the child functions within the work as simultaneous aspects of the heroine's good and bad selves. The psychoanalytic critic attempts to communicate a disciplined and profound understanding of a work of art.

Even when the critic, either apparently or frankly, takes the corpus of an author's work as signifying conscious, preconscious, or unconscious processes and then writes about them, he is not dealing with a biological author. Wayne Booth (1961, p. 63) has introduced the term "implied author" into the critical lexicon to distinguish what, in fact, the critic moves toward when he uses the work to discuss the creator. The psychoanalytic critic, by extension, discusses not an historic, biological being replete with drives, but what might be called an "implied mind." Surely this implied mind is but one more convention that facilitates interpretation.

In the strictest sense, it follows that verification of a psychoanalytic literary interpretation on the basis of historical evidence is a contradiction in terms. Not that comparison of clinical and literary interpretation lacks interest, quite the contrary: nevertheless, to compare out of interest is not to verify. Because the interpretation functions not as a signifier of clinical truth, but as a communication about what the work produces in the competent reader, a literary interpretation is properly confirmed only by a reading of the text or texts upon which it is based. When, however, the critic looks for real evidence, he seeks extratextual assurance of clinical acumen and runs away from the community of readers who await his interpretation in order to judge its value.

Moreover, the belief in one right and confirmable answer implied by belief in verification is potentially dangerous. If a new reading opens up to us previously unacknowledged aspects of a work, it is because, like the psychoanalytic patient ready for an interpretation, we are ready for the new reading though resistant to articulating it ourselves. To accept the possibility of new readings is to accept the existence of defensive blind spots, to accept, that is, individual limitation; to assert that a literary interpretation is capable of quasi-scientific confirmation is to deny that limitation. Thus, no matter how the critic is tempted to move from the text to a discussion of an historical rather than an implied mind, the task of psychoanalytic literary interpretation must remain distinct from that of clinical diagnosis. The first admits the existence of fiction, preserves its autonomy, and seeks to increase the understanding of the unconscious patterns evoked by the text in the competent reader. The second posits the existence of a real subject, adopts conventions that dissolve the text, and requires historical confirmation to buttress what otherwise, given the fact that the clinical situation itself is a fiction, might appear tenuous evidence. The first aspires to communication, the second to science.

To draw a distinction is by no means to claim mutual exclusivity. Rather, once the distinction is understood the possibilities for cross-fertilization are considerably expanded. If the analyst's understanding of an author made the critic differently aware of a particular work, the critic would still need to translate his understanding of that insight into a literary interpretation that illuminates the work for others. Conversely, the critic's sensitivity to the text may just as easily open new areas of clinical interest to the psychoanalyst.

Surely the real value of Greenacre's work for the critic is not to be found in its dubious reconstructions of the events of Swift's infancy, but in the way her suggestions about his character illuminate our reading of his work. We might go further and speculate that in reality her skillful "listening" to the text, not her occasionally questionable methodology, led her to re-create the latent fetishistic nature of Swift's sexuality and make his life intelligible in its terms. What then appears misleading is the demand of her conventions for genetic interpretation and historical reconstruction, the requirement that clinical intuition be supported by history rather than text, for these requirements cause the text— the source of her intuition—to be obscured by the fiction of clinical truth.

13 Radical Simplicity and the Impact of Evil

Several of Voltaire's best-known tales are similar in shape and plot, apparent variations on an inner theme. *Zadig* (1741), *Candide* (1759), and *L'lngénu* (1767) all involve a naive or idealistic protagonist wandering the world in search of a woman who had been denied him by fate and authority, grappling the while with the frustration imposed by arbitrary and powerful men and carried out through their often impersonal and cruel institutions. At the chronological center of the tales *Candide* has an emotional impact lacking in the others; it has been frequently asserted that it is the product of personal crisis and represents the author's confrontation with the existence of evil (Wade 1969). Philosophic and biographical implications aside, for these have been frequently discussed elsewhere, what formal factors, absent in the other tales, compel this impression of the impact of evil?

Like any other attempt to explore the emotional aspect of fiction, this one requires assumptions about a reader, that literary figure who of late has become more controversial than the literature he reads. Critics of several persuasions, while in agreement on the interdependence of reader and text, have been divided over whether the reader should be considered an objective or subjective entity.[1] Such differences threaten to cloud the valuable perspective that the participatory model has opened for us and might best be resolved by recognizing a spectrum of response encompassing both individual differences and (not necessarily conscious) collective experience engendered by a literary text. It is the latter end of the spectrum that concerns me.

The assumption that readers not only react idiosyncratically to a text but also share in a collective experience seems justified on the grounds of their participation both in the human condition itself and in a particular culture where, inter alia, common educational practices, language, history, mythology, values, and ideals foster a more specific communality. Freud (1908) has pointed out the role of unconscious fantasy shared between the creative writer and his audience, and Hans Sachs (1942) has described a community of daydreams. More recently Beres and Arlow (1974) have suggested that a reservoir of shared experience as it is elaborated in fantasy forms the basis of empathy, that quality of feeling with another that lies at the root of esthetic participation.

It is not, however, my intention to explore the emotional impact of *Candide* by searching for an unconscious fantasy. The search for latent content raises methodological questions outside the scope of this chapter (see Chapter 10). Rather, I shall follow a suggestion of Hutter (1977) and relate collective response to the structure of the text utilizing psychoanalytic knowledge of normal development as a guide. Accordingly, I shall make no attempt to discern what latent wish or accompanying fantasy might under-

---

1. Among those who objectify response and for whom an objective reader follows logically: Culler (1975), Iser (1974), Nelson Jr. (1968). Among those who hold response and the reader to be subjective: Crosman (1980), Bleich (1978), Holland (1975). For an excellent general survey of varieties of reader-response criticism see Suleiman (1980).

lie the manifest content of *Candide*. It suffices that the representation of that wish, the hero's pursuit of a woman who combines maternal and sexual qualities, sets in motion a plot characterized by the interplay between the realization of a representation of desire and its frustration. Although the represented wish may conceivably furnish a symbolic structure for several individual wishes, the experience of wish and frustration, which characterizes a reading of *Candide*, is universal.

The problem of defining a collective experience on the basis of an emotional response that will in many be unconscious remains difficult. Not all readers react in the same conscious way to elements in a literary work. For example, the sequence of wish and frustration of wish present in *Candide* tends to evoke anger. The small child will have a tantrum when the frustration of a wish results in an increase of undischarged tension that is experienced as "unpleasure" (Freud 1914b). Some readers, however, may derive gratification from the frustration itself and be consciously immune to the anger it engenders. Others, to avoid experiencing the anger, may idealize the philosophical resolution at the end, concentrate entirely on historical issues, or see only the ironic overlay that minimizes the considerable sadism especially present in the first half of the work. These defensive and characterological responses do not necessarily contradict the assertion of a particular collective experience involving frustration; to the psychoanalytically informed they rather confirm the presence of something consciously unknown.

What is at work in reading is akin to what psychoanalysis calls countertransference in its broadest sense, the emotional responses of the analyst to the patient that, scrutinized, may provide him with valuable information about the patient or, unscrutinized, may interfere with his understanding of and response to the patient. Freud's original description of countertransference was narrower in scope, concerned with interference from the analyst's unconscious exclusively (Freud 1910c). Gradually, however, definitions have broadened to include the patient's contribution. Several modern theoreticians even hold that in the severer pathologies countertransference reactions are induced, an effort on the part of the patient to re-create his early experiences or to rid himself of his most fragmenting feelings.[2] The relative merits of these various theoretical developments need not concern us here. What is useful to remember is that certain aspects of countertransference phenomena are not unique to a treatment situation. Conscious response often represents a distortion of the underlying experience, and these distorted reactions may occur in all experiences of everyday life, including reading. In fact, such reactions may well account for the strident passion with which rival groups of critics hold fast to contradictory interpretations when the more interesting question remains whether something in the text inspires this disagreement.

The emotional flexibility to explore rather than interpret and hold fast, however, requires the same vigilance to unconscious response as the clinician must exercise: scrutiny of feeling and fantasy, of intense reactions or their absence, of silence or over-talkativeness. Knowledge derived from clinical practice and observations of development shows that certain forms of presentation, certain sequences, certain types of material ought generally to evoke a particular response. Since there is no entirely objective standard by which to identify countertransference reactions, knowledge of hypothetical tendency must be supplemented by self-knowledge, intuition, and experience. We will need, then, to be satisfied with a rather subjective standard after all, a hypothetical reader whose reading experience represents a hypothetical collective experience (see Chapter 10). If this uncertainty flies in the face of wishes for scientific rigor, it should be recalled that accepting uncertainty is a necessary corollary to accepting the unconscious.

One may, however, be reasonably certain of the intensity of

---

2. For recent writing about countertransference, see, among others, Giovacchini (1979), Klein (1946), Searles (1965), Winnicott (1975).

Candide's emotional impact on the reader (Vanden Heuval 1967, Marsland 1966, Thacker 1968), despite both the balance achieved as the second half progresses and the ever-present element of ironic distance. To describe this impact in terms of manifest theme, one is drawn to the horrifying—because arbitrary—weight of "civilized" evil. Surely the critical debate over whether Voltaire solves the problem of evil reflects this impact (Brooks 1964, Coulet 1960, Pappas 1968, and Wolper 1969). Whatever the substance of critics' disagreements, it is much less significant than the fact that they conceive of Voltaire's success or failure in these terms, as though by solving the problem he could in some way protect them from the feeling of vulnerability his work awakens.

What factors in *Candide* could account for this impact of evil? One is the organization of the plot. Beneath the distancing and mitigating ironic tone that characterizes the narrator's presentation, the world of *Candide* is built upon a fundamental rhythm of expectation and betrayal. *Candide* is a dialectic of desire and punishment, of trust and the brutal deception of that trust. The hero, innocently desiring Cunégonde and faithfully believing his tutor, is cast out into a best of all possible worlds that proves a mutilating inferno. Despairing, cold, hungry, and penniless, he finds his flagging faith restored by two strangers who treat him to dinner—then brusquely trick him into military servitude where he is robbed of any modicum of individuality and freedom, and finally stripped of his skin in a beating. His fellow sufferer, the old woman, in her parallel journey through life, is deprived by murder of a princely husband at the moment when she joyously anticipates marriage, then ravished, enslaved, and made witness to the dismemberment of her mother and attendants. A eunuch she believes kind fortunately rescues her from the bloody pile of corpses onto which she has collapsed, then quickly sells her anew into slavery.

These betrayals, rhythmic norms rather than exceptions in *Candide*, frustrate fulfillment; within the fiction they break down the characters' integrity; without, they assault the reader's sense of security through continual frustration of his conventional ex-

pectations of the marvelous. The two travelers, so often brutal-
ized and betrayed, withdraw into a state of numbness in which,
separate from their bodies, they feel neither physical nor emotional
pain; they merely endure. Candide wordlessly traverses a war-torn
countryside, the objective correlative to his burnt-out inner state;
the old woman, less and less desired, becomes first concubine, then
slave, then an object dispatched from city to city, until her body
is reduced to its most concrete physicality and becomes food. In a
final bitter irony, buttock replaces breast in a gruesome parody
of the primordial experience of security.

One result of this catastrophic rhythm is the intensified search
for warmth and safety. The main characters yearn for protection,
for a magic circle of comfort, security, and satiety, as is attested
to by their frequent hunger, their stubborn innocence and comic
grandiosity, their idealization of Westphalia, and their constant
and oft-contradicted assertions that they are infallible, perfect,
or deserving of the best. Characters and reader are temporarily
granted that protection in Eldorado.

Another and parallel result is the release of destructive forces.
Indeed the fictional reality of the tale does not permit retreat for
long. Outside that magic circle of perfection resides the social
world into which the characters are constantly propelled. And this
evil outside world is a place where the social institution seeks out
the individual to destroy him. Children are castrated to sing in
operas, slaves dismembered for disobedience, the military takes
brutal possession of Candide's body. In fact, the double row of
soldiers poised to club him becomes a giant devouring maw. In
this evil social world, sadism, rationalized, runs rampant. There are,
of course, the overt acts of individuals who enslave, rob, rape, and
disembowel, but the esthetically pleasing ritual of an auto-da-fé
camouflages equally sadistic yet socially sanctioned wishes. When
brutality is committed in the name of good, when justice condones
robbery and charges a fee, when freedom involves a choice between
death by clubbing or firing squad, then language becomes the
agent of social deception and the social world beyond the magic

circle a place of uncertain perception as well as of danger. Deceiving characters emerge from its midst conferring names on themselves, promising uniqueness and coveting riches, and then merge back into its anonymity. Thus the false Cunégonde is only "une friponne" (Voltaire 1959, p. 185) ("a shyster"). Candide also becomes part of the universe of shifting forms—separated from his name—stepping back from naive candor into the socially conferred guise of mercenary. In rapid succession he offers his loyalty to the Spanish, then the Jesuits, avows his German birth and finds Cunégonde's brother, then disguises himself as Jesuit in order to flee, and is held prisoner and threatened with death by the Oreillons because accoutrements designate him as Jesuit. He escapes with his life only by slipping out of the clothing of his assumed identity. This social world, representing the individual's rage at frustration, destroys the self. In becoming part of its spreading insubstantiality, the individual momentarily ceases to exist.

One way in which the evil realm incorporates the self is by undermining the individual's perceptions and thus depriving him of his ability to anticipate, judge, and experience himself as a subjective continuity in time. Encountering Candide, the major characters emerge out of the treacherous social world in continuously changing shapes. The "femme tremblante, d'une taille majestueuse, brillante de pierreries, et couverte d'une voile" (VII, 107) ("a woman, trembling, of majestic stature, shimmering in jewels, and covered by a veil") is Cunégonde, though the other veiled woman is a fraud. One of the women "qui étendaient des serviettes sur des ficelles pour les faire sécher" ("who spread out napkins on a line to dry") is also Cunégonde "rembrunie, les yeux éraillés, la gorge sèche, les joues ridées, les bras rouges & écaillés" (XXIX, 217) ("sun tanned, eyes bloodshot, neck dried out, cheeks wrinkled, arms red and tough"). The commander, "le bonnet à trois cornes en tête, la robe retroussée, l'épée au côté, l'esponton à la main," ("three-corned hat on his head, gown tucked up, sword at his side, dagger in his hand,") is the young Baron (XIV, 136). He metamorphoses into friend, then into arrogant aristocrat, changes effected with a chameleon-like speed paralleled by Candide's confusion of names: "'Mon révérend père, . . . mon ancien maître, mon ami, mon beau-frère'" (XV, 140–41) ("'My holy father, . . . my old master, my friend, my brother-in-law'"). Pangloss reappears as an ineffective galley-slave, as a corpse dissected back to life, and most frighteningly as that phantom who throws himself on Candide: "un gueux tout convert de pustules, les yeux morts, le bout du nez rongé, la bouche de travers, les dents noires, & parlant de la gorge, tourmenté d'une toux violante, & crachant une dent à chaque effort" (III, 94) ("a beggar all covered with pustules, eyes dead, end of nose gnawed, mouth skewed, teeth black, speaking in a croak, tortured by a violent cough, and spitting up a tooth with each attempt.")

The destructiveness represented by the instability of the social realm and of the self here intersect, for Pangloss's ghostly "disguise" is a mutilation that ordinarily belongs to nightmare. By making disguise a matter of body, the text turns the possible illusion of the ghost into the fictional reality of a disfigured tutor. As the physical body yields its integrity, the character becomes his disguise, becomes, that is, other.

Both the savageness of the fictional reality and the rhythm of the plot depend on the radical simplicity of the hero for their full effect. An appropriate accompaniment to the cruel and unstable reality that surrounds him, the characteristics united by the name of Candide designate him incomplete. The oscillations of his spirits according to the fullness of his stomach, his taking in of Pangloss's teachings because of the facilitating presence of the beautiful Cunégonde, his profound dependence on her to give his life shape and direction, his belief that a high degree of happiness consists in *being her*, all suggest that Voltaire has constructed a developmentally primitive literary character. So much, in fact, is Candide's simplicity coupled with devices that suggest infantile experience that it shocks us to discover in the last chapter that as he has reached maturity he has acquired a beard.

Despite this growth—for much of the tale Candide is so lacking in self-definition that he is "incapable of irony," as Coulet (1960) aptly notes—he is devoid of judgment. Thus, he is dependent on guides to judge for him. Whether they prove trustworthy, like Cacambo, or treacherous, like Venderdendur, is a hazard of his radical simplicity, for his lack of differentiation manifests itself in uncritical, open-mouthed, passive receptivity.

It is this infantile openness, moreover, that involves the reader in the fictional world and thus in its brutal betrayals. Nothing masks Candide's primitive yearning for Cunégonde, or for that best world promised by Pangloss, and these wishes, emerging contrapuntally against the cruel deceptions of the plot, tend to elicit the reader's empathic wishes for food, warmth, and protection. Thus, when Candide's are abruptly frustrated, so too, our own.

The reader's subjective participation in Candide's desires is facilitated in a number of ways. Among the most important is the adroit use of "internal focus,"[3] Genette's (1972) term for the restriction of the reader's field of vision to that of a given character. Of course, internal focus is not the norm of *Candide* where the narration, like that of most tales, is omniscient. Rather, internal focus represents a temporary shift of perspective away from narrative omniscience. Sometimes nearly imperceptible, such a shift may also involve the reader quite dramatically and subjectively in fictional danger. Immediately after the safe arrival in Buenos Aires where Cunégonde and Candide have fled together, new danger supervenes: "Elle court sur le champ à *Candide*. 'Fuyez,' dit-elle, 'ou dans une heure vous allez être brûlé.' Il n'y avait pas un moment à perdre; mais comment se séparer de *Cunégonde, &* où se réfugier?" (XIII, 133) ("She runs immediately to *Candide*. 'Flee,' she says, 'or in one hour you are going to be burned.' There

---

3. Genette's reciprocal term is "zero degree focalization." I have used omniscience in its place for stylistic not theoretical reasons.

wasn't a moment to lose; but how could he separate from *Cuné-gonde* and where could he find refuge?") Objective description cedes to an internal focus upon Candide's experience of his predicament. At this point, the chapter ends, the danger unresolved and under-distanced.

The reader's vision is reduced to a restricted internal focus that limits his knowledge of the fictional world as severely as Candide's and renders him equally helpless. Thus the reader becomes temporarily one with a character of neither judgment nor knowledge, and the force of that sadistic reality through which the child-hero is deprived of wished-for security increases. The sense of helplessness is complemented by the frustration of the chapter break,[4] a device that as a formal analogue to Candide's sense of being trapped, places the reader in the same position of powerlessness in relation to the narrator as the hero finds himself in vis-à-vis the causal events of the fiction.

Nor is this the only instance in which a formal analogue furnishes the reader with the fictionally appropriate response. Just as within the fiction the characters' perception of self is threatened by the menacing transformation of the body, so the reader's perception of the fictional world is undermined by the use of an ambiguous signifier. During the carnival in Venice Candide encounters six men who are addressed as kings. "'Tout n'est qu'illusion & Calamité'" (XXIV, 190) ("'All is nothing but illusion and calamity'") he has earlier sighed, preparing to consider the six kings as part of the locally sanctioned disguise. Since Cacambo, so closely allied to Vice and his classical counterpart the slave who manages the comic plot, also appears incognito, the dinner seems designated as theater. What appears to be disguise, however, turns out to be calamity. The kings are exiled and impoverished sovereigns with neither status nor power who cling to meaningless social forms and designations. When one of them actually begs for money, the signifier "King"

_____

4. For a differently oriented discussion of chapter division see Danahy (1973).

becomes dissociated from its conventional connotation of money and power. Fictional reality redefines language.

In this way, the reader shares in attenuated fashion in an experience of disorganization. Fooled by the carnival and Cacambo, then disoriented by the redefinition of the signifier "King," the reader's hold on fictional reality becomes somewhat precarious. The question arises for him: What is real carnival if what appears to be carnival is reality? Although it is not answered, the implied answer is the unsettling one that there is no distinction: fictive illusion and fictive reality merge. Which events are then reliable, asks the reader, the hanging and murder of Candide's friends, either witnessed or committed by Candide, or their existence as galley slaves before his eyes? And if these slaves with disfigured faces are named Pangloss and the Baron, are they, like the kings, Pangloss and the Baron in name only?

What spares the reader too much disorientation is the distancing effect of the omniscient narration. The narrator, reliable, objective, in control, gives a counterbalancing stability to the unstable fictional world and authority to the events he describes. The breadth and scope of his vision create a distance from fictional event that permits the reader the anticipation of danger, the illusion of safety, and the luxury to appreciate irony. With this broader perspective, the narrator exposes the naivete of Candide and the self-importance of his companions, enabling us, *Dieu merci*, to find release in laughter.

Yet this relief is not so complete as we might suspect. It alleviates, but does not prevent, our subjective reaction to the dangers of the fictional world. In the presentation of the earthquake, for instance, disaster strikes mimetically: "A peine ont-ils mis le pied dans la ville en pleurant la mort de leur bienfaiteur, qu'ils sentent la terre trembler sous leurs pas; la mer s'élève en bouillonnant dans le port, & brise les vaisseaux qui sont à l'ancre." (V, 101) ("Hardly have they set foot in the city, lamenting their benefactor's death, when they feel the ground shake beneath their feet; the sea heaves up boiling in the port and breaks up the ships at anchor.")

The restrained description of upheaval in and of itself hardly moves. Rather, its placement in a sequence in which natural disaster and human cruelty follow each other precipitously surprises. When Plangloss and Candide set foot on shore after the death of Jacques and the shipwreck, reader and characters alike prepare for a respite. But safety is accorded only an introductory subordinate clause—in the main clause new disaster shocks.

Only after the reader is startled into subjectivity does the narrative present the exaggerated and idiosyncratic reactions of the victims: the sailor looks for booty, Pangloss for a way of justifying his philosophic system, Candide for solace. Shock is countered by comedy. Yet these stylized descriptions are dependent on the reader's initial surprise for their comic effect. They afford him release secondarily because they allow him to escape his subjective involvement and to regard the beleaguered characters objectively.

Nor is the earthquake scene an exception. For the first half of the tale, over and over again, deftly and economically, the narrative moves the reader from safety to new danger: Candide and Cunégonde tell leisurely and objectively of the horrors of their lives in the comfort of a sea journey only to be separated the moment they come to port. Further, the narrative moves the reader from safe objectivity to the intimacy of the subjective not only by means of such formal devices as shifts of focus and manipulation of chapter divisions but also by means of a play with convention that turns the events of the fiction into versions of chance as haphazard and out of control as the fictional world itself (Price 1965).

The rhythm of trust and betrayal, safety and danger thus finds its counterpart in the oscillation of the reader between participation in the danger of the fictional world and a more comfortable sharing of the omniscient narrator's objectivity. Until Candide begins to grow in the second half of the tale, his radical simplicity, evoking as it does a universal infantile defenselessness, emerges as a crucial subjective focus from which objective narration must rescue us before the boundaries of comedy are transgressed.

Through the structure of the text, then, the reader of *Candide* is engaged in a cycle of wish, frustration, and reactive anger that facilitates a transient identification with an infantile hero, on the one hand, and lends the impact of anger to the arbitrary external authority that assails him, on the other. The plot itself and formal elements such as the ordering of the action, the handling of narrative focus, and the syntax all contribute to the reader's identificatory wishes for warmth, safety, and security. When these wishes, apparently realized, are abruptly frustrated, the resultant anger fosters an experience of outside authority—whether fictional destiny or social institution—as cruel and implacable. The power that anger confers upon frustrating authority, in turn, increases the experience of powerlessness through which the reader, identified with the hero/victim, confronts his own vulnerability. Thus the transient identification with the hero is reinforced and the cycle of wish, frustration, and anger renewed. This reciprocal relationship between literary structure and the affect—conscious or not—that that structure evokes in the reader is an essential and complex element in the esthetic experience of *Candide*.

References

Abend, S. (1979). Unconscious fantasy and theories of cure. *Journal of the American Psychoanalytic Association* 27:579–595.

Arlow, J. (1961a). Ego psychology and the study of mythology. *Journal of the American Psychoanalytic Association* 9:371–393.

―――― (1961b). A typical dream. *Journal of the Hillside Hospital* 10:154–158.

―――― (1963). The supervisory situation. *Journal of the American Psychoanalytic Association* 11:576–594.

―――― (1969a). Unconscious fantasy and disturbances of conscious experience. *Psychoanalytic Quarterly* 38:1–27.

―――― (1969b). Fantasy, memory, and reality testing. *Psychoanalytic Quarterly* 38:28–51.

―――― (1971). Character perversion. In *Currents in Psychoanalysis*, ed. I. W. Marcus, pp. 317–336. New York: International Universities Press.

―――― (1979a). Metaphor and the psychoanalytic situation. *Psychoanalytic Quarterly* 48:363–385.

———— (1979b). The genesis of interpretation. *Journal of the American Psychoanalytic Association* 27 (suppl):193–206.

———— (1980). The revenge motive in the primal scene. *Journal of the American Psychoanalytic Association* 28:519–541.

———— (1981). Theories of pathogenesis. *Psychoanalytic Quarterly* 50:488–513.

———— (1987). The dynamics of interpretation. *Psychoanalytic Quarterly* 56:68–87.

———— (1990a). *Aggression and prejudice: the blood libel.* Paper presented at the Conference on Aggression, American Friends of Hebrew University, November 18.

———— (1990b). Methodology and reconstruction. *Psychoanalytic Quarterly* 60:539–563.

Atlas, J. (1988). The case of Paul de Man. *New York Times Magazine*, August 25.

Auerbach, E. (1942–1945). *Mimesis: The Representation of Reality in Western Literature,* trans. W. Trask. Garden City, NY: Doubleday, 1957.

Balter, L., Lothane, Z., and Spencer, J. H., Jr. (1980). On the analyzing instrument. *Psychoanalytic Quarterly* 49:474–504.

Bass, A. (1985). On a history of a mistranslation and the psychoanalytic movement. In *A Difference in Translation,* ed. J. Graham. Ithaca, NY: Cornell University Press.

Beres, D. (1962). The unconscious fantasy. *Psychoanalytic Quarterly* 31:309–328.

———— (1968). The role of empathy in psychotherapy and psychoanalysis. *Journal of Hillside Hospital* 17:362–369.

Beres, D., and Arlow, J. (1974). Fantasy and identification in empathy. *Psychoanalytic Quarterly* 43:26–50.

Bergmann, M. S. (1991). Why reconstruction remains controversial. Paper presented at a meeting of the Institute for Psychoanalytic Training and Research, March 15.

Bleich, D. (1978). *Subjective Criticism.* Baltimore: Johns Hopkins University Press.

Blum, H. P. (1977). The prototype of preoedipal reconstruction. *Journal of the American Psychoanalytic Association* 25:757–785.

—————— (1978). Reconstruction in a case of postpartum depression. *Psychoanalytic Study of the Child* 33:335–362. New York: International Universities Press.

—————— (1980). The value of reconstruction in adult psychoanalysis. *International Journal of Psycho-Analysis* 61:39–52.

—————— (1986). The concept of the reconstruction of trauma. In *The Reconstruction of Trauma: Its Significance in Clinical Work,* ed. A. Rothstein, pp. 7–29. Madison, CT: International Universities Press.

Boesky, D. (1973). Déjà raconte as a screen defense. *Psychoanalytic Quarterly* 42:491–524.

—————— (1990). The psychoanalytic process and its components. *Psychoanalytic Quarterly* 59:550–584.

Booth, W. C. (1961). Distance and point-of-view: an essay in classification. In *The Theory of the Novel,* ed. P. Stevick, pp. 87–107. New York: Free Press, 1967.

Bottiglia, W. (1964). *Candide: Analysis of a Classic,* 2nd ed. rev. Geneva: Institut et Musée Voltaire.

Brenner, C. (1982). *The Mind in Conflict.* New York: International Universities Press.

—————— (1992). *Modern conflict theory: or beyond the ego and the id.* Paper presented at the New York Psychoanalytic Institute, December 8.

Brooks, P. (1979). Fictions of the Wolfman. *Diacritics* 9:72–83.

Brooks, R. A. (1964). *Voltaire and Leibniz.* Geneva: Droz.

Buie, D. (1981). Empathy: its nature and limitations. *Journal of the American Psychoanalytic Association* 29:281–307.

Bunyan, J. (1678). *The Pilgrim's Progress.*

Burlingham, D. (1935). Empathy between infant and mother. *Journal of the American Psychoanalytic Association* 15:764–780, 1967.

Butor, M. (1966). Diderot le fataliste et ses maîtres. *Critique* 22: 387–418, 619–641.

Chasseguet-Smirgel, J. ed. (1964). *La sexualité feminine: recherches psychoanalytiques nouvelles.* Paris: Payot.

———— (1984). *Creativity and Perversion.* New York: Norton.

Chesnau, A. (1968). La structure temporelle de *Jacques le Fataliste. Revue des Sciences Humaines* 131:401–413.

Coen, S. (1981). Notes on the concepts of selfobject and preoedipal object. *Journal of the American Psychoanalytic Association* 29: 395–412.

———— (1992). *The Misuse of Persons.* Hillsdale, NJ: Analytic Press.

Cohen, H. (1976). La figure dialogique dans *Jacques la Fataliste.* In *Studies on Voltaire and the Eighteenth Century,* 162. Oxford: Taylor Institute.

Coulet, H. (1960). La candeur de Candide. *Annales de la Faculté des Lettres et Sciences Humaines d'Aix* 34:87–99.

———— (1967). *Le Roman Jusqu'à la Révolution.* Paris: Armand Colin.

Crocker, L. (1961). *Jacques le Fataliste,* an "expérience morale." *Diderot Studies* 3:73–99.

Crosman, R. (1980). Do readers make meaning? In *The Reader in the Text,* ed. S. R. Suleiman and I. Crosman, pp. 149–164. Princeton: Princeton University Press.

Culler, J. (1975). *Structuralist Poetics: Structuralism, Poetics and the Study of Literature.* Ithaca, NY: Cornell University Press.

———— (1980). Prolegomena to a theory of reading. In *The Reader in the Text,* ed. S. R. Suleiman and I. Crosman, pp. 46–66. Princeton: Princeton University Press.

———— (1981). *The Pursuit of Signs: Semiotics, Literature, Deconstruction.* Ithaca, NY: Cornell University Press.

———— (1982). *On Deconstruction: Theory and Criticism after Structuralism.* Ithaca, NY: Cornell University Press.

Curtis, H. C. (1983). Construction and reconstruction: an introduction. *Psychoanalytic Inquiry* 3:183–188.

Danahy, M. (1973). The nature of narrative norms in *Candide.* In *Studies on Voltaire and the Eighteenth Century* 114:113–140. Banbury, Oxfordshire: Voltaire Foundation.

References   265

De Man, P. (1969). The rhetoric of temporality. In *Blindnesss and
Insight: Essays in the Rhetoric of Contemporary Criticism,* 2nd ed.
Minneapolis: University of Minnesota Press, 1983, pp. 187–
228.

——— (1988). *The Wartime Journalism of Paul de Man.* Lincoln:
University of Nebraska Press.

Diderot, D. (1771, 1778). *Jacques le Fataliste et son Maître.* Geneva:
Droz, 1977.

Easser, R. (1974). Empathic inhibition and psychoanalytic technique. *Psychoanalytic Quarterly* 43:557–580.

Ehrard, J. (1970). Lumières et roman, ou les paradoxes de Denis
le fataliste. In *Au Siècle des Lumières,* pp. 137–155. Paris: Publications de l'Education Nationale.

Ehrenpreis, I. (1962, 1967). *Swift: The Man, His Works, and the Age,*
vols. 1 and 2. Cambridge: Harvard University Press.

Ekstein, R., and Wallerstein, R. S. (1958). *The Teaching and Learning of Psychotherapy,* rev. ed. New York: International Universities Press, 1972.

Etchegoyen, R. H. (1991). *The Fundamentals of Psychoanalytic Technique,* trans. P. Pitchon. London: Karnac Books.

Fellows, O. (1968). *Jacques le Fataliste* revisited. *L'Esprit Créateur*
8:42–52.

Felman, S. (1977). Turning the screw of interpretation. *Yale
French Studies* 55/56:94–207.

——— (1980). On reading poetry: reflections on the limits
and possibilities of psychoanalytic approaches. In *The Literary Freud: Mechanisms of Defense and the Poetic Will,* ed. J. H.
Smith, pp. 119–148. New Haven: Yale University Press.

Fine, B. D., Joseph, E. D., and Waldhorn, H. F., eds. (1971). *Recollection and Reconstruction: Reconstruction in Psychoanalysis.*
New York: International Universities Press.

Fliess, R. (1953). Countertransference and counteridentification.
Journal of the American Psychoanalytic Association 1:268–284.

Freud, A. (1936). *The Ego and the Mechanisms of Defense.* New York:
International Universities Press, 1966.

Freud, S. (1900). The interpretation of dreams. *Standard Edition* 4/5.

——— (1901). Fragment of an analysis of a case of hysteria. *Standard Edition* 7:7–122.

——— (1907). Delusions and dreams in Jensen's *Gradiva*. *Standard Edition* 9.

——— (1908). Creative writers and day-dreaming. *Standard Edition* 9.

——— (1910a). The antithetical meaning of primal words. *Standard Edition* 11.

——— (1910b). Leonardo da Vinci and a memory of his childhood. *Standard Edition* 11.

——— (1910c). The future prospects of psychoanalytic therapy. *Standard Edition* 12.

——— (1914a). Remembering, repeating and working-through: further recommendations on the technique of psycho-analysis. *Standard Edition* 12.

——— (1914b). Instincts and their vicissitudes. *Standard Edition* 14:111–140.

——— (1917). Introductory lectures on psychoanalysis. Part III. *Standard Edition* 16.

——— (1918). From the history of an infantile neurosis. *Standard Edition* 17.

——— (1921). Group Psychology and the Analysis of the Ego. *Standard Edition* 18.

——— (1923). The ego and the id. *Standard Edition* 19.

——— (1925). Negation. *Standard Edition* 19.

——— (1927). Fetishism. *Standard Edition* 21.

——— (1937a). Analysis terminable and interminable. *Standard Edition* 23.

——— (1937b). Constructions in analysis. *Standard Edition* 23.

——— (1940a). An outline of Psycho-Analysis. *Standard Edition* 23.

———— (1940b). Splitting of the ego in the process of defence. *Standard Edition* 23.

———— (1950 [1895]). Project for a scientific psychology. *Standard Edition* 1:295–397.

Friedman, L. (1980). Kohut: a book review essay. *Psychoanalytic Quarterly* 49:393–422.

———— (1983). Reconstruction and the like. *Psychoanalytic Quarterly* 3:189–222.

Gediman, H. (1983). Annihilation anxiety: the experience of deficit in neurotic compromise formation. *International Journal of Psycho-Analysis* 64:59–70.

Gediman, H., and Wolkenfeld, F. (1980). The parallelism phenomenon in psychoanalysis and supervision: its reconstruction as a triadic system. *Psychoanalytic Quarterly* 49:234–255.

Genette, G. (1972). *Figures III*. Paris: Editions du Seuil.

Giovacchini, P. (1979). *Treatment of Primitive Mental States*. New York: Jason Aronson.

Glover, E. (1929). Communication: the "screening" function of traumatic memories. *International Journal of Psycho-Analysis* 10:90–93.

———— (1932). The relation of perverse-formation to the development of reality-sense. In *On the Early Development of Mind*. New York: International Universities Press, 1956, pp. 216–234.

Goldberg, A., ed. (1978). *The Psychology of the Self: A Casebook*. New York: International Universities Press.

Gray, P. (1982). "Developmental lag" in the evolution of technique for psychoanalysis of neurotic conflict. *Journal of the American Psychoanalytic Association* 30:621–655.

Greenacre, P. (1950). The prepuberty trauma in girls. *Psychoanalytic Quarterly* 19:298–317.

———— (1953). Certain relationships between fetishism and faulty development of the body image. *The Psychoanalytic Study of the Child* 8:79–98. New York: International Universities Press.

———— (1955). *Swift and Carroll: A Psychoanalytic Study of Two Lives*. New York: International Universities Press.

———— (1956). Re-evaluation of the process of working through. In *Emotional Growth. Psychoanalytic Studies of the Gifted and a Great Variety of Other Individuals*, vol. 2, pp. 641–650. New York: International Universities Press.

———— (1975). On reconstruction. *Journal of the American Psychoanalytic Association* 23:693–712.

Greenson, R. R. (1960). Empathy and its vicissitudes. In *Explorations in Psychoanalysis*, pp. 147–161. New York: International Universities Press.

———— (1968). Disidentifying from mother. *International Journal of Psycho-Analysis* 49:370–374.

Grossman, L. (1992). An example of "character perversion" in a woman. *Psychoanalytic Quarterly* 61:581–589.

———— (1993). The perverse attitude toward reality. *Psychoanalytic Quarterly* 62:422–436.

Grossman, W. (1967). Reflections on the relationships of introspection and psychoanalysis. *International Journal of Psycho-Analysis* 48:16.

———— (1982). The self as fantasy: fantasy as theory. *Journal of the American Psychoanalytic Association* 30:919–938.

Grossman, W., and Simon, B. (1969). Anthropomorphism: motive, meaning and causality in psychoanalytic theory. *Psychoanalytic Study of the Child* 24:78–114. New York: International Universities Press.

Grossman, W., and Stewart, W. (1977). Penis envy: From childhood wish to developmental metaphor. In *Female Psychology*, ed. H. Blum, pp. 193–212. New York: International Universities Press.

Hanly, C. (1990). The concept of truth in psychoanalysis. *International Journal of Psycho-Analysis* 71:375–383.

Hartmann, G., ed. (1978). *Psychoanalysis and the Question of the Text*. Baltimore: Johns Hopkins University Press.

Hartmann, H. (1939). *Ego Psychology and the Problem of Adaptation.* New York: International Universities Press, 1958.

Heuval, J. V. (1967). *Voltaire dans ses Contes.* Paris: Armand Colin.

Hoffer, A. (1993). Is love in the analytic relationship "real"? *Psychoanalytic Inquiry* 13:343–356.

Holland, N. (1975a). *Five Readers Reading.* New Haven: Yale University Press.

——— (1975b). Unity identity text self. *Publications of the Modern Language Association* 90:813–822.

Hutter, A. (1977). The high tower of his mind: psychoanalysis and the reader of *Bleak House, Criticism* 29:296–316.

Iser, W. (1974). *The Implied Reader: Patterns of Communication in Prose Fiction from Bunyan to Beckett.* Baltimore: Johns Hopkins University Press.

Jakobson, R., and Halle, M. (1956). *Fundamentals of Language.* The Hague: Mouton.

Joseph, B. (1971). A clinical contribution to the analysis of a perversion. In *Psychic Equilibrium and Psychic Change: Selected Papers of Betty Joseph,* ed. E. Spillius and M. Feldman, pp. 51–67. London: Tavistock/Routledge, 1989.

Karush, A. (1979). Introductory remarks on the role of empathy in the psychoanalytic process. *Bulletin of the Association of Psychoanalytic Medicine* 18:62–63.

Katan, M. (1969). The link between Freud's work on aphasia, fetishism, and constructions in analysis. *International Journal of Psycho-Analysis* 50:547–553.

Kavanaugh, T. (1973). The vacant mirror: a study of mimesis through Diderot's *Jacques le Fataliste.* In *Studies on Voltaire and the Eighteenth Century,* 104. Banbury, Oxfordshire: Thorpe Mandeville House.

Kermode, F., ed. (1952). *English Pastoral Pastry from the Beginnings to Marvell.* London: George G. Harrup.

Kernberg, O. (1975). *Borderline Conditions and Pathological Narcissism.* New York: Jason Aronson.

270

References

———— (1976). *Object Relations Theory and Clinical Psychoanalysis.* New York: Jason Aronson.

———— (1979). Notes on empathy. *Bulletin of the Association of Pyschoanalytic Medicine* 18:75–80.

Klein, M. (1946). Notes on some schizoid mechanisms. *International Journal of Psycho-Analysis* 27:99–110.

Kofman, S. (1980). L'énigme de la femme: la femme dans les textes de Freud. Paris: Flammarion.

Kohler, E. (1970). "Est-ce-que l'on sait où l'on va? L'Unité structural de *Jacques le Fataliste et son Maître* de Diderot. *Philologica Pragensia* 13:186–202.

Kohut, H. (1959). Introspection, empathy and psychoanalysis. *Journal of the American Psychoanalytic Association* 7:459–483.

———— (1966). Forms and transformation of narcissism. *Journal of the American Psychoanalytic Association* 14:243–272.

———— (1971). *The Analysis of the Self.* New York: International Universities Press.

———— (1977). *The Restoration of the Self.* New York: International Universities Press.

———— (1979). The two analyses of Mr. Z. *International Journal of Psycho-Analysis* 60:3–28.

———— (1984). *How Does Analysis Cure?* ed. P. Stepansky. Chicago: University of Chicago Press.

Kris, A. (1981). The conflicts of ambivalence. *Psychoanalytic Study of the Child* 39:213–234. New York: International Universities Press.

———— (1983). Determinants of free association in narcissistic phenomena. *Psychoanalytic Study of the Child* 38:439–458. New York: International Universities Press.

Kris, E. (1952). *Psychoanalytic Explorations in Art.* New York: International Universities Press.

———— (1956). The recovery of childhood memories in psychoanalysis. *Psychoanalytic Study of the Child* 11:54–88. New York: International Universities Press.

Lacan, J. (1956). The function of language in psychoanalyses. In

The Language of the Self, trans. A. Wilden, pp. 3–87. Baltimore: John Hopkins University Press.

———— (1966). Le séminaire sur la lettre volée. In *Ecrits I.* Paris: Editions du Seuil.

Langs, R. (1981). *Classics in Psychoanalytic Technique.* New York: Jason Aronson.

Laplanche, J., and Pontalis, J.-B. (1967). *Vocabulaire de la psychoanalyse.* Paris: Presses Universitaries de France.

Laufer, R. (1963). La structure et la signification de *Jacques le Fataliste. Revue des Sciences Humaines* 112:517–535.

Leavy, S. (1973). Psychoanalytic interpretation. *Psychoanalytic Study of the Child* 28:305–330. New Haven: Yale University Press.

Lecointre, S., and Le Galliot, J. (1971). Pour une lecture de *Jacques le Fataliste. Littérature* 1:22–30.

Le Guen, C. (1982). The trauma of interpretation as history repeating itself. *International Journal of Psycho-Analysis* 63: 321–330.

Lehman, D. (1992a). *Signs of the Times: Deconstruction and the Fall of Paul de Man.* New York: Poseidon.

———— (1992b). Paul de Man: the plot thickens. *New York Times,* May 24, Section 7, p. 1.

Leov, N. (1965). *Jacques le Fataliste,* poème parabolique. *Journal of the Australian Universities Language and Literature Association* 23:24–48.

Levin, H. (1966). Notes on convention. In *Refractions, Essays in Comparative Literature,* pp. 32–61. London: Oxford University Press.

Levine, F. J. (1977). Review of the *Restoration of the Self,* by H. Kohut. *Journal of the Philadelphia Association of Psychoanalysis* 4:238–247.

Lewin, B. D. (1948). The nature of reality, the meaning of nothing, with an addendum on concentration. *Psychoanalytic Quarterly* 17:524–526.

Loewald, H. (1949). Ego and reality. In *Papers on Psychoanalysis,* pp. 3–20. New Haven: Yale University Press, 1980.

———— (1970). On psychoanalytic theory and the psychoanalytic process. *Psychoanalytic Study of the Child* 25:45–68. New York: International Universities Press.

———— (1975). Psychoanalysis as an art and the fantasy character of the psychoanalytic situation. *Journal of the American Psychoanalytic Association* 23:277–299.

London, N. (1985). Review of *The Restoration of the Self* by H. Kohut. *Journal of the Philadelphia Association of Psychoanalysis* 66:95–107.

Lowenstein, R. (1957). Some thoughts on interpretation in the theory and practice of psychoanalysis. *Psychoanalytic Study of the Child* 12:127–150. New York: International Universities Press.

Loy, J. R. (1950). *Diderot's Determined Fatalist.* New York: King's Crown Press.

Mahler, M. S., Pine, F., and Bergman, A. (1975). *The Psychological Birth of the Human Infant.* New York: Basic Books.

Mallarmé, S. (1865). *L'Après-Midi d'un Faune(églogue).* In *Ouevres Complètes,* ed. H. Mondor and G. Jean-Aubry, pp. 50–53. Paris: Gallimard, 1961.

———— (1891). *Sur l'évolution litteraire.* In *Oeuvres Complètes,* ed. H. Mondor and G. Jean-Aubry, pp. 866–872. Paris: Gallimard, 1961.

———— (1894). *La musique et les lettres.* In *Oeuvres Complètes,* ed. H. Mondor and G. Jean-Aubry, pp. 642–657. Paris: Gallimard, 1961.

Marsland, A. (1966). Voltaire: satire and sedition. *Romantic Review* 57:35–40.

Marvell, A. (1681). "On a Drop of Dew." In *The Poems and Letters of Andrew Marvell,* vol. 1, ed. H. M. Margoliouth. Oxford: Clarendon Press, 1952.

Mauzi, R. (1964). La parodie romanesque dans *Jacques le Fataliste. Diderot Studies* 6:89–132.

McDougall, J. (1985). *Theaters of the Mind.* New York: Basic Books.

————— (1986). Identification, neoneeds and neosexuality. *International Journal of Psycho-Analysis* 67:19–32.

Mitchell, S. (1993). *Hope and Dread in Psychoanalysis.* New York: Basic Books.

Modell, A. (1979). Empathy and the failure of empathy. *Bulletin of the Association of Psychoanalytic Medicine* 18:70–75.

Mukařovský, J. (1977). *The Word and Verbal Art: Selected Essays.* New Haven: Yale University Press.

Nelson, L., Jr. (1968). The fictive reader and literary self-reflectiveness. In *The Disciplines of Criticism*, ed. P. Demetz, T. H. Greene, and L. Nelson Jr., pp. 173–191. New Haven: Yale University Press.

Olden, C. (1953). On adult empathy with children. *Psychoanalytic Study of the Child* 8:111–126. New York: International Universities Press.

Ornstein, P. H. (1979). Remarks on the central position of empathy in psychoanalysis. *Bulletin of the Association of Psychoanalytic Medicine* 18:95–108.

Ostow, M. (1979). Letter to the editor. *International Journal of Psycho-Analysis* 60:531–532.

Paget, V. (1909). *Laurus Nobilis: Chapters on Art and Life.* London: Lane.

————— (1913). *The Beautiful.* Cambridge: Cambridge University Press.

Pappas, J. (1968). *Candide* rétrécissement ou expansion? *Diderot Studies* 10:241–263.

Pinsky, R., trans. (1994). *The Inferno of Dante.* New York: Farrar, Straus, and Giroux.

Pontalis, J. B. (1977). *Frontiers in Psychoanalysis: Between the Dream and Psychic Pain*, trans. C. P. Cullen. New York: International Universities Press, 1981.

Price, M. (1964). *To the Palace of Wisdom: Studies in Order and Energy from Dryden to Blake.* Garden City, NY: Doubleday, 1965.

Propp, V. (1928). *Morphology of the Folktale*, trans. L. Scott, 2nd ed. Austin: University of Texas Press, 1969.

Pruner, F. (1970). *L'Unité Secrète de Jacques le Fataliste*. Paris: Minard.

Rangell, L. (1963a). The scope of intrapsychic conflict. *Psychoanalytic Study of the Child* 18:75–102. New York: International Universities Press.

———— (1963b). Structural problems in intrapsychic conflict. *Psychoanalytic Study of the Child* 18:103–138. New York: International Universities Press.

———— (1982). The self in psychoanalytic theory. *Journal of the American Psychoanalytic Association* 30:863–892.

Reed, G. (1994). *Transference Neurosis and Psychoanalytic Experience: Perspectives on Contemporary Clinical Practice*. New Haven: Yale University Press.

Reich, A. (1951). On countertransference. In *Psychoanalytic Contributions*, pp. 136–154. New York: International Universities Press, 1973.

———— (1966). Empathy and countertransference. In *Psychoanalytic Contributions*, pp. 344–360. New York: International Universities Press, 1973.

Renik, O. (1992). The use of the analyst as a fetish. *Psychoanalytic Quarterly* 71:197–204.

———— (1993). Analytic interaction: conceptualizing technique in the light of the analyst's irreducible subjectivity. *Psychoanalytic Quarterly* 4:553–571.

Richards, A. (1981). Self theory, conflict theory and the problem of hypochondriasis. *Psychoanalytic Study of the Child* 36:319–337. New York: International Universities Press.

———— (1982). The superordinate self in psychoanalytic theory and in the self psychologies. *Journal of the American Psychoanalytic Association* 30:939–958.

Ricoeur, P. (1970). *Freud and Philosophy: An Essay on Interpretation*, trans. D. Savage. New Haven: Yale University Press.

Roelens, M. (1973). *Jacques le Fataliste* et la critique contemporaine. *Dix-Huitième Siècle* 5:119–137.

Rothstein, A. (1980). Toward a critique of the psychology of the self. *Psychoanalytic Quarterly* 49:425–455.

Roustang, F. (1984). *The Quadrille of Gender: Casanova's Memoires,* trans A. C. Vila. Palo Alto, CA: Stanford University Press, 1988.

Sachs, D. M., and Shapiro, S. H. (1976). On parallel processes in therapy and teaching. *Psychoanalytic Quarterly* 45:394–415.

Sachs, H. (1942). *The Creative Unconscious: Studies in the Psychoanalysis of Art.* Cambridge, MA: Science-Art Publication.

Said, E. (1972). *Abecedarium culturae:* structuralism, absence, writing. In *Modern French Criticism,* ed. J. Simon, pp. 341–392. Chicago: University of Chicago Press.

Saussure, F. de. (1916). *Course in General Linguistics.* New York: McGraw-Hill, 1966.

Schafer, R. (1959). Generative empathy in the treatment situation. *Psychoanalytic Quarterly* 28:342–373.

——— (1980). Narration in the psychoanalytic dialogue. In *Essential Papers on Literature and Psychoanalysis,* ed. E. Berman, New York: New York University Press, 1993, pp. 341–368.

——— (1982). The relevance of the 'here and now' transference interpretation to the reconstruction of early development. *International Journal of Psycho-Analysis* 63:77–82.

——— (1992). *Retelling a Life: Narration and Dialogue in Psychoanalysis.* New Haven: Yale University Press.

Schapiro, M. (1956). Leonardo and Freud: an art-historical study. *Journal of the History of Ideas* 17:145–178.

Scholes, R. (1982). *Semiotics and Interpretation.* New Haven: Yale University Press.

Schwaber, E. (1983). A particular perspective on analytic listening. *Psychoanalytic Study of the Child* 38:519–546. New York: International Universities Press.

Schwartz, L. (1974). Narcissistic personality disorders—a clinical discussion. *Journal of the American Psychoanalytic Association* 22:292–306.

——— (1978). Review of *The Restoration of the Self* by H. Kohut. *Psychoanalytic Quarterly* 47:436–443.

Searles, H. F. (1955). The informational value of the supervisor's emotional experiences. In *Collected Papers on Schizophrenia and Related Subjects.* New York: International Universities Press, 1965, pp. 157–176.

Shapiro, T. (1974). The development and distortions of empathy. *Psychoanalytic Quarterly* 43:4–25.

——— (1981). Empathy: a critical reevaluation. *Psychoanalytic Inquiry* 1:423–448.

Sherman, C. (1976). *Diderot's Art of Dialogue.* Geneva: Droz.

Silber, A. (1983). A significant "dream within a dream." *Journal of the American Psychoanalytic Association* 31:899–915.

Skura, M. A. (1981). *The Literary Use of the Psychoanalytic Process.* New Haven: Yale University Press.

Smith, I. H. (1962). The Madame de la Pommeraye tale and its commentaries. *Journal of the Australasian Language and Literature Association* 17:18–30.

Spence, D. (1982). *Narrative Truth and Historical Truth: Meaning and Interpretation in Psychoanalysis.* New York: Norton.

Spenser, E. (1596). *The Faerie Queene.* In *The Poems of Spenser,* ed. J. C. Smith and E. De Selincourt. London: Oxford University Press, 1963.

Spitz, R. (1965). *The First Year of Life.* New York: International Universities Press.

Spitzer, L. (1948). *Linguistics and Literary History.* Princeton: Princeton University Press.

Steele, B. (1986). Child Abuse. In *Reconstruction of Trauma: Its Significance in Clinical Work,* ed. A. Rothstein. New York: International Universities Press, 59–83.

Stoller, R. (1973). *Splitting.* New York: Quadrangle.

———— (1975). *Perversion: The Erotic Form of Hatred.* New York: Pantheon.

Strachey, J. (1934). The nature of the therapeutic action of psycho-analysis. *International Journal of Psycho-Analysis* 15: 127–159.

Suleiman, S. R. (1980). Introduction. In *The Reader in the Text,* ed. S. R. Suleiman and I. Crosman, pp. 3–45. Princeton: Princeton University Press.

Terr, L. (1991). Childhood traumas: an outline and interview. *American Journal of Psychiatry* 148:10–20.

Thacker, C. (1968). Introduction. In *Candide ou l'Optimisme: Edition Critique.* Geneva: Droz.

Thomas, R. P. (1974). *Jacques le Fataliste, Les Liaisons Dangereuses* and the autonomy of the novel. In *Studies on Voltaire and the Eighteenth Century* 117:239–250. Banbury, Oxfordshire: Thorpe Mandeville House.

Ticho, E. (1982). The alternate schools and the self. *Journal of the American Psychoanalytic Association* 30:849–862.

Tillyard, E. M. W. (1943). *The Elisabethan World Picture.* London: Chatto and Windus.

Todorov, T. (1971). *Poétique de la Prose.* Paris: Editions du Seuil.

Treurniet, N. (1980). On the relation between the concept of self and ego in Kohut's *Psychology of the Self. International Journal of Psycho-Analysis* 61:325–333.

———— (1983). Psychoanalysis and self psychology: a metapsychological essay with a clinical illustration. *Journal of the American Psychoanalytic Association* 31:59–100.

Tyson, P. (1993). *Neurosis in childhood and in psychoanalysis: a developmental reformulation.* Paper presented at the meeting of the American Psychoanalytic Association, San Francisco, May 20.

Vanden Heuvel, J. (1967). *Voltaire dans ses contes.* Paris: Armand Colin.

Van Laere, F. (1973). *Jacques le Fataliste:* un problème de coherence structurelle. In *Studies in the Eighteenth Century III*. Canberra: Australian National University Press, 1976.

Vartanian, A. (1970). *Jacques le Fataliste*: a journey into the ramification of a dilemma. In *Essays on Diderot and the Enlightenment in Honor of Otis Fellows*, ed. J. Pappas, pp. 325–347. Geneva: Droz.

Vidan, G. (1967). *Jacques le Fataliste entre l'amour et le hasard*. Studia Romantica et Anglica Zagrabiensia 24:67–95.

Viderman, S. (1970). *La Construction de l'Espace Analytique*, 2nd ed. Paris: Gallimard, 1980.

——— (1977). *La céleste et le sublunaire*. Paris: Presses Universitaires de France.

Voltaire (1959). *Candide ou l'Optimisme, Edition Critique*. Paris: A. G. Nizet.

Voigt, M. (1962). Swift and psychoanalytic criticism. *Western Humanities Review* 16:361–367.

Wade, I. O. (1969). *The Intellectual Development of Voltaire*. Princeton: Princeton University Press.

——— (1986). Organic unity in Diderot. *L'Esprit Createur* 8:3–14.

Waelder, R. (1936). The principle of multiple function: observations on over-determination. *Psychoanalytic Quarterly* 5:45–62.

——— (1960). Psychoanalysis, scientific method and philosophy. *Journal of the American Psychoanalytic Association* 10:617–637.

Wagner, J. (1977). Code et histoire dans *Jacques le Fataliste*. *Revue des Sciences Humaines* 165:23–31.

Wellek, R. (1966). Vernon Lee, Bernard Berenson, and aesthetics. In *Discriminations: Further Concepts of Criticism*, pp. 164–186. New Haven: Yale University Press.

Werner, S. (1975). Diderot's Great Scroll: Narrative arts in *Jacques le Fataliste*. In *Studies on Voltaire and the Eighteenth Century*, 128. Banbury, Oxfordshire: Thorpe Mandeville House.

Wimsatt, W. (1963). What to say about a poem. In *Hateful Contraries*, pp. 215–244. Lexington: University of Kentucky Press.

Wind, E. (1963). *Art and Anarchy*. London: Faber & Faber.

Winnicott, D. W. (1947). Hate in the countertransference. In *Through Paediatrics to Psycho-Analysis,* pp. 194–203. New York: Basic Books, 1975.

Wolper, R. S. (1969). Candide, gull in the garden? *Eighteenth Century Studies* 3:265–277.

Credits

The author gratefully acknowledges permission to reprint material from the following sources:

"Dr. Greenacre and Captain Gulliver: Notes on Conventions of Reading and Interpretation," by Gail Reed, in *Literature and Psychology* 26:185–190. Copyright © 1976 by Richard Feldstein.

"The Two Analyses of Mr. Z," by H. Kohut, in *International Journal of Psycho-Analysis* 60:3–28. Copyright © 1979 *International Journal of Psycho-Analysis*.

"Candide," by Gail Reed, from *Literature and Psychoanalysis*, edited by Edith Kurzqeil and William Phillips. Copyright © 1983 by Columbia University Press. Reprinted with permission of the publisher.

"Toward a Methodology for Applying Psychoanalysis to Literature," by Gail Reed, in *The Psychoanalytic Quarterly* 51:19–42. Copyright © 1982 *The Psychoanalytic Quarterly*.

Index

286   *Index*

Halle, M., 17
Hanly, C., 14
Hartmann, G., 33
Hartmann, H., 198
Heuval, J. V., 261
Hierarchy
    clinical work and, 61
    meaning, absolute relativity
        and, 45–46
    narrative, explicit
        reconstruction and, 39–
        40
History, Freud and,
    psychoanalytic
    understanding, 186–188
Hitler, A., 48
Hoffer, A., 35
Holland, N., 216, 258n1
Homosexuality, transference
    perversion, clinical material,
    65–68
Hutter, A., 258

Individual differences,
    psychoanalytic
    understanding and, 4
Infantile neurosis, concept
    replaced, 129
Interpretation
    classical psychoanalysis, self-
        psychological interpretation
        compared, 148–156
    discrimination and, 36–37
    literature as analogy,
        psychoanalytic
        understanding, 166–
        175
    in self-psychology, 137–148

of transference, explicit
    reconstruction, clinical
    illustration, 21–22
Isakower, O., 165
Iser, W., 258n1

Jacques le Fataliste et son Maître
    (Diderot), 219–231
Jakobson, R., 17
Jung, C. G., 187

Karush, A., 203
Katan, M., 17
Kavanaugh, T., 223, 224, 226
Kermode, F., 241
Kernberg, O., 76, 202
Klein, M., 13
Koch, S., 48n7
Kofman, S., 33
Kohler, E., 222, 223
Kohut, H., 13, 76, 136, 137, 141,
    145, 146, 148, 156, 158, 202,
    204, 205, 206, 208, 209, 213
Kris, A., 76
Kris, E., 14, 135, 205

Lacan, J., 172, 218
Langs, R., 260n2
Language
    assumptions about,
        psychoanalytic
        understanding, 161–165
    primary process and, 16–18
Laplanche, J., 199
Lauffer, R., 223
Leavy, S., 196, 198, 206
Lecointre, S., 224, 226
Le Galliot, J., 224, 226

Index

289